DATE DUE

Wonderland

By the same author

The Green Road Home
To the Linksland
Bart & Fay (a play)

Wonderland

A Year in the Life of an American High School

Michael Bamberger

ATLANTIC MONTHLY PRESS
New York

Published simultaneously in Canada
Printed in the United States of America

Permission to quote from Nelly's "Hot in Herre" by Hal Leonard Corporation. Words and
Music by Pharrell L. Williams, Cornelius Haynes and Charles L. Brown © 2002 EMI
BLACKWOOD MUSIC INC., WATERS OF NAZARETH, BMG SONGS, INC.,
JACKIE FROST MUSIC, SWING T PUBLISHING, ASCENT MUSIC INC. and
NOUVEAU MUSIC COMPANY. All Rights for WATERS OF NAZARETH Controlled
and Administered by EMI BLACKWOOD MUSIC INC. All Rights for JACKIE FROST
MUSIC Administered by BMG SONGS, INC. All Rights Reserved International.
Copyright Secured. Used by Permission.

Excerpt from "The Hollow Men" in COLLECTED POEMS 1909–1962 by T.S. Eliot,
copyright © 1936 by Harcourt, Inc., copyright © 1964, 1963 by T.S. Eliot,
reprinted by permission of the publisher.

Library of Congress Cataloging-in-Publication Data
Bamberger, Michael, 1960-
Wonderland : a year in the life of an American high school / by Michael Bamberger.
p. cm.
ISBN 0-87113-917-0
1. Youth—Pennsylvania—Pennsbury (School district)—Social conditions.
2. High school students—Pennsylvania—Pennsbury (School district)—Social
conditions. 3. Proms—Pennsylvania—Pennsbury (School district)
4. Bucks County (Pa.)—Social life and customs. I. Title
HQ799.72.P4B35 2004
305.235'09748'85—dc22
2003069501

Atlantic Monthly Press
841 Broadway
New York, NY 10003

04 05 06 07 08 10 9 8 7 6 5 4 3 2

For *Mark Bowden*,
who opened the door,
and the window, too.

Contents

Contents

In a Wonderland they lie,
Dreaming as the days go by,
Dreaming as the summers die:

Ever drifting down the stream—
Lingering in the golden gleam—
Life, what is it but a dream?

—Lewis Carroll
Through the Looking-Glass

Prologue: The Day of the Prom

Saturday, May 17

Mike Kosmin and his friends started talking about her in September, the hot girl in the hot car, and now Mike's father was finally seeing her, on the day of the prom. The girl was a senior, and from the start of the school year, Mike and his buddies called her Jeans, for the low-cut, faded blue jeans she wore once a week or so, acid-washed and faded at the hips, with the zipper in the back. Mike was a junior at Pennsbury High, not a nerd, though he loved computers; not a jock, though he had made himself a good hockey player. He was a little chunky, funny, new to driving and the world of girls. On Labor Day weekend, his parents had surprised him with the ultimate gift, a car, not some ratty old clunker but a brand-new triple-black Acura RSX. Mike was saving up to improve the sound system. Still, some ride.

Mike's father had handed the virgin car keys to his only son and said, "When I was your age, I had an old Ford Falcon that took a quart-a-oil just to drive down the shore." He wasn't Mike's genetic father, but they shared a first name, and they were as close as any father and son. "The next generation should have something better, ya know?"

Only the most connected juniors could get a space in the oversubscribed Pennsbury student parking lot, so Mike Kosmin was forced to rent one at the pizza place next to the school. Each day, when the final school bell rang at 2:10 P.M., Mike and a buddy or two would trek across the school lot and across a baseball diamond over to Marcelli's Pizza, turn on the car radio, and watch Jeans walk to her black Corvette. She'd flip her long blond hair over one shoulder, slip into her sleek car, and drive off to places unknown.

Someday, Mike knew, he'd be in the main parking lot, in the thick of things. One of his best friends, Bob Costa, didn't even have a car but somehow had snagged a permit for student parking. Bob held it out as something he'd give his friend, someday.

Costa was well connected and unusually sharp. He was the president of the junior class and the second-best debater on the Pennsbury forensics team. He always seemed a step ahead of everybody else.

He was also a movie buff, and he quickly identified Jeans's cinematic ancestor. She was Pennsbury's version of the mystery girl in the white Thunderbird in *American Graffiti*, the one played by Suzanne Somers, the blond goddess with the shimmering lips whom earnest Richard Dreyfuss, in his short-sleeved madras plaid summer shirt, can never quite catch up to. Once Costa said it, everybody agreed: The girl in the T-bird was Jeans.

None of them knew where Jeans lived, what middle school she had attended, where she worked, how she got her Corvette, what guy she saw. They didn't even know her name until Dan Bucci finally spoke up. "She's Alyssa Bergman," he said one afternoon. "I sit next to her in D period. Modern media, with Mr. Mahoney. He does alphabetical seating. She talks to me. She's got a boyfriend. He's, like, twenty-five years old. He's in college or something."

And now here was Mike's father, practically face-to-face with the hot girl in the hot car, on the third Saturday in May, the day always reserved for the Pennsbury prom.

Mike's parents were doing the annual prom-day walk-through, when Pennsbury is on public display and hundreds of locals tour the school lobby, gym, and hallways. It is the day the locals judge for themselves the quality of the transformation from ordinary middle-class suburban high school to some sort of dance-party fantasyland, to decide for themselves if this year's kids had outdone last year's kids.

Nobody else, not one of Pennsbury's booming rivals, had anything like the Pennsbury prom. At Council Rock North and Central Bucks East and Neshaminy, along with most every other place you could think of, they all did the same thing: They held their proms in a Marriott ballroom or in some ghastly catering hall. The whole country had gone that way years ago. A prom in the gym? How low-rent can you get? How *ghetto*! At Council Rock and everyplace like it, the kids—that is, the kids who actually went to their proms—hired shiny limos for the night. They mocked the Pennsbury kids when Action News sent a reporter to do a feature on their prom: how the dates arrived by helicopter or pogo stick or in the back of a brightly painted cement mixer, how the sidewalks around the school were teeming with spectators. . . .

The Pennsbury kids, most of them from Levittown, in the heart of working-class Lower Bucks County, pretended not to care about what the rich kids said. *Yer mad*, they'd say, *'cause we're on TV and yer not.*

Mike Kosmin's mother and stepfather, the buyers of the triple-black Acura RSX, were not Levittowners. By Pennsbury standards, they were rich. They could have bought a home in any school district. Big Mike—the stepfather, Mike Mackrides—was a successful house builder. Cyndi Mackrides sold real estate. They could have sent their son to private school. They chose Pennsbury because they wanted Mike to go to a large public high school with every sort of kid you could imagine. They chose Pennsbury because it had some kids applying to Princeton and many more heading off to the military or trade school or Bucks County Community College or work. They chose Pennsbury because it had its own traditions, because it had a prom so out of the ordinary that Action News covered it every third year or so.

The Mackrides ambled down the school's hallways, savoring their first walk-through, awed by the creative skills of kids who looked so unexceptional when you passed them in the mall.

The theme was Hollywood Nights. The entrance to the school was now a red carpet that stretched from the parking lot to the front door. Each wall, every last circa-1965 brick, was covered with movie posters and Hirschfeld drawings and murals painted by students showing John Travolta in *Pulp Fiction* and Julie Andrews in *The Sound of Music* and Mike Myers in *Austin Powers: The Spy Who Shagged Me*. There were red-and-white-striped popcorn boxes that stood six feet tall, and over-size candy stands, and a sixteen-foot-high papier-mâché Oscar statue, painted gold. They were in promland. Big Mike and Cyndi stopped ev-ery few feet to inspect something, as if they were touring the Smithsonian, or to say hello to somebody: a teacher, an administrator, a neighbor, a friend of their son's.

After a while, big Mike wandered off, away from Cyndi, to get some fresh air and gather his emotions. He was a strong man, a man who knew music, cars, movies, women, himself, his stepson. He'd often say of Mike, "He's looking for his cool." Big Mike had found his years ago. But the memories of what it was to be young and inept and excited had over-whelmed him for a moment.

Near the end of the walk-through, he came upon a cardboard cutout of Alyssa Bergman, Jeans, the hot girl in the hot car, the girl who epito-mized cool to his son. A local amateur photographer, who had retired from the phone company and was Alyssa's next-door neighbor, had set up life-size cardboard pictures of Britney Spears, Justin Timberlake—and Alyssa. A promgoer could pose with one of the cutouts for a picture and show it off for years to come. *Yeah, my prom date.*

"So this is her?" big Mike said. "This is the hot girl in the hot car?"

He looked at the Alyssa cutout for a long moment. He curled his lips and nodded. He could see it. She was stunning.

"She doesn't do anything for me," he said coyly.

He took hold of his wife's elbow and led her through the growing crowd, opened the door of his big black BMW, and headed them home. They were leaving Fairless Hills and driving out to the farthest reaches of the Pennsbury school district, past the modest ranch houses of Levittown, past garden apartments and mobile homes, past the former farmland of Yardley and Newtown, now speckled with suburban pal-aces. All of it was Pennsbury.

Chapter

One

Taking Attendance

September

I. Principal Katz

The roles must be filled. A high school must have politicians, athletes, beauties, scholars, musicians, poets, actors, clowns, insiders, outsiders, and large numbers of the unexceptional. At the start of the school year, there may be any number of vacancies, but over the course of the year, the positions will be filled. It was true at my school and it was true at yours and it was true at Pennsbury. A school with no athletes will somehow identify sports stars. Celebrities of some sort will always emerge. The common trait of a school's most famous students—celebrated for *something*, good or bad—is their exalted sense of themselves. But the status of the prominent is ultimately conferred by all the ordinaries who make up the great middle in any student body. These anonymous souls, passing through school with shuffling feet and quiet voices, have no idea how important they are. Who would the notables play to if this great middle-class audience did not exist? Finally, there must be a person seeking to direct the populace. The school must have a principal, its mayor and police chief in one. It's a rule.

The hands of Bill Katz, the principal at Pennsbury High, the lone high school of the Pennsbury school district, trembled slightly whenever he lifted the microphone to make the morning announcements. The kids who took the microphone after him—Matt Fox, the school president, and Bob Costa, the junior-class president—didn't get it. What could Mr. Katz possibly be nervous about?

He towered over everybody. Except for his paunch, Mr. Katz still looked like the basketball star he once was. When he graduated from Pennsbury in 1967, he was a stick. His picture, in black and white, had been plastered all over *The Falcon*, the school yearbook. Soon after, *The Falcon* went color. The yearbooks from the 1970s were done in Kodachrome, and the children of those kids were present-day students. Mr. Katz's yearbook was from a distant era, even though he'd been in the second class to graduate from the new building, as people still called it decades after it had opened.

His prom date became his first ex-wife. His second ex-wife was the mother of his two boys, one at Boston University, the other at MIT. That was what the teachers at Pennsbury knew about Mr. Katz. Beyond that, he was a mystery. His devotion to the Pennsbury prom—and to the idea that the prom should always remain in the Pennsbury gym, to hell with what the rest of the country was doing—was well known throughout the school district. But other things, like who he spent his weekends with, were unknown. Nobody at Pennsbury had ever seen him eat.

Young teachers were timid around him. He had a low, raspy voice that made people work hard to hear him. He wore button-down shirts daily, always with a sport coat and tie. His clothes were exceedingly sturdy and vaguely retro, as if he had raided a men's department at Sears years before and stocked up for life. His only concession to the sadistically hot days at the start of the school year was short-sleeved shirts.

For most of his adult life, the most reliable address for Mr. Katz had been Pennsbury High, 705 Hood Boulevard, Fairless Hills, PA, 19030. He had been the assistant principal or the principal at Pennsbury for two decades, plus his four years as a student. He knew his school. He knew the kids and how they lived. Mr. Katz, the son of a career army man, had spent his high school years in Levittown. Even though Pennsbury was massive—Mr. Katz's building housed the junior and senior classes, with fifteen hundred kids, while the ninth- and tenth-graders were in a neighboring building—it was intimate to him and to very few others.

He knew where the kids would go "on campus," as he liked to call it, to try to cut class or smoke cigarettes or engage in "inappropriate physical behavior." He was privy to the most private details of the students' lives. He knew about their health issues, their sex lives and drug problems and learning difficulties. He knew about their parents' problems, too: unemployment, spousal abuse, gambling addiction, alcohol and drug abuse, credit-card debt. No different than anywhere else. He was exceedingly discreet about what he knew, just as he was about himself. If he dated at all, the teaching staff didn't know about it.

What they knew was that he drank coffee from the time he came in, shortly after six A.M., until the time he left, ten or twelve or more hours later. He kept a coffee warmer on his desk, in an office that was crowded with manuals and textbooks and industrial furniture. Behind his desk he kept a tall thermos filled with coffee. He lived on cashews and Hershey's Kisses and peanut M&M's. His diet could only have contributed to his trembling hands.

As he took the microphone on September 11, 2002, the first anniversary of the terrorist attacks, Mr. Katz's hands were shaking more than usual. As principal, he worried most about the safety of his kids. After that there was an endless list of things that kept him busy. How did his students compare to the state norm on standardized tests? How did they behave on the class trip to Washington, D.C.? Would the football team make the play-offs? But safety came first. September 11 was a painful reminder to Mr. Katz that there were forces in the world beyond his control.

The attacks had hit close to home. There were Pennsbury kids who had older siblings or fathers who worked in the World Trade Center, seventy miles away from Yardley and Newtown, the two wealthy pockets of the Pennsbury school district. (From Yardley or Newtown, a commuter crossed the Delaware River to Trenton, New Jersey, a ten-minute car trip. From there it was an hour-long train ride to Penn Station, in Manhattan.) There were kids whose fathers flew for American or United. Soon after the attacks, Mr. Katz learned that the father of a girl in the district had been the pilot of the Boeing 767 that crashed into the south tower.

And now it was the first anniversary. He had thought hard about the best way to recognize the date. He had considered asking his teachers to devote the day to studying issues related to the attacks. But in the end, he decided a little would go a long way: a moment of silent meditation followed by the reading of a poem written by the daughter, now a ninth-grader, of the pilot, Victor Saracini.

"President Matt Fox will now read Kirsten Saracini's poem 'Years Gone By,'" Mr. Katz said. His voice was solemn. He was a foot taller than Matt, to whom he handed the microphone.

Matt Fox was being asked to do something out of character. Suddenly, he needed to be serious.

When he ran for president, everybody figured it was a joke. He was the short, funny Jewish kid with yellow sideburns who had run a for-profit boxing club in his backyard until the school shut him down. *You don't have insurance*, an assistant principal had told him. *You're promoting your private enterprise on school walls. Young man, this will not fly!*

The two girls he ran against were good-looking and popular. They played sports. They took honors classes. They were in the service clubs. Matt Fox, he was just a prankster. Once Fox and his little prankster crew went to the mall, put a diaper on the ground, poured chocolate syrup in it, placed a $5 bill underneath the diaper, and waited for some kid to retrieve the bill, watching from a distance and recording the event with a video camera.

On another occasion Matt and four accomplices went to the Red Robin—a restaurant near the mall, and a Pennsbury hangout—dressed as a family. Matt was the daughter, in a wig. Another kid, Zach Woods, was the father, with talcum powder in his hair. The mock family sat down and engaged in a simulated family feud while ordering Cokes and lunch. But Matt's wig wouldn't stay on straight and he couldn't get beyond the line "But *Dad*." The old-gal waitress just stared at them, her order pad frozen at midchest, not laughing or smirking or doing anything except looking at Matt and his buddies as if they were very strange. That was the Matt Fox who ran for school president.

Late in Matt's junior year, there was an assembly for the candidates. The first girl gave a speech about how their class should have the biggest homecoming day, the most spirit, the best prom, the most exciting this, the most exciting that. The second girl followed with the exact same speech.

When it was Matt's turn, something occurred to him. He was going to win. The girls would split the girl vote, and if he could just show a pulse and be funny, he'd have the boy vote and the presidency. He ditched his prepared speech and winged it. "If you vote for me, I promise you a future brighter than . . ." He named a noted Pennsbury pothead. The student voters roared. "If you vote for me, I promise free admission to Matt Fox Boxing!" More cheers. Right then and there, Matt vowed to himself not to put up any posters. *Let the girls plaster the halls with their signs*, he thought, *I'm running as an outsider.* "If you vote for me, I promise you this: Your senior year will be *one big party!*" Even the Goth kids in the back of the auditorium, drawing cubist pictures with gnawed Bic pens on their skinny, veiny arms—even they looked up at that. The election was his.

It was May then, the May of his junior year. Summer was coming. Everything was easy.

Now it was September, the September of his senior year, and everything was serious.

At lunch, the senior girls were already making lists of potential colleges and prom dates. Matt couldn't believe it. His plan was to apply to Penn State and only Penn State. The idea of lining up a prom date more than a half-year before the event struck him as bizarre. But that was what the girls were doing, ranking their potential dates as if they were college choices, with a Safe date, a Reach, and a useful boy somewhere in between. It was unsettling.

And now he had to read a poem written by a girl whose father was killed in the September 11 attacks. This was different. This wasn't trumped-up seriousness. This was the real thing.

Matt cleared his throat, lowered his already deep voice, now the voice of his school, took the microphone from Mr. Katz's quivering hands, and read Kirsten Saracini's poem "Years Gone By."

At 0 you wanted Victoria to be my name forevermore
At 1 you bought me Ernie while in a Japanese toy store
At 2 you called me "Big Nea" and helped me to learn to read
At 3 you let me hold Brielle and taught me to do good deeds
At 4 you wrote me letters when you went away

At 5 you made me go to church and taught me how to pray
At 6 you bought me a Mexican backpack and waved 'bye as I went to school
At 7 you took me to Jamaica (which by the way was totally cool)
At 8 you played catch with me and taught me to play ball
At 9 you took me to get my hair cut in the mall
At 10 you brought me cookies and bars from your trips
At 11 you took me to Cancún and gave me bargaining tips
At 12 you taught me how to survive in middle school, and for that I soared
At 13 you took me to the beach and taught me how to Boogie-board
And for all the years that come I know one thing will never change
You will always be my daddy and I will always feel the same
I love you

Matt ad-libbed nothing. The president handed the microphone back to the principal, who nodded his approval. The secretaries were crying. Mr. Katz gave Matt a pass so he could return to his class, photography with Mr. Lefferts, without harassment from the hall monitors. The hallways were empty, and Matt's sneakers squeaked on the linoleum floor, still shined to high buff from a late-summer waxing. He made his way past the empty cafeteria. He turned a corner and practically bumped into a girl carrying her books the old-school way, in a pile, her arm underneath them, resting them on her perfect hip. Matt could see her navel. There was no jewelry in it. The girl was a well-known senior, a beauty, an athlete. They lived near each other.

"Nice job, Matt," she said in a low voice.

Matt Fox was speechless. He had known the girl since kindergarten. For years they had ridden a bus together. She had never initiated a conversation with him, not even a hello. Now she was saying *nice job*.

Maybe, just maybe, Matt Fox thought, he was on her list.

II. Lindsey "Peanutface" Milroy

Lindsey Milroy was a frenetic girl, but the fall of her senior year was particularly hectic for her, because of her competing allegiances to field hockey and her social life.

Her mother and father had gone to Pennsbury, graduating a few years after Mr. Katz. They went to the prom, although not together. Lindsey had grown up knowing all about the prom. She had gone to the prom the previous year, with a twelfth-grade date, and she of course would be going again in her own senior year. And naturally, she would be going with Win, who had taken her as a junior and later that weekend, in the back bedroom in a beach house at the Jersey Shore, had taken . . . Well, no; he didn't *take* it. It was a mutual decision made by consenting teenagers.

She told her closest friends—including her mother—that it wasn't much of an event. But everybody figured Lindsey was kidding herself, because the first time was always a big deal. If nothing else, it cemented her relationship with Win. She didn't know where she'd be going to college, but she was all set for the prom, right from the start of the school year. She was a little haughty about this, but that was her nature. Her friends didn't mind that quality in her. Her enemies had a field day with it.

Lindsey had worked on the Prom Committee as a junior, and she knew she'd return to it as a senior. She would do whatever was necessary to make her prom (and her prom-day self) as spectacular as possible.

As a junior, working nightly on prom decorating in the weeks before the big dance, she caught the eye of Jim Minton, one of the two Prom Committee faculty advisers. He liked the way she bossed around the other kids, even though she was only a junior. Some of the other girls thought Lindsey was a bitch, but Mr. Minton didn't care. He needed someone pushy as an overall Prom Committee co-chair.

Mr. Minton, an art teacher with a long gray ponytail and tattoos, had a poor memory for names, so he took to calling Lindsey Cabbage Patch, after her small, scrunched face. She looked like a Cabbage Patch doll, with narrowly spaced eyes and an unusually small mouth; but she also had the long, lean, athletic body of a J. Crew model and gorgeous, expertly cut hair. Her hair was her calling card. It was a thick, lively blond mane, just short of her shoulders. It swooped over half her forehead in the same hairdo that Jennifer Aniston had made famous. The other girls noted how often Lindsey ran her hands through her hair.

Lindsey was a member of Pennsbury's athletic elite and a central figure in its social ruling class. But she was beloved in neither. There was a group of athletes at Pennsbury called the Brew Crew, and orbiting around the Brew Crew was a satellite girls' group named for a movie, the Spy Kids. One of the Spy Kids had been seeing Win, a popular Pennsbury hockey player. Then Lindsey entered Win's life, and suddenly, he was hanging out only with her. The Spy Kids blamed Lindsey for that. They decided to make her life wretched. They started calling her Peanutface, for her crowded face. They scrawled *Peanutface* with paint across one of the prom murals she'd painted. Later, Lindsey emerged from a prom-decorating session and found the steering wheel of her car covered with peanut butter. These events just gave Lindsey more resolve.

Mr. Minton liked her energy. One night in her junior year, while everybody else was working on prom murals, Mr. Minton sat Lindsey down in the bleachers of the gym. In the bright lights, Lindsey's unblemished skin had a yellow glow. Mr. Minton asked Lindsey if she thought she had the stuff to be an overall Prom Committee co-chair her senior year. He needed somebody willing to be a tyrant. "Oh, yeah," Lindsey answered without hesitation. "I can be your prom Nazi."

She proved it soon after when Mr. Minton, the prom's artistic heart, announced that he was working on his last prom. He said that working on the prom had become too demanding, that he needed time for his own family and his own art. Lindsey got in his face immediately. "You're coming back, Minton," she said. Some of the kids called him Ozzy. He looked like Ozzy Osbourne, the heavy-metal legend. He even signed his e-mails to students that way. But no student, especially a fetching girl one third his age and half his weight, called him by his last name right to his face, not in a serious way, anyway. Mr. Minton found something exciting in her boldness, and in her backhanded recognition of his artistry. "I'm not going to have my senior prom ruined just because you've got to run back to your family and your potter's circle or whatever the hell you call that thing." She was dynamic, even tantalizing. Her imperfect face on her perfect body had a lot to do with it.

III. Bob Costa, Junior-Class President

His father, a lawyer, had a business card, and the junior-class president saw how useful it was, so he ordered some for himself. His card read:

BOB COSTA

PENNSBURY HIGH SCHOOL

Costa worked to get the school wired from the start of his junior year. The first item on his agenda was securing a parking space, even though he didn't own a car, didn't even have a driver's license. The parking space, that was just the start. Every morning, while reading the daily announcements over the PA system, Costa was making a study of Pennsbury from the inside. He saw how Mr. Katz had cordoned himself off, how the private door that led from the school lobby to Mr. Katz's office was for exiting only—it had no outside knob. Costa saw the daily lists of the kids assigned to what passed for the school jail, ISS (in-school suspension), whose warden was a cute Levittowner named Jen Snyder—Miss Snyder—fresh out of college and only a half-decade out of Pennsbury herself. Costa had access to the schedule of every kid in the school. Useful! Whenever Costa wanted to casually happen upon somebody, he could.

Costa had Pennsbury Pride, a term he used without irony. He and his family were devout Catholics—Mass every Sunday, without fail—and his twin brother, James, attended a small private Catholic high school. Costa was glad his school was public and immense. He figured if he could make a mark at Pennsbury, he could make a mark anywhere. His father, Tom, a former police officer and a no-nonsense man, was an in-house lawyer of high rank for Bristol-Myers Squibb, the giant pharmaceutical company based in Princeton, New Jersey. His mother, Dillon, was also a lawyer, but with four kids (the twins plus a younger sister and brother) in a big house, she was too busy as a chauffeur, cook, housekeeper, and crisis manager to work billable hours as well.

Bob's lack of a driver's license didn't make things easier for Dillon Costa, but she knew what came with teenage driving, so she wasn't eager for either of her twin sons to get behind the wheel. Tom Costa had the boys on an incentive program: Get through high school without drinking—not even a sip of beer—and receive a $1,000 bonus at graduation. In September of their junior year, Bob and James were still in line for the reward. Bob was in it for the money, but more because he hated even the idea of disappointing his father. Anyway, he was usually out of temptation's way. Bob had big, flat feet (the residue of youthful clubfeet) that worked hard to support his heavy legs. He had a cheeky, round face that was freckled with birthmarks. There was nothing in his look or striving personality that got him on the invitation list for the Pennsbury keg parties. Being the second-best debater on the forensics team gave him status only in certain circles, and he knew it.

To accommodate Tom Costa's work, the family had lived in London when the twins were in seventh and eighth grades. They returned to Yardley the summer before Bob and James entered ninth grade. While in London, Bob applied to Lawrenceville, an elite prep school near Princeton. Lawrenceville rejected him. The rejection turned Bob into a fourteen-year-old populist. Before long, he had renounced his parents' Republican politics (although he didn't tell them). He turned his back on all things preppy. He decided he would embrace the public high school experience and get everything he could out of it. He vowed to live a life out of *Fast Times at Ridgemont High*, out of *Risky Business*, out of the *American Pie* movies.

The big event at Pennsbury was the senior prom. All the juniors had was a dinner dance, held each year in November. Costa hadn't given it much thought. He was getting his life together piece by piece, and the girl part wasn't there yet. Then one day there was startling news, deemed unbelievable by Costa and Mike Kosmin and their cadre of nice-boy juniors. Dan Bucci, with his beak nose and angular face and quiet, nervous manner, had asked Alyssa Bergman, the hot girl in the hot car, to the junior dinner dance.

Jeans! A senior! Corvette girl! With the twenty-five-year-old boyfriend in college! With the unbelievable . . . *everything*! Bucci didn't even have a learner's permit. He was *way* out of his league. And her answer was . . . *yes!*

Costa had been pushing Bucci at lunch to ask her, but he never figured his friend would actually do it. He certainly never imagined she would say yes. And now Bucci was taking the most gorgeous of all the gorgeous seniors at Pennsbury to the crappy little junior dinner dance, maybe even in her Corvette.

"We're not gonna do anything," Bucci said.

"How do you know?" Costa asked.

Bucci made a face. He was resistible and he knew it. "Think about it. She's got a boyfriend. He's like twenty-five. She's already got the word out. We go to the dance, we go home. That's it."

"Yeah, well, still," Costa said. He had to admit it: Bucci was *way* ahead of him.

Costa decided then that he'd go to the junior dinner dance, to see Bucci, if nothing else. He wondered if, come May, Bucci might wind up at *her* prom. A junior boy, from Costa's own schlubby circle, at the senior prom. It was a preposterous idea. Costa loved it.

IV. Alyssa Bergman, Corvette Girl

Alyssa Bergman's first boyfriend was a hood. That's how her parents thought of him. He smoked, wore an imitation leather jacket, didn't have an after-school job, showed no ambition, had no college plans, ate poorly (and it showed), did no schoolwork, cut school routinely, even though he had no chance of getting away with it. (He was her alter ego.) His father was a Pennsbury janitor, and he kept tabs on his son, but there was only so much he could do. Alyssa's parents, Frank and Denise Bergman, a chiropractor and a nurse, didn't talk about the boyfriend, Nick Driscoll. They figured Alyssa's relationship with him was an act of rebellion. They knew if they complained about Nick, it would only push their beautiful daughter closer to him.

So they said nothing. They watched and worried. Alyssa's mother worked in the delivery room at Lower Bucks Hospital. She taught classes in prenatal care. Every year she saw scores of girls, teenagers like Alyssa, carrying unwanted babies. She knew teenagers had sex. She had two daughters. She didn't pry into their lives. Instead, she told them about contraception early. She didn't believe in abortion, and her daughters inherited that belief.

Denise Bergman had once helped deliver a baby without a brain. The baby's life would be brief and joyless. The doctor didn't understand why the mother wanted to go through with the delivery. Nurse Bergman did: The mother wanted to be with her child, even if the infant's life was barely an hour. The baby was born in silence, and Denise Bergman was there, stroking the mother's hair, creating a bond for life with a woman she did not know.

Frank Bergman was a driven man, hardworking and disciplined, devoted to his enthusiasms, most particularly martial arts, healthy eating, Chevy Camaros, and his thriving practice as a chiropractor. He was tall and slender, with penetrating eyes that scared some of the boys who called on Alyssa and her older sister, Dianna. He could spend forty minutes eating a bowl of whole-wheat pasta. He rushed nothing, including the raising of his daughters. He wanted them to graduate from Pennsbury, then from Bucks County Community College, then from Temple University in Philadelphia. Those schools he was willing to pay for. Anywhere else, they were on their own. After they got their degrees, he wanted them to work with him in his practice. In an ideal world, they would live at home, comforted by the familiar, by the barking dog and the plush carpeting. If they got married, their husbands could live in the house, too. Dianna's boyfriend already lived with them, in a basement bedroom. He paid $140 a month in rent.

Frank Bergman's patience was close to boundless, and he figured he'd ride out Alyssa's relationship with Nick. Then he received a call from one of Alyssa's teachers.

"You know I had Dianna, and I know what a good student she was," the teacher began. "I'd always heard that Alyssa was a worker, too." Alyssa was not scholarly, and the classes she chose were far from the school's most demanding, but she had always done neat work and handed it in on time. "Alyssa's not doing her assignments, and her classwork is poor."

Frank Bergman wasn't going to blame Nick. That would be too easy. He was deciding how to address the schoolwork issue when a more urgent crisis emerged: He caught his daughter smoking. His patience vanished.

"You want to smoke?"

"So what if I do?"

"Fine, then smoke."

"Whatever."

"Get in the car."

"Why?"

"Just get in."

They got in the car, each slamming the door. They drove to the 7-Eleven near their house in Fairless Hills.

"Buy two packs of cigarettes," Frank Bergman told his daughter. "If you're gonna smoke, you're not gonna do it behind my back."

The father had miscalculated. Alyssa actually bought the cigarettes, *two* packs of Marlboro Lights. They drove home in silence. He sat her down at the kitchen table.

"Smoke a cigarette in front of me."

Another misjudgment. She smoked a cigarette.

"Fine, smoke another one."

Another silent smoke.

"Smoke another!"

Alyssa ran off to her bedroom, crying. It was her final cigarette.

Soon after, she and Nick drifted apart. Her schoolwork improved. She started going with another guy, older but warmly received by Alyssa's parents. She was still dating him as her senior year began.

One day in September, she came home from school with news for her mother.

"I can graduate in January instead of June."

"Why would you want to do that?" Denise Bergman asked. But she knew the answer. Alyssa had always been in a rush: to get her first job, to get her first car, to get her homework done, to get on with her life.

"Mom, I've got the credits, why should I be in high school in January when I can be in college?"

"But you'll miss out on your senior year." Alyssa's mother had gone to Christ the King, a large Catholic high school in New York City, in the early 1970s. The girls and the boys were kept separate, but all the rules went to hell by the end of senior year. A good time. "What about prom and graduation and all that?" The Bergmans lived a mile from the school. They knew Pennsbury's traditions well. Dianna had gone to the prom with the guy who now lived in the Bergman basement.

"Mom, I can still go to prom. I can still go to graduation."

Her mother offered no other argument. It wasn't her nature. Anyway, she knew her Alyssa. If you stood in her way, you were the enemy.

V. Rob & Stephanie

Once a week at Pennsbury, midmorning on Wednesdays, the regular school day came to a stop for a program called EOP. It was the brainchild of Mr. Katz, and it stood for Educational Opportunity Period. (In its early days, when EOP was held at the end of the day, the kids said it stood for Exit Opportunity Period.) When Mr. Katz was a student at Pennsbury, many kids stayed at school after the final bell, to play chess and attend meetings of the National Honor Society. Things had changed. Half the kids at Pennsbury, and an even higher percentage of the Levittown kids, worked after school, making $7 an hour at fast-food restaurants or at mall stores.

The kids at Pennsbury wanted cars, stereos, DVDs, dinner out. To pay for it all, to pay for the things they figured lots of kids got from their parents, they were willing to work. Lindsey Milroy, the Prom Committee co-chair, with the Jennifer Aniston hairdo, worked at a nursing home run by the Grey Nuns of the Sacred Heart, wheeling around old folks. Alyssa Bergman, commuting from school in her black Corvette, was a waitress at the T.G.I. Friday's near the mall.

Because of after-school jobs, the kids had money, but the school's club life suffered. EOP was Mr. Katz's answer to that. During EOP, a student could play chess or Scrabble or guitar, develop photographs, attend a Prom Committee meeting, hang out with a group of gay students, build stage sets, study the Bible, or learn how to raise a child.

Each Wednesday morning, six or eight or ten Pennsbury girls attended Lynn Blakesley's teen-parenting EOP session. The girls were always urged to bring their boyfriends, or the fathers of their children. But every week, the classroom was all girls and just one boy. The boy who came was Rob Stephens, a big kid with bright red hair and multiple earrings and a playful manner. He was a senior and a Levittowner, once a football player and a wrestler, but not after he discovered girls and certainly not after he got his girlfriend, Stephanie Coyle, a junior from Levittown, pregnant. Each week, from the start of the school year, Stephanie was at the child-care EOP session with Rob beside her. In September, Stephanie was sixteen years old and seven months pregnant. She was a serious, lovely girl, with the skin of a child.

Rob and Stephanie had met at the mall. Immediately, they felt they could talk to each other about anything. For a while that's what the relationship was—talking. And then it evolved. Soon they couldn't wait for the school day to end because they knew what was next. Their days were boring, but their after-school activity wasn't. It was thrilling, it was adult, and it belonged to them.

Rob always carried condoms. You had to use a contraceptive, they both knew that, especially if you were having sex practically daily. Some kids did it in cars or in the woods, but Rob and Stephanie often had not one but two empty Levittown houses from which to choose. They thought anything other than a real bed was cheap. Stephanie, especially, felt a thing should be done the right way or not at all.

For the first four and a half months, Stephanie did not know she was pregnant. Her cycle had never been regular, and she didn't feel pregnant, and they had always used protection. One day she called Rob on her way to Wildwood, at the Jersey Shore, where her family had a vacation home in a wooded trailer park. At first she was coy.

"Lemme guess," Rob said. "You got your period."

"No," Stephanie said. "The opposite. I'm pregnant." She started to cry.

Holyshitholyshitholyshit, Rob thought.

"What do you want to do?" he asked her. He didn't need to ask. He knew the answer. Neither was a devout anything—Rob didn't know if Stephanie was Catholic or Protestant or what—but both felt that abortion was murder. They had talked about that when the conversation was theoretical. They had seen pictures of fetuses in school. They both believed that life began in the fetus.

"I want to keep it," Stephanie said.

Ron immediately sent an e-mail to an old friend, Harry Stymiest, the kindest and most religious kid he knew.

"I hope you're going to stand by that girl," Harry wrote back.

Rob knew Harry's simple instruction was correct. He also knew his life as a seventeen-year-old high school senior enthralled with video games was over. He held his breath and found his parents and prepared himself for the worst.

Rob had been conceived when his father was a senior at Pennsbury and his mother a junior. His father had graduated in 1985, his mother in '86. The father's nickname was listed next to his yearbook picture: Spliff, code for a pot smoker. Rob's parents were both able to graduate on time, but their lives had been nothing like easy.

"She's what?" the father yelled.

"Pregnant," the son said again.

"Are you a fucking idiot?" Rob's father screamed.

Stephanie lived with her mother and stepfather. When she told them she was pregnant, her mother asked if she wanted to give the baby up for adoption, but Stephanie knew she couldn't. Her mother was supportive. Her stepfather stopped talking to her. He pretended Stephanie didn't exist, not at the dinner table, not on the driveway, not when they passed each other in the small, neat house they shared.

When Stephanie returned to school in September, obviously pregnant, she felt student eyes upon her. To Rob's old football teammates, Stephanie's pregnancy confirmed their view of him, that he was a loser. (Only one player, the quarterback, did not drop him.) Rob and Stephanie felt like everybody in the world was allowed to have secrets, except them. Their privacy was gone.

Mrs. Blakesley's teen-parenting EOP session was their refuge, a place where they could talk about the things important to them that almost nobody at Pennsbury could understand. They felt comfortable with Mrs. Blakesley, who seemed never to judge anyone, who brought pretzels, apple juice, and brochures to each session. They talked about who should be the baby's godfather, and the name of the kindly and devout Harry Stymiest came up. They talked about their desire to go to the prom, in the faraway month of May.

"I know it's not the highest priority, and I know the tickets are expensive and everything, but I don't think our lives should come to a stop because we're having a baby," Rob said.

"We're going," Stephanie said. "I'm going to yours this year, and next year you're coming to mine."

"As long as we can find somebody to watch the baby," the expecting father said.

VI. Quarterback Bobby Speer

The quarterback, Bobby Speer, lived in Levittown, near Rob Stephens. Bobby's mother had told him to drop Rob as a friend long before Rob got Stephanie pregnant. But Bobby felt his mother was being too harsh and, years later, his teammates too unjust. What did they really know about Rob?

Bobby refused to be judgmental about Rob or anybody else. He had to live with a burden of his own, the burden of being perfect. No, worse than that: the burden of everyone *thinking* you're perfect. Of course, he had no one to blame but himself for his public image. The kids at Pennsbury, the teachers, even his coaches, they knew only what Bobby wanted them to know. And he wanted to keep his story simple.

Bobby was a senior and a football captain, the quarterback of a team that would be as good as Bobby could make it. He was a wrestler at a school with a rich wrestling tradition. He was the center fielder on a baseball team that went to the play-offs year after year. He was a solid B student with the sedentary goal of returning to Pennsbury as a teacher and coach. He was the polite-to-all kid with a long-standing girlfriend, Lauren Cognigni, a junior and a star pitcher on the softball team. Bobby had a wholesome appearance, with a strong chin, blond hair, and kind, wide eyes. Lauren was thin, muscular, dark-haired, unusually attractive. They were Pennsbury's most famous couple. When the senior girls made their prom-date wish lists, they didn't bother putting Bobby on them, not even under the heading of Reach. They all knew he was spoken for.

Bobby's father was at the school often. Kirk was out of work on medical disability—he had been struck by a forklift—and attended nearly every game, in every season. The coaches were always deferential because he had done such a good job with Bobby. The younger coaches would say, "Hello, Mr. Speer." The older ones would nod and say, "Kirk."

They didn't do anything to engage him. They knew he was a bleacher coach filled with opinions, and they knew he had one agenda: what was best for Bobby.

Bobby never corrected anybody who called Kirk "Mr. Speer," and Kirk didn't, either. It was too complicated, it wasn't anybody's business, and it screwed up the Bobby Speer story. Kirk wasn't Bobby's father, not technically. He wasn't even married to Bobby's mother. But his devotion to Bobby was fanatical.

Kirk and Bobby, along with Bobby's brother and mother and her father, lived under one roof. They were a family. Bobby never spoke of his biological father, even though he carried his last name. He hadn't seen him since he was five. As far as he knew, his blood father was a drug addict or an inmate or both, somewhere in the Midwest.

Bobby considered Kirk Safee his real father, all 280 pounds of him, one hundred pounds under his all-time high. It was Kirk who was managing Bobby's college recruitment. Kirk figured a good football season would give Bobby his pick of colleges and a full athletic scholarship.

What would happen with Bobby's kid brother, Danny, four years younger, the family did not know. Danny had been born with spina bifida, with his spinal cord protruding through his skin. From birth he had been paralyzed from midchest down. When Karen Speer was eight months pregnant, she had a sonogram. A doctor took her into a private room and told her if she wanted the baby to die, she should insist on a vaginal delivery. Her response was to demand a cesarean.

Danny's bedroom had to be modified, a special bathroom built, the family van fitted for him. The lives of the family members were adjusted to his needs. They thought nothing of that. It was their norm. On weekends Kirk often took Danny to wheelchair basketball tournaments or to play wheelchair baseball. In summer he took him to a camp for kids in wheelchairs. The state paid for Danny's wheelchairs. Karen wished she and Kirk could get married, but she worried that marriage would endanger her state medical benefits and put an end to Danny's free wheelchairs.

The Pennsbury kids knew Bobby's brother was in a wheelchair, but that was all they knew. They didn't know Bobby lifted his brother out of the wheelchair and into bed every night. They didn't know Bobby got him to the bathroom, that he changed his brother's diaper, that he cleaned up after him. Bobby didn't talk about those things.

The idea that Bobby would someday be going off to college weighed on Danny. So much of Danny's identity was wrapped up in being Bobby Speer's kid brother. And who else in the house had the strength to lift his 150-pound body in and out of the wheelchair? Not his grandfather, not his mother, not his father. Nobody.

"You're gonna go to college and then to the pros, and Danny's gonna be your agent," Karen Speer told Bobby. It was a snapshot from the future in the photo album of her mind.

Danny was around the corner in his wheelchair, listening. They lived in a house, as many Levittowners did, where kitchen conversations could be heard by everybody. Danny was not yet in high school, but he knew his mother was dreaming. He knew Bobby would someday leave for college, and thereafter his life would never be the same again. Each would take his own path.

But Bobby nodded in silent agreement. He was in high school. Is there a time when fantasy is richer? You're old enough to see a real glimpse of your adult self, but young enough to dream. Somehow you meld the two, the glimpse and the dream.

Bobby knew the picture his mother carried ultimately came not from her mind but from his. He gave it to her, and she gave it back to him. Back and forth it went, back and forth.

VII. Harry Stymiest, PHS-TV *Personality*

Harry Stymiest, pious and kind, had always been an outsider at Pennsbury. His German surname was pronounced STY-mist. He'd been born with cerebral palsy, and accommodations had been made for him all his school life. He was a big, round senior with a buzz cut, and his left leg dragged slightly behind him as he shuffled down the Pennsbury hallways. He had almost no strength in his left hand, and it flapped around when he wasn't mindful of it. His right hand wasn't much stronger. Shaking hands or gripping a pencil was work for him. His face had a distinctive curve to it. He had large, sleepy hazel eyes. His appetite was astonishing, and he always had food nearby. The kids did not mock him. He was nice to them, and they were nice to him, particularly the ones who lived in Pennwood Crossing, the mobile-home park where he had lived all his life with his father and mother. Mostly, though, he was left to do his own thing.

Harry was desperate to become an Eagle Scout, and he would if he could somehow get through the knot-tying requirement. On Sundays he went to Emilie United Methodist Church with his parents, morning services followed by Bible study in the afternoon. Scouts and church, these were not the common interests of most Pennsbury kids. Sundays were spent sleeping, watching football, parading through the mall. Harry was doing his own thing.

He was fascinated by TV production and had been since he was six, when his mother took him to see a taping of *Bozo the Clown* in Philadelphia. He was taken with the prodigious cameras and the men behind them and how the men and their cameras glided silently and effortlessly across the darkened studio floor on wheeled dollies, connected to the world by thick rubber-coated cables. By the time he was a senior at Pennsbury, Harry had become a fixture at PHS-TV, the school's in-house cable-TV channel that reached sixty thousand homes in Lower Bucks County. PHS-TV was operated by Pennsbury kids and managed by a teacher, Al Wilson, who had been at Pennsbury for thirty years, staying sane only by means of a droll and acerbic wit. He treated Harry like a real person.

Mr. Wilson needed kids to cover night school-board meetings. He needed kids to cover homecoming, visits by local pols, school plays and concerts, the annual wing-eating contest, Sports Nite, the prom, all the events that defined the Pennsbury year, year after year. Harry could not be overworked. The more the better. He had found a role for himself. He was the outsider looking in. He saw the world of his school through the viewfinder of his PHS-TV video camera. Editing a sanitized vision of that world in the PHS-TV studio for sixty thousand cable-ready homes helped give his life meaning. Mr. Wilson was his main link to the real world.

"Mr. Wilson, I'm going to grab lunch down at the cafeteria, but don't worry, I'm coming right back to Studio 230," Harry said one morning.

"God bless ya, Harry," Mr. Wilson said.

"You want that school-board meeting edited down to fifteen minutes?"

"The shorter the better, Harry."

"I'll get it down to ten!"

"Knock yourself out, my man."

The PHS-TV studio was where Harry ate most of his meals. It was home. Mr. Wilson wondered if Harry would ever be able to move beyond the studio, or if he had adopted the boy for life.

Chapter
Two

Our Town

There are two Levittowns: the one in Pennsylvania, the center of the universe for most Pennsbury students; and another in New York, on Long Island. They were both named for Bill Levitt, the great assembly-line builder who constructed affordable homes for men returning from war and starting families and working in union factories. In the 1950s Pennsylvania Levittown, you could buy a brand-new home for as little as $99 down and $59 a month for thirty years. Thousands of people did just that.

All through the 1950s and 1960s, right through the early 1980s, Lower Bucks County was a little pocket of the old industrial Northeast. Levittown had little to do with Philadelphia, even though it was only thirty miles from the Liberty Bell, and nothing to do with New York City. You could have dropped it in alongside the factory towns on the Monongahela River, on the outskirts of Pittsburgh, and nobody would have blinked. Levitt built his houses in four models, none of which had basements. There was the Levittowner, a one-story, three-bedroom, one-bathroom house with a carport. There was the Rancher, a one-story house with four bedrooms, two bathrooms, and a carport. There was the

Jubilee, built for supervisors, which had four bedrooms on two stories, a dining room, and a garage. And then there was the grandest Levitt house of all: the Country Clubber, a Jubilee with more square footage.

Originally, the conformity of the Levittown house was a major part of its appeal, but a half-century later, most every home owner in Levittown had put a personal touch on his or her home: dormers, chimneys, stockade fences, year-round Christmas decorations, bathrooms with extra-wide doors to accommodate wheelchairs. Almost every house had a garage, and inside many of the garages were shiny muscle cars—a Camaro, a Corvette, a Mustang—used only for special occasions. There were no Saabs in Levittown, not that I ever saw.

The original system by which Levitt named his sections and streets suggested a well-ordered man. Bobby Speer and his family lived on Elm Lane in the Elderberry Pond section, where all the street names begin with *E*. Bobby's teammate Rich Moore stayed with his mother on Easter Lane during the school year; they were the only black family on the street. (In Levittown, maybe one house in fifteen was owned by a black, Hispanic, or Asian family.) Rob Stephens and his young parents lived around the corner, on Ember Street. Stephanie Coyle, Rob's pregnant girlfriend, lived on Pond Lane in the Pinewood section. Mr. Minton, the art teacher and prom adviser, lived on the same street. Mr. Katz, the principal, had grown up in the Elderberry section, on Elderberry Drive, where his parents still lived.

In the fall of 2002, there were Levittown homes, spruced up and expanded, selling for over $200,000, but $98,500 was a far more common asking price. In other parts of Bucks County, in the new developments north of Route 1—where Mr. Katz and Bob Costa (the junior-class president) and Lindsey Milroy (the prom co-chair) and Mike Kosmin (the kid with the Acura but no parking spot) lived—houses routinely sold for $350,000 and sometimes double or triple that. Six or seven miles south of those developments, Bill Levitt's houses continued to serve their original purpose. They were homes for workaday people.

The original Levittown breadwinners worked in the paper mills and breweries and factories on the Delaware River, most commonly at the sprawling 3M plant or at Rohm and Haas or at a U.S. Steel mill called the Fairless Works, named for Benjamin F. Fairless, the president of

U.S. Steel during World War II. The steel mill had employed more than ten thousand people in its peak years, before the Vietnam War. The disposable income of these workers spawned bakeries, pizzerias, barbershops, and beauty parlors. It also built bowling alleys and taverns and family-owned garages and strip malls. To a passerby, these ugly little roadside malls were unremarkable in every way. But they were important to Levittowners. They continued to employ people, Levittown kids and their mothers in particular, in the early years of the twenty-first century, even after the factory jobs had all sailed overseas. These centers of commerce were survivors, and so were the shoppers who used them.

By the fall of 2002, many Levittown women worked in health care—as nurses, as dental hygienists, as office receptionists, as cooks in hospital kitchens. Others were secretaries at small law firms or insurance offices. Some worked for the school system or at the local branch of a national superstore—Rob Stephens's mother worked at Toys "R" Us—where an important fringe benefit was a 10 percent employee discount, even on sale items.

Roughly one Levittown house in four was headed by a single woman. Many of them had grown up in Levittown. They stayed because they were given the house by their parents, with the mortgage settled. They had gone through the local schools and turned out all right, so why shouldn't their children do the same? This had a lot to do with why the Pennsbury prom was still held in the gym, even though most everybody else had moved their proms out and into mirrored ballrooms. The prom tradition was handed down. It came with the deed to the house.

The living arrangements in Bobby Speer's house, where three generations lived in one cramped Levittown house, were not uncommon. Many Levittown houses had one or two grandparents, one or two parents, and two or three kids living in them. You could drive by those houses late at night and see the glow of competing TVs in different rooms.

What the postindustrial Levittown father did for work was harder to say. It was no one thing. Many worked in construction. Or, when the Bucks County construction boom was in its periodic hibernation, they found work maintaining the new houses north of Route 1. That work would take them to the Yardley and Newtown developments. Men worked as roofers or as plumbers' assistants or as day laborers or on municipal road crews. Most were paid hourly wages, making double minimum wage if they had a particular skill. Over a year, $30,000, maybe. Typically, one income alone couldn't keep a house up and the cars running and the cell phones on and the cable TV plugged in. So the mothers and children often worked, too.

The new-development houses, built on mowed-down cornfields in the 1970s and 1980s, were nothing like the Levittown houses. They were big and boxy, with central air-conditioning and finished basements. Five over four with a door, Mike Kosmin's builder father, big Mike, called them: five windows on the second floor, four on the first, with a door right in the middle, generally closed and locked. In the early 1990s, when those ample houses started to look passé, the first McMansions went up seemingly overnight: houses with five bedrooms or more, blacktop drive-ways, and pro-quality backboards with adjustable rims, so the rush of slam-dunking a basketball could be known to any seventh-grader. Most of the owners of these homes, the supersized ones and the more ordinary ones, had gone to college. They were doctors, building contractors, law-yers, accountants. Or they sold something: insurance, plumbing supplies, cable systems. Or they were highly ranked hospital or school adminis-trators with two children, like Mr. Katz. They worked in Philadelphia or Trenton or Newark or New York, or in suburban corporate campuses where the windows did not open but parking was ample.

The developments where they lived were assigned the quaint mail-ing addresses of Yardley and Newtown, but the main streets of those old villages were inadequate for their shopping needs. To accommo-date them, the massive Oxford Valley Mall was built right off Route 1. It was at this mall that Rob Stephens met Stephanie Coyle, outside Kahunaville, a restaurant near the food court. The Red Robin, where Matt Fox and his buddies staged their mock family fight, was in the Oxford Valley Mall complex. So was the T.G.I. Friday's where Alyssa Bergman worked. Everyone went to the mall for movies or dinner out or big-ticket shopping. Newtown and Yardley people, Fairless Hillers, the Levittowners—everybody. You couldn't go to the mall without see-ing Pennsbury kids or teachers, working or shopping. They kept the place humming.

II.

Feeling prosperous, the original 1950s Levittown home owners—the men who worked in the mills and factories—spawned babies, large numbers of them, presumably with some cooperation from their wives. As the first batch of babies headed toward fourteen, the local school districts realized they needed new high schools. (The Neshaminy school district ran through Levittown, too.) Before long the old redbrick Pennsbury High, built in 1950, was overwhelmed. In the mid-1960s a new Pennsbury High was built on a vast vacant field in Fairless Hills, adjacent to Levittown. The architecture firm of Vaughn and Associates won the commission, based on its previous success, the design for the Bucks County Prison.

The most notable features of the new Pennsbury High were that very few of the classrooms had windows, and the two main entrances to the building were protected by a wavy foot-thick cement canopy that the Pennsbury kids have always called *The Noodle*. Inside the school, the ceilings were low, particularly in the cafeteria. So were the plastic desks and the chairs; even short kids felt tall. Pennsbury looked like the kind of school you see all over the country: in the new suburbs outside Houston, in South Florida, and especially in California. There were distinct smells associated with certain parts of the school. The bathrooms smelled like grapefruit disinfectant, and the cafeteria like sauerkraut and nachos, and the weight room like old socks. There were lockers, owned by junior girls and festooned with pictures of the singer John Mayer, emitting the aroma of eau de strawberry.

In the years right after Mr. Katz graduated, the baby boom went berserk. The graduating class swelled to twelve hundred in the early 1970s. To accommodate the crowds, the school day was held in shifts, starting at six in the morning. When the shifts overlapped, the corridors were so thick with students that you could see nothing in front of you but, say, a plaid flannel shirt. In the '74 *Falcon*, one student wrote, "Many of us will remember the sun rising over the steel mill in B period." The school was woefully understaffed, and many teachers were being hired right out of college. (In the new century, that kind of hiring was rare; Miss Snyder, of Levittown and ISS, was an exception.)

In 1970, amid the population explosion at Pennsbury, Jim Cunningham was hired as a history teacher (only later did his field become social studies). He was twenty-two, four years older than some of his students, saving up to get married. The prom was in need of a faculty adviser, and the pay was $300. Mr. Cunningham was pleased to get the gig. He needed the money.

At the age of fifty-four, he would tell his friends while sipping Scotch and smoking cigarettes at the old Yardley Inn on Friday afternoons, he was ready to do something else, ready to start his adult career. He knew he had been teaching too long when he found himself sitting next to people who were both former students and the children of former students. More than once he had been tempted to say to them, "What are you doing in *my* bar?" But he held his tongue, because the person next to him was a fellow adult, a man with a briefcase full of problems, a woman with her engagement ring turned upside down, people with as much right to the bartender's ear as he had.

Mr. Cunningham had always liked proms. He had gone to one of Pennsbury's rivals, Woodrow Wilson, class of '66. He picked up his prom date, Sandra Locklear, in a sky-blue '65 Rambler Classic that belonged to his father, a welder. She was wearing a full-length olive-green satin skirt and an aqua silk blouse. He slipped an orchid corsage around her wrist and took a long look at her. She looked gorgeous. He was wearing black tuxedo trousers, a white dinner jacket, a clip-on black bow tie. He was a Levittown boy. (The Cunninghams lived on Kindle Lane; they'd been the fifth family to buy a home in the Kenwood section.) The rich had always had their cotillions and assemblies, but after World War II, the grand social occasion became the birthright of the masses, too. Across the country, the prom—the tuxes, the flowers, the shiny cars, the parade of pretty girls in pretty dresses—became the coming-out party for the working class. The name was an abbreviated version of *promenade*. La-de-da. Leisure for everybody.

Jim Cunningham's prom was held in the school gym, the norm in those days, and the theme was Ebb Tide. Everywhere you looked, there were dinghies and driftwood. The dancing went from nine to midnight. Then there was a full-length movie and after it a hypnotist. The idea was to keep the kids so occupied, so late into the night, that they would forget their other impulses. Naturally, the scheme failed.

By the thirty-third September of his teaching career, Jim Cunningham had been married to the former Sandy Locklear for thirty years. The afternoon when he was a bachelor teacher and a female student had left a note on his desk that read *I want to fuck you* seemed like a different lifetime. It had been years since he'd had his overall Prom Committee cochairs to his house for cocktails before the prom. It had been years since a student had called him at home, running from a drunk, angry father. His career had spanned eras. When he began teaching, the role of the teacher, as Mr. Cunningham saw it, was to get inside the lives of the students and shape them. Now the job was all about, he said, "covering your ass."

For years, he had been one of those teachers found at almost every school, the teacher who shapes lives, the teacher whom former students talk about at their twenty-fifth reunion. If you're lucky, you had such a teacher, his or her strong personality lingering in your memory still. Typically, these unforgettable teachers are more than willing to express opinions or to appear eccentric. Mr. Cunningham's students, the ones paying attention, knew about his obsessive interest in the White House, his objection to abortion on moral grounds, his loyalty to the Republican Party. The kids who remembered him, the kids who were changed by him, were the ones able to argue with him in a time when teacher-student debate was viewed as a good thing. In the American public high school, that was a long time ago.

Still, Mr. Cunningham had had many excellent years. The proms, the good ones, were his proudest moments. In 1995 his son, Matt, in his senior year at Pennsbury, was a co-chair. The father and son battled but produced a superb prom. In 1999 his daughter, Tracy, was a co-chair in her senior year. An altogether sweeter experience. Mr. Cunningham thought the '73 prom, the Wizard of Oz, was one of his best. He also had a deep fondness for the '81 prom, New York, New York. The '92 prom, Treasures of the Deep, reminded him of his own. A very fine prom.

Eventually, the prom job became too big for one person, and Mr. Cunningham took on a deputy, a math teacher named Lou Schragen.

They were a harmonious team until one night in their tenth year together, in the throes of the pre-prom chaos, when Mr. Schragen lifted a heavy ceramic coffee mug, looking to heave it at his colleague. Mr. Cunningham saw a deep tiredness in his friend's face and said, "Let me drive you home." The math teacher explained that he had an inoperable brain tumor and that his medications sometimes produced psychotic behavior. Mr. Cunningham accompanied Mr. Schragen to the prom that year. That was in 1988. The theme was Under the Sun. When the gym got too hot, Mr. Cunningham brought Mr. Schragen home and hugged him good night at his front door. A few weeks later, Lou Schragen was dead.

Later, Mr. Cunningham took on a young English teacher and a life-long Levittowner, Dan Mahoney, as his deputy. After Tracy's prom, Mr. Cunningham turned the prom over to Mr. Mahoney. For the 2000, 2001, and 2002 proms, Mr. Cunningham was the committee consultant. He was at large. Mr. Mahoney enlisted the help of Mr. Minton, the art teacher with the gray ponytail, whose father had been a Levittown barber and who himself worked in the U.S. Steel mill before it closed. Mr. Minton had been a year ahead of Mr. Cunningham at Woodrow Wilson but had come to teaching years after. He was still going strong. Mr. Cunningham had handed off the prom, the thing in his professional life that had brought him the most pride. "I inherited a nice dance," he told them. "I turned it into the Pennsbury prom."

Once a year for many years, an old-time school photographer named Jerry, from Varsity Studios in Ossining, New York, would drop by Pennsbury High and give Mr. Cunningham a $1,000 check for prom decorations. It was a payment in kind: Every year on prom night Jerry took prom portraits, an important payday for Varsity. One day Jerry said, "I've traveled up and down the East Coast shooting proms. No school can match what you guys do." Maybe it was a sales line. Mr. Cunningham chose to believe it was not. He had helped create a prom that eight or nine out of ten seniors attended. The scholars and the athletes went, the cool crowd, the druggies, the disabled kids—everybody went. He had helped create a prom that unified and defined the school.

Mr. Cunningham believed that high school was adult life in concentrated form. In the important ways, the high school kid and the high school experience had not changed during his years at Pennsbury. High school had always been about the search for love, for sex, for various highs, for independence, for acceptance.

To Mr. Cunningham, the Pennsbury prom was a five-day experiment in adulthood, steeped in ritual and pattern. The prom was always on the third Saturday in May. The Friday before it was a day reserved for primping. The Sunday after it many of the kids drove down to the Jersey Shore, where they stayed in inexpensive motels and empty summer homes. The Monday after the prom was always a senior skip day, when cutting school was decriminalized for a day. The following day was always a teacher workshop day, which meant there was no school. A five-day prom. Five days of partying: drinking beer, smoking pot, having sex, making noise, getting tattoos, getting sun, sleeping in the afternoon and staying up all night long.

What had changed over the years, Mr. Cunningham observed, were attitudes: toward blacks, toward gays, toward the disabled and the different. Along the way, there were defining episodes. In 1987 two openly gay boys tried to buy prom tickets to go as a couple. The school board got itself all knotted up, but Mr. Cunningham put his own conservatism in check and resolved the dispute. "Let them come," he told the board. "If you make a big fuss over it, you'll ruin the prom for the other kids. If a boy wants to go with another boy, if a girl wants to go with another girl, what's it to us? The prom is special because it's run by the kids, and it's for the kids. The kids don't care. Why should we?"

His words carried the day. He liked to tell people the prom was his, but he knew the deeper truth: The Pennsbury prom was what children on the cusp of adulthood could do when left to their own devices. The prom was about the better selves deep within the kids, the better selves deep within them yearning to get the hell out.

III.

When you first go back to school as a middle-aged man—married, children, station wagon, dog, lawn in need of mowing; need I say more?—you find you can't stop staring at the kids. They're on display, like mating birds. Everywhere you look, there are barely dressed girls in a back-to-school heat wave, not even eighteen and all dolled up. The boys are even more obvious, with their untucked shirttails and unchecked testosterone. The whole scene is horribly distracting.

It wasn't just me, suddenly back in a classroom many years after my final school lunch. Teachers at Pennsbury, male and female, knew what I was talking about. Parents, deluded as usual, think teaching takes place in some sort of isolation chamber. The teachers know better. They'll tell you that just because you're handing out hallway passes now doesn't mean you're any different than you were in high school. If you're going to make it in teaching—and some, of course, do not—you learn to bury your feelings and get on with your lesson plan.

In 1978 I graduated from Patchogue-Medford High School, a large public high school on the South Shore of Long Island, about sixty miles from Manhattan. When I enrolled at Pennsbury in September 2002, it was twenty-five years after I had begun my senior year. Pennsbury seemed familiar to me, in its size and in other ways. Patchogue-Medford—like the village of Patchogue, where I grew up—was economically diverse in my day, but with a substantial blue-collar middle-class Italian population. Pennsbury was the same way, except for the Italian part. The white kids at Pennsbury were a mishmash of ancestries. They could often find Irish, Italian, German, Jewish, Catholic, and Protestant ancestors in their family trees. There was a senior at Pennsbury named Blair Maloney. Naturally, she was Jewish.

Pennsbury was about 85 percent white and 15 percent black, Hispanic, and Asian. My class at Patchogue had been roughly the same. At both schools, a kid could push himself or not, according to the courses he took. Many more from Pennsbury went to college; about half of the graduating class went directly to four-year schools. In my class, about one in ten was college-bound.

I had never heard of Pennsbury High until I saw a minute-long item on the eleven o'clock news one night, at home in Philadelphia. That was in 2002, on the third Saturday in May. The clip showed a parade of kids lined up to get into the school, transporting themselves in boats and floats, a little red wagon, dressed-up work trucks. The sidewalks in front of the school were packed with waving people. I was fascinated. The cheerful spectators looked like something from my Patchogue past. They looked like townspeople. But I knew they couldn't be. I knew the only place townspeople existed anymore was in the movies.

IV.

If proms have any particular importance to me, I don't know about it. It is true that on the night I met the woman who is now my wife, at a crowded party in a small apartment, I asked her if she had attended her high school prom. But I was just nervous and knew that question sent you down one of those national rite-of-passage conversational roads. (Who'd you go to *your* prom with?) Football's the same way; it gives you something to talk about. I went to my prom with the girl who was the editor of our yearbook. Many of the yearbook's sponsors were businesses on Main Street, Patchogue, L.I., N.Y., 11772.

My mother, a retired English teacher, has my prom pictures in a well-ordered album. My brother's, too. My brother, class of '75, is posed near a tree wearing a cream-colored rental, with a ruffled shirt and an enormous black bow tie. The next day my father, a half-foot shorter than my brother, put on the tuxedo before it was due back and stood on our front lawn for a photo, the arms of the jacket covering most of his hands, the pant cuffs trampling the grass. A funny shot. My own snaps, from 1978, are suitably ridiculous: six feet, 130 pounds, black pants, black shoes (stolen for me by a West Point–bound friend from our high school's ROTC supply room), bright white coat, Jewish Afro, red plaid clip-on bow tie.

My date, editor of *Record '78*, was a cheerleader, a flutist in the school orchestra, a prominent member of the National Honor Society. We both thought highly of a bearded English teacher, Bill Sullivan, who taught, among other things, Thornton Wilder's *Our Town*. (Talk about your townsfolk.) Lienne was adored by teachers but maybe too perfect to be elected homecoming queen, if you know what I mean.

We started dating in the spring of our senior year, and it was all extremely innocent—dinners at the Steak Loft, movies—not just by today's standards but by any. I always had Saturday-night money because I mowed lawns, caddied for our principal on weekends, and ran a successful football betting pool, which my calculus teacher, Mr. Caggiano, played weekly.

When I started going to Pennsbury, I began an e-mail correspondence with Lienne, the first contact we'd had in years. She got out a tucked-away prom packet. Our prom's theme song was "We May Never Pass This Way Again" by Seals & Croft. The live music was provided by the Noblemen, but neither Lienne, who has an excellent memory, nor I, blessed with a good memory myself, could recall such a band. The prom was held at the wood-paneled Narragansett Inn, in faraway Lindenhurst. We sat with—oh, does anybody care who we sat with?

Lienne wrote that when she had informed Bud Mazura, the assistant principal in charge of making my life miserable, that we were going to the prom together, he did not mask his disappointment: "You're going with that JD?" I may not have been the yearbook editor or an orchestra member, but I was not a juvenile delinquent. I think he unfairly blamed me for the school's rampant gambling. The librarians allowed us to play poker on the reading tables. Was that *my* fault?

After the prom, Lienne and I stopped at a diner off Sunrise Highway and changed into civilian clothes and drove to Westhampton Beach. I laid out a blanket. It was cold and windy and, before long, sand was in our hair and mouths and we were shivering. We headed home. I know there were others who had grand plans for that night. We did not.

But for whatever reason, the prom memory leaves me in a warm glow. "You were a good sport," Lienne wrote. No, she was. My dancing, I'm certain, was horrible, and I struggled to get the orchid corsage around her left wrist. Her mother helped.

"We were innocents," I wrote to Lienne.

She wrote back, "We were."

V.

When I was in high school, everybody played air guitar. Everybody had a fantasy life. With a snow shovel in your hand, you were Peter Frampton or Eric Clapton or the lead guitarist from Lynyrd Skynyrd. Or, with different props, you were Pete Maravich or Angie Dickinson or Bobby

Kennedy. I think Lienne imagined herself lecturing to a packed hall of Harvard undergraduates, like the professors in *Love Story*.

We dreamed, grew up, made adjustments. When I realized I wasn't going to become Cleon Jones (the best hitter on the '69 Mets), I set my sights on making a living with a typewriter. In my day job, as a writer for *Sports Illustrated* (take that, Bud Mazura), I see the rare exceptions, the high school air guitarists who graduated to the main stage. There's a wide range there. Western High's Tiger Woods, class of '93; Darryl Strawberry of Crenshaw High, class of '80. When they were hotshot schoolboys, Hall of Fame lives were predicted for both of them. I know this because at *SI* we often dust off the memories of old high school coaches and teachers and friends when we're trying to take the measure of the notable. We want to know: Who, really, was he then, and who is he now? If you've ever been to a reunion, you've done the same thing. Who, really, was the girl sitting next to you in Typing II senior year, and how did she become . . . whatever.

I went to Pennsbury—I went back to school—to take the measure of the girl in Typing II *now*, a decade before her tenth-year reunion, before she becomes a dental hygienist or a computer programmer or whatever thing she will go on to do. No examined life is ordinary. If there's any one thing I took from *Our Town*, it's that.

Chapter
Three

Homecoming

October

I.

The school year continued. Early each morning a secretary ripped off a page from a desk calender, and a new day was under way. Changes were coming daily. Alyssa Bergman, the girl in the black Corvette, was nominated for homecoming queen. Mike Kosmin and Bob Costa and Dan Bucci laughed. The rest of the school had discovered her. Kosmin was still parking at the pizza place, off in no-man's-land, but in chemistry he was discovering how to engage a girl, or his lab partner, anyhow: tell her jokes, keep her laughing. Rob Stephens, with his baby coming, had taken a job at Babies "R" Us. His job, like his mother's position at Toys "R" Us, came with the 10 percent employee discount, although it could not be applied to formula or diapers. When Rob's shifts were over, he and Stephanie went shopping for the baby, due in mid-November. The job, the shopping, the pregnant girlfriend made Rob feel more adult, even if his primary urge was to get home to his computer and his video games.

Bobby Speer was trying to adjust to the rookie football coach, who did not like to pass the ball, which was a problem for Bobby, because passing the ball was what he did best and what college recruiters wanted to see him do. Mr. Minton and Mr. Mahoney, the two faculty advisers

to the prom, had been conducting EOP meetings every Wednesday
morning. There was never a morning announcement about the meetings, yet two dozen or more girls and a smattering of boys were attending the sessions. The faculty advisers wanted kids who were so eager they
could find their way to unadvertised meetings. For the most part, the
kids who showed up were like Lindsey Milroy, kids who had worked on
the previous year's prom. As for Milroy, she was severely overextended.
She was playing field hockey, fighting with her boyfriend, hanging out
with her friends, looking at colleges, working at the Grey Nuns, feuding
with her enemies, shopping, tending to her hair and body, talking on
her cell phone, partying on the weekends, and snoozing through her
morning classes. Her usual refrain was "I need *sleep!*" She'd groan the
final word. She felt something weird going on in her chest—right in her
heart, it seemed to her—but she didn't talk about it.

One morning Mr. Minton and Mr. Mahoney convened a special
meeting to tell Milroy and another girl, Alicia Fuscellaro, that they
would be the two overall Prom Committee co-chairs. Alicia was flushed
with excitement. Milroy looked ready to go back to bed. The two girls
knew each other only in passing.

"How's field hockey going?" Alicia asked Lindsey.

"Terrible," Lindsey said.

"Really? I thought you guys were so good."

"We suck."

"You guys seem so close."

"We hate each other."

Mr. Minton and Mr. Mahoney had an idea that the two girls would
complement each other.

The fledgling Prom Committee's first order of business was to select
a theme. The committee was to nominate five themes, and the senior class,
by popular vote, would choose one. The two overall co-chairs had to select the area chairs, who would be in charge of decorating specific regions
of the school: the gym, the hallways, the bathrooms, the lobby. Mr. Minton
and Mr. Mahoney had to sign off on the choices, but that was a formality.
They had chosen co-chairs who could assess talent.

Still, the two advisers were the authority figures. They didn't know
it, but they were already having their first problem. A group of four or

five black girls with no prom experience had been attending the weekly
EOP prom meetings. Mr. Mahoney was thrilled, because very few black
kids had been involved in the Prom Committee over the years. But in
the previous year, both the prom king and queen had been black. It made
sense. Pennsbury was overwhelmingly white, but culturally, the kids
embraced black life. The emergence of black prom stars had encouraged
a dynamic girl of Liberian descent, Nemadia Knuckles, and a group of
her friends to join the Prom Committee. Getting started was hard for
them. They didn't know what to do. They were looking for direction
and weren't getting it. "I don't think they like us," Nemadia said at the
third Prom Committee meeting. "They never ask us anything. Don't they
want our ideas?" Her friends nodded in agreement. They shared her
dissatisfaction.

Mr. Mahoney saw the whole scene differently. He saw the black girls
sitting in a group away from the others (whom they did not know). When
he talked, they flipped through prom catalogs. He read that as lack of
interest, while they thought they were following directions, looking for
decorating inspirations. Whatever Mr. Mahoney was talking about was
unfamiliar to them. By the time the suggested themes were placed on a
ballot, none of them particularly exciting to Nemadia and her friends,
they were gone from the committee. You could attribute no part of the
problem to racism. You could attribute all of it to race relations.

The white kids at Pennsbury were enamored of black city life. Allen
Iverson, the elfin superstar guard on the Philadelphia 76ers basketball team,
his black skin covered in tattoos and his life story an outsize saga of urban
living, was a hero to many of the Pennsbury kids, both boys and girls. So
was Eminem, the white rapper who could pass for black, particularly to
the Levittown boys. They played his music so loud you could hear it out
of their headphones as they ambled home from school, smoking cigarettes,
oblivious to the oncoming traffic. They dressed like the black kids in North
Philadelphia, with their cargo pants low and their plaid boxer shorts high.
Some of their fathers, working as plumbers' assistants or other knee-pad
jobs, sported the same look, although not intentionally.

The committee, with no input from the black girls, came up with
these five themes: Arabian Knights, Aztec, Asian Wonders, Hollywood
Nights, and Cities Around the World.

In general, the committee members were most excited by Aztec, for which they wrote this impassioned description on the ballot that would soon be distributed to the seniors:

> Through the jungle, guided by the bright moon over Central America, you come upon the old ruins of an ancient tribe. The humid air sweeps over your skin as you examine this temple further. Under the heavy vegetation that has overgrown the stones, you find a door. Through that door lies the beauty, treasures, intrigue, and passion of the long-forgotten culture that will be brought back to life.

Two dissenting committee members, Priscilla Chung and her friend Kim Lenhart, saved their enthusiasm for Asian Wonders:

> Transform PHS into a hologram. Turn it one way and you see the American high school. Turn it the other way and you see the Asian wonders. Meet a different world where tradition, simplicity, and tranquility whisper in our ears. A night that will surely be our best.

The description for Hollywood Nights was willfully ordinary:

> It's Oscar time again and this time you're invited. Spend the evening in Tinseltown and experience the thrill of the red carpet. Get to see the landmarks and spend time in scenes from your favorite movies. So grab your camera and don't forget your autograph book as Pennsbury goes Hollywood!

The concluding exclamation mark was planted in sarcasm.

"Hollywood is so cheesy," one girl said.

"So, *so* lame," said another.

"I promise you it can be done without cheese," Mr. Mahoney said. "No cheese factor."

The girls were offering up Hollywood without enthusiasm. They were offering it because they knew the tastes of their classmates. They knew it would win, and it did, handily. They counted the votes one afternoon with resignation. They took it for granted that almost three-quarters of the seniors had made the effort to vote for a theme for a prom that was almost eight months away. At first their disappointment was profound. They were describing the winning theme with words like *sorry* and *pathetic*.

Lindsey Milroy was thumbing through *People*, whizzing by pictures of Ben and J.Lo and Jennifer and Brad, in Mr. Mahoney's windowless, overheated classroom. She decided to put an end to the whining. "Hollywood," the Prom Committee co-chair said, "will kick ass!" And she was gone, out the door, no hallway pass, no good-bye.

II.

When Harry Stymiest, the pious boy with the buzz cut and the dragging left leg, heard about the prom theme, an idea immediately struck him, an idea he shared with nobody but his computer: He would get the DeLorean from *Back to the Future* for his ride to the prom. As for a date, he was determined to get one of those, too. He went online and began to search.

III.

And then another brash idea sprang forth, this one from Mr. Mahoney: The prom should have a name musical act. He needed to hire a new band, anyhow. The go-to Pennsbury prom band, a funked-out reggae group, had done well for years, filling the dance floor through the night. But Mr. Mahoney had grown uncomfortable with the band members. They seemed stoned, more so every year, and during their breaks, they would leer at the Pennsbury girls, more brazenly every year. Mr. Mahoney was nervous about anything that even hinted of sexual impropriety. "Thirteen years of Catholic school," he said. "There's guilt galore." The Rasta men would not be coming back.

"You could have anybody you want play your prom," Mr. Mahoney asked his Prom Committee one day. "Who would it be?"

The committee girls were smiling. *This is cute.* No names were forthcoming. They knew Mr. Mahoney was going way outside the box. He didn't think so. After all, he had a budget. There was $3,000 earmarked for a band, but he knew there was room to play with that number.

"Seriously, just name names. We're a big prom. We've had name acts before. We pay. One year Robert Klein performed at the prom." Normally, Mr. Mahoney knew the references the kids would get, but the comedian's name was meaningless to them. The big acts who had once played the Pennsbury prom—the Ink Spots, the Dell-Vikings, Barry Manilow—were irrelevant now.

Finally, one girl shyly mentioned Nelly, a rapper who wore a Band-Aid across his left cheek, who just then had a hit with an impossibly catchy refrain:

It's getting hot in here
So take off all your clothes
I am getting so hot,
I wanna take my clothes off.

After that, names were forthcoming. Somebody mentioned Pink, a female singer who had grown up in Doylestown, the county seat of Bucks County. Somebody mentioned Boyz II Men. Somebody mentioned Britney Spears, and there was hissing. Somebody mentioned Eminem, but he was immediately deemed too expensive. Somebody mentioned John Mayer. There was murmuring.

John Mayer was a young white guitarist starting to establish himself as the next Dave Matthews, the folkie guitarist who had been selling out stadiums for over a decade. John Mayer was nothing like famous, but the Pennsbury kids were on to him. Earlier in the year, he had played a small club on South Street in Philadelphia in front of 350 people, and Pennsbury was well represented. There was a group of Pennsbury kids, Bob Costa and Blair Maloney among them, who knew the lyrics of songs Mayer had not even recorded yet, songs that had made the rounds over the Internet. One of those songs was called "No Such Thing." As the school year started to unfold, the official version of the song, from a CD called *Room for Squares*, was becoming a college-radio hit. To the kids at Pennsbury, the refrain struck home, and more than once I heard small groups of girls singing these lines:

I wanna run through the halls of my high school
I wanna sing at the top of my lungs.

"He's so hot," a girl said.

"Maybe we could get him," said Mr. Mahoney.

There was a discussion of what it would take. Certainly more than $3,000, they all agreed. Still, there could be car washes, bake sales, fund-raisers.

The first step, Mr. Mahoney said, would be to write an irresistible letter to Mayer. He asked the girls to each draft a sample. Within days, he had merged the compositions into a single letter, which he printed on Pennsbury High School stationery. The letter was dated October 11, signed by Alicia Fuscellaro, and sent to Mayer's agents:

Dear Mr. Mayer,

When you played in Philadelphia last spring, a bunch of us from our school, Pennsbury High, left that concert as your biggest fans. Usually artists sound so much different live than they do on an album, but you hit every note! You wouldn't believe how popular you are at our high school. Just the mere mention that I was writing this letter got everyone excited. When you sing, "I want to run through the halls of my high school, I want to scream at the top of my lungs," we want to scream at the top of our lungs.

We're writing to you because we would love for you to play our Senior Prom on Saturday night, May 17, 2003. Now, we know you normally don't play proms, but this is far from some cheesy affair at some hotel or catering hall with cheap balloons and the Chicken Dance. Our senior prom at Pennsbury High is, we think, like no prom anywhere else. We hold our prom right in our gym, but it's decorated so magically you'd hardly recognize it. Dozens of kids, along with a few teachers, work all year to make the night special. At most schools maybe half of the kids go to their prom, if that, and it's usually the cool kids and the popular kids. At Pennsbury High, almost everybody goes to the prom, the "in crowd" and everybody else. Single-sex couples, pregnant seniors, computer nerds, football stars—everybody! The prom lasts from seven o'clock at night to three in the morning! Not only is there a band and a DJ, but the students may attend a hypnotist show during the evening. Our senior class this year

contains 750 kids, with every type you could imagine. We'll
probably have around 1,200 people at the prom. We've included
a video that shows last year's prom, because the uniqueness of
our prom is hard to describe if you've never seen it.

On prom night, the whole community comes out, behind
barricades, just to watch the prom dates make their entrances.
People arrive at the prom by everything from a fire truck to a
little red wagon. It's like Oscar night. In fact, the theme for this
year is "Hollywood." We would do everything in our power to
make sure your stay in Philadelphia is great. We'd arrange for
your transportation, we'd put you up wherever you wanted to
stay; we'd arrange a driver for you if you needed one—anything
to make your stay enjoyable. We would do whatever necessary to
pay your fee, just please tell us what it is. We'd raise the money
from our prom ticket sales, car washes, and other fund-raising.

Could you or your manager give us a call or write or e-mail
us to say whether you'd like to play our prom? We would love to
hear from you. If you played, everyone would remember the '03
Pennsbury Senior Prom forever! Trust us, there's plenty of "room
for squares."

"If he doesn't respond to that letter, I wouldn't want him playing
our prom," Alicia said.

Overnight an invention spread through the school with giddy and
uncontrollable speed. *John Mayer is playing the prom.* There was some
grumbling from some of the Levittown boys, the kids who listened to
Eminem on their way home from school, kids who said John Mayer was
"gay," a word they used not just for homosexuals but for anything that
even hinted at effeminacy. But mostly the kids were awed. Someone with
real talent, someone on TV, would be coming to their school. When
Costa heard about it, he made a vow: He'd get himself to the prom.

Mr. Mahoney was always impressed by how news, accurate or not,
swept through the school. He made no effort to quash the John Mayer
rumor. Buzz about the prom was good for the prom, he reasoned.

He read the letter one last time, put it in an envelope, patted the
package, and sent it off.

IV.

Alyssa Bergman did not have a good sense of herself. She was shocked when she was nominated for homecoming queen and certain she would never be elected. The other girls were more beautiful, she reasoned. They were involved in school activities. (Alyssa was not.) She was unaware of how famous she was for her jeans, for her car, for her beauty, and for her boyfriend nobody knew.

She regarded the nomination alone as a great accomplishment. She wanted people to take notice of her. That's why she paid such close attention to her hair and clothes and body. That's why she had a convertible. She *enjoyed* stopping at a red light and having a guy pull up beside her and behold her. Alyssa's dream was to become a famous swimsuit model. What she lacked was a star's attitude. She said yes to Dan Bucci, yes to his little junior dinner dance, because, she told people, "If he's willing to ask me, who am I to say no?"

Alyssa told her friend Danielle Nutt, another nominee for homecoming queen, that she had no chance of winning. Danielle was dismissive: "Can't you hear people talking?" But Alyssa could not.

Then there was a serious irregularity in the homecoming king and queen election, and it threw the cafeteria handicapping out of whack. At first there were five king nominees and five queen nominees, as always. But then the ballot for king was expanded by one. The confusion came because of a Pennsbury rule that prohibited football players from being nominated for king. (Years earlier, a coach had decided that the homecoming hubbub was disruptive to player performance.) One senior, Sean Adams, was not on the ballot because the teachers overseeing the election thought he was playing football, as he had while a junior. But he wasn't, and his objection was heard and sustained, and instead of the usual ten candidates on the homecoming court, Adams made eleven. To even up the court, another female nominee, Andi Glick, was added. Nobody objected to Andi's late inclusion, even though she immediately became one of the front-runners. She was a track star and an excellent student and popular in various segments of the student body. Adams's support was less widespread but centered in a powerful group nobody was eager to take on, the Brew Crew.

The winners were announced on a Saturday night in October, under the lights of the football field, right before the homecoming game. Before Matt Fox announced the winners, Alyssa was chanting to herself: *Please call my name, please call my name.* Her name was called but she didn't hear it. Sean Adams, her processional escort, gave her a congratulatory hug, and the magnitude of what had happened finally reached her. Mr. Katz placed a tiara on her head.

One frenzied moment later, she was in the hands of her king, the gangly Zach Woods, the father of the Pennsbury pranksters, the boy who had led his mock family, Matt Fox among them, to the Red Robin by the mall. Zach, a foot taller than his queen, was as ironic as Alyssa was guileless. He wore a peculiar, twisted expression on his face for his official king-nomination glossy. He was a smart, funny kid. The main thing he had in common with Alyssa was that he, too, had no interest in extracurricular activities. The other nominees for king played sports, ran clubs, campaigned for the throne. Zach was opposed to obvious effort for anything. He already knew he would be skipping the prom. It was too much work, emotional and otherwise: finding a date, getting a tuxedo, arriving amid the hoopla. Just thinking about it wore him out.

"Where is my queen?" he demanded at homecoming, adopting an accent from Monty Python. "I must gather my court immediately!" He was seventeen and an expert in satire. King Zach was a member of a burgeoning group, not just at Pennsbury but everywhere: children who had grown up on *The Late Show with David Letterman.* For them, irony was a language. By turning everything into a gentle joke, a kid could achieve fame as a nonconformist without rejecting all local values.

The newly crowned king and queen marched across the field. Alyssa, with a black sash across her gowned homecoming-queen body, was beaming. Her father stood in the stands and videotaped her every step. The next week at school, she stopped at the main office to speak to one of the assistant principals.

"What are my special responsibilities?" she asked.

"What?"

"As homecoming queen."

"Special responsibilities?"

"Don't I have to visit sick children in hospitals?"

"No."

"Or distribute food to the poor?"

"No."

"Be a role model or something?"

She was taking Dan Bucci to the junior dinner dance, that was something.

As her stature in school increased, Alyssa's decision to go with Bucci to his junior dinner dance was being viewed as an act of charity. People said it showed Alyssa had heart. Before homecoming, Alyssa had refused to see it that way. After, she started to see herself, for the first time, as others did. One day in modern media she looked at Bucci, ever stammering in her presence, and said, "The only reason you want me to go to your junior dinner dance is so you can go for a ride in my car." There was a hint of guile in her voice. It was a first.

She kept Bucci in the dark about her boyfriend, Michael Castor. The only people at school who knew anything about him were her close Pennsbury friends, Danielle Nutt and Jaime Schaffer, most notably. They felt he slowed her down.

"You've been going out, what, for two years?" Danielle asked one day.

"Yeah."

"You two are like an old married couple," Jaime said.

"What's wrong with that?" Alyssa asked.

But she knew. She knew her relationship with Michael was oddly mature. It felt like an arranged marriage. But after Nick, it was comfortable. It was easy.

Michael's father was a chiropractor, and his mother was a nurse, just as Alyssa's father and mother were. When the two men were starting their practices in Bucks County in the early 1980s, they were involved in the same professional organizations. They became close friends. Their wives became close, too. They were pregnant with their first children at the same time. Long before Alyssa and Michael started going out, Dianna and Michael were an item. They played together regularly when they were five. They were a cute little couple. The parents joked that someday they would get married.

But then, without rancor, the Castors and the Bergmans went their separate ways. The fathers got busy with their work and their homes, and the mothers became pregnant again. The opportunities to get together seemed to vanish. The families were no longer making time for each other. The Castors lived in Newtown, and their three kids went to the Council Rock schools. The Bergmans lived in Fairless Hills and sent their two daughters to the Pennsbury schools. The lives of the two families were unfolding in different parts of Bucks County. The distance was not significant, but it seemed so. They no longer shared the dramas of their daily lives. The Castors barely knew Alyssa. They certainly knew nothing about the smoking episode or her boyfriend with the fake leather jacket or how she had stopped doing her schoolwork for a while. In Newtown, where the Castors lived, the houses were guarded by shiny shrubs. In Fairless Hills, people didn't spend their money on automatic sprinkler systems. They were just trying to keep things going.

The Bergmans, financially, were way ahead of many of their neighbors. They weren't strapped for cash. Nothing like it. They were savers. Frank Bergman had a thriving practice, with many Pennsbury teachers and administrators as patients, Mr. Mahoney among them. Denise Bergman was making $50,000 a year as a veteran nurse, working three twelve-hour shifts per week. They could have bought a home in the Council Rock school district. They could have bought in Newtown or Yardley. But they were happy where they were, close to the school, in a house with no mortgage.

Frank Bergman managed the family finances. For college, he did not go away to school and had made all his own tuition payments. He did not believe in expensive, faraway colleges. He did not believe in the stock market. He despised debt. When the family built a four-bedroom Victorian-inspired vacation home on ten acres in upstate New York, near Lake George, Frank had it paid off within a decade. When he bought himself a brand-new limited-edition 2002 bright-red Camaro for nearly $38,000, it was mostly with cash. When Alyssa decided she *had* to have a Corvette, her father found a gorgeous black '98 model listed for $29,000. Frank offered $28,000. The salesman said that would not get it done. *Fine*, Frank said. He walked out of the showroom, his crying daughter beside him. The guy came running after him. He took Frank Bergman's won't-budge offer.

On their street, people thought the car was a gift from father to daughter. It wasn't. Alyssa contributed $8,500 from selling her first car, a Firebird, which she had bought herself, to her neighbor. She took out $10,000 from her own savings account. (Frank Bergman had taught his daughters about the joys of compounding interest at a very young age.) She borrowed the rest. The only thing her father did was cosign the loan. She knew she would have to work two jobs to make her car and insurance payments, to pay for gas, repairs, and upkeep. She was willing to do it. That was how good the car made her feel, and that was how much she had bought in to her father's life philosophy: You appreciate only that for which you work. When he took his family on luxurious vacations, cruises especially, Frank had a good time. He figured he had earned the right to relax in style.

A few months after Alyssa broke up with Nick, the Bergmans went on one of their luxurious family cruises. When it was over, they flew back to Philadelphia, tanned and relaxed. At the baggage carousel, Cheryl Castor spotted Denise Bergman, an accidental reunion of long-lost friends. Several weeks later, the families went out for dinner together—Italian, in Trenton—and retired to the Castor home. That night Michael Castor took Alyssa to the basement and taught her how to shoot pool. He was no Nick. He was tall, slender, a starter on the Council Rock basketball team, looking for a college where he could play.

Before long they were inseparable. Some nights Alyssa stayed at the Castors' and some nights Michael stayed at the Bergmans'. Each had his or her own room for the sleepovers, but the parents knew what was going on. The Bergman parents were not worried. They knew their daughter would never be reckless. They liked Michael—so dutiful, so ambitious, so serious. He drove a Camaro. He was careful with his money. He was right out of the Frank Bergman mold. Nick was becoming a memory.

By the fall of 2002—when a band of junior boys started tracking Alyssa, when her Corvette became the most famous car in the student lot, when she was voted homecoming queen—Michael Castor was trying to figure out what to do next. He was twenty. He had completed two years at Bucks County Community, where he had been on the basketball team. He was living at home. His hair was thinning. He was working at Romano's Macaroni Grill, a chain restaurant near the Oxford Valley Mall. And his hot girlfriend was going to the pathetic Pennsbury junior dinner dance with some dweeby guy.

"You could have checked with me first," he said.

She knew he had a point. But Bucci had caught her by surprise with his attention, and she had said yes on the spot. Michael and Alyssa were a traditional boyfriend and girlfriend. There wasn't much of that.

"It's nothing," Alyssa said.

"Nothing—well, I'm gonna be there when he comes by."

Alyssa thought that was cute.

V.

There was a new football coach. Pennsbury had hired him without so much as a call to the quarterback, Bobby Speer, or his surrogate father, Kirk Safee. Kirk was not happy. A new coach meant a new playbook and a new philosophy, right at the start of Bobby's senior year. If Bobby had any chance for a full ride to a Division I school, he needed to have a spectacular senior season. He needed to be calling plays from the line of scrimmage and throwing perfect bombs when his first three options vanished. He needed to take hits and pop right up again. The recruiters had to see it, live or on tape. There had to be moral victories, close games against the superior teams of the Suburban One League, and the systematic decimation of inferior teams. And now there was a brand-new bull-necked coach, Galen Snyder.

Coach Snyder had played on the undefeated '85 Falcon team during a time when Pennsbury was grittier, when there were still sons of factory workers on the team. Those kids were coarse. They were natural linebackers who enjoyed hitting. They were natural fullbacks, human bulldozers. Snyder wanted to return Pennsbury to that kind of team, a team that didn't need a quarterback with a spectacular arm to succeed. He wanted a team that *hit*.

Bobby, Kirk would tell recruiters and sportswriters and other parents, was a quarterback out of the modern NFL West Coast offense model, a quarterback who made things happen by putting the ball in the air. The thing about Bobby, Kirk told his audiences, was his quick release. Look at him, Kirk would say, a videotape running, about to get to the good part. He was so proud of Bobby, so eager to see him get the attention and opportunity he deserved.

That's him there, number 1. Watch him, just watch him. What's he gonna do? Watch this. BAM! See him fire that pass over the middle? Did you see that? Did you see that quick release? Receiver didn't even see the ball coming at him. You're not gonna have that problem at the college level. The new coach here, he plays the game on the ground. How can you get a passing rhythm going when you're throwing ten times a game?

It was a nervous time in the Speer-Safee home. The season was played over ten consecutive weeks in September, October, and November (plus play-off games, if the team went that far). Those ten games, Kirk proclaimed, would dictate Bobby's college career and his life after.

The recruiters and the local sportswriters knew what Bobby Speer was: a short (six even), slow, immobile high school quarterback who had two qualities that might let him play football at a small college: an above-average arm and an unusually resilient body and personality. You didn't see that much anymore, not in the suburbs. Bobby could get whacked from two sides and still not go down. He would get trampled by a pack and hop right up. Playing in pain was no problem for him. When recruiters and sportswriters talked to him, he had little to say. He was the opposite of Kirk. He explained nothing.

They didn't know how Bobby carried his handicapped brother, Danny, to bed each night. Or the pressure he felt to be Danny's hero. They didn't know that Kirk was not his actual father. They didn't know the void Bobby felt, not knowing if his biological father was behind bars or inhaling drugs or what.

School was a joy for Bobby, an escape. There were teachers at Pennsbury who knew how well Bobby could do if you just gave him a system. There were girls at school, lots of them, who fawned over Bobby. When he walked down the Pennsbury hallways in his varsity jacket, he knew people were looking at him. He was Bobby Speer. He was, in Pennsbury vernacular meant as high praise, not gay. He knew there were girls waiting for him to break up with Lauren. Once, at a football game, a girl held up a sign that read I WANT TO HAVE SEX WITH BOBBY SPEER. He could not be tempted. He didn't go to Brew Crew parties. He didn't go to the parties where there was drinking, smoking, strip poker, wild times.

Nobody knew why.

VI.

The girl with the sign, she was a good friend of Bobby's. Lauren's, too. The sign was a joke, that's what Bobby figured. The sign girl was a jock, a tomboy, thin and exuberant. She bled orange and black, the school colors. She was friends with a lot of the Pennsbury athletes, both boys and girls.

One night, when they were both sophomores, the girl was at Rob Stephens's house. This was before Stephanie became pregnant with Rob's baby. But it was after Karen Speer had ordered Bobby to end his friendship with Rob. (Bobby's mother had long thought Rob was heading down a reckless road. She assumed that Bobby, so quiet and obedient, had followed her instructions. He had not.)

Rob and the girl were on a sofa watching TV, just the two of them. Intimate overtures turned into an argument. The girl left the house screaming that her older brother would be returning to kick Rob's ass.

Rob, anticipating a violent confrontation, called the police, who took his statement and later the girl's. The incident spiraled from there. Rob was charged with assault, and his case was adjudicated in a juvenile court. Rob spent everything he had on legal fees. He was placed on probation and ordered to attend group-therapy sessions, once a week for several months. Rob described the meetings as a complete waste of time.

To his former teammates, there were now three strikes on Rob. First he quit wrestling and football. Then he had a murky episode with a girl beloved by Pennsbury athletes. The third strike was becoming a teenage father. He was no longer one of them, not in any sense. They froze him out.

Only the most important athlete of them all, Bobby Speer, ignored the ban on Rob Stephens. Rob had once been Bobby's center, the player who snapped the football to him on every down. Bobby had known Rob all his life. What if their stations in life were reversed? Bobby was not a churchgoer, but he lived his life by two biblical injunctions: *Do unto others as you would have them do unto you*; and *Judge not, lest ye be judged*.

Early in the school year, Rob bumped into Bobby in a hallway. They hadn't seen each other over the summer.

"You heard about me and Steph?" Rob asked.

"Yeah," Bobby said. He didn't know what to say next. Bobby knew it was traditional to congratulate an expecting father, but that didn't seem like the right thing to do.

"I'm gonna be a father."

"You ready for this?"

"No."

"You'll be all right," the quarterback said assuredly. He was a leader of boys. They were both seventeen. "When that baby comes, I want to see it, okay?"

VII.

The word spread from one faculty room to another. Mr. Cunningham, father of the Pennsbury prom and one of the best-paid teachers in the district, one of the few teachers making over $90,000 a year, was retiring. He was making no secret of it. He was counting down the days until his final day, except he didn't know when that would be. He knew he could not wait until the end of the school year. More than once, he had visited Mr. Katz's office, trying to work out the complicated union accounting of vacation, sick, and personal time owed him. He wanted out, the sooner the better.

Mr. Katz knew it made no sense to have Mr. Cunningham teach a day longer than he wished. He treated his teachers as adults, until they gave him reason not to. A couple of years earlier, Mr. Cunningham had come to Mr. Katz and said he needed to take a nine-week leave of absence for personal reasons. They went into it just enough so that Mr. Katz could understand the underlying issue, and no further. Mr. Katz did not consult with the administrators above him, the assistant principals below him, the officials from the teachers' union. He simply gave the veteran teacher the time off, with pay. And now Mr. Cunningham was telling him he had to get out.

Mr. Katz understood why. They were the same age. They had both seen the profession change. Mr. Katz thought most of the changes had improved education. Mr. Cunningham did not.

Mr. Cunningham believed the teacher should be an authority figure. That was how he ran his house, how he ran his classroom, how he ran his diving team in his years as coach, how he ran his proms. When his son, Matt, was overall Prom Committee co-chair in '95, he had come upon his father counting the votes for prom theme. Mr. Cunningham didn't decide on the theme the way his successor had, as an open process. He guarded the procedure closely, because if the vote came out in a way he didn't like—for a prom theme he could not decorate—a recount might show that another theme had actually won. Ancient Egypt and the Nile always sounded so enchanting, but Mr. Cunningham knew all that brown made for a dull lobby, and your lobby presentation was critical to the success of your night.

"Dad," Matt said urgently, seeing the tidy ballot piles on his father's desk, "as your overall co-chair, I need to know what won."

The father continued to distribute the ballots. He was not a man easily interrupted. "Matt," he said, "as prom faculty adviser, I'm telling you, you'll find out when I want you to find out."

He was that way in all things.

He believed the ever-growing list of rules for teachers existed to keep the inept in line. Mr. Cunningham found particularly galling a district mandate that required calls from parents to be returned within forty-eight hours.

"How dare they tell me when I have to return a call," he said. "Never in my life have I ever taken more than *twenty-four* hours to return a call. If you're doing the job right, you're calling them way before they're calling you, anyway."

It made him want to get out.

He hated electronic grading. He felt the modern teacher had been turned into a self-esteem counselor, that the modern teacher's role was to make the student feel good about himself. If the student couldn't spell or use proper grammar, that really didn't matter.

He felt teaching had become less personal. From the 1970s right through the mid-1980s, there was a social life between teachers and select students. Or there was for Mr. Cunningham. "You'd see the kids on a Saturday night, but come Monday morning it was all business again," Mr. Cunningham said. "Out of school you got to know students as people." As prom faculty adviser, Mr. Cunningham had been taught the pleasures of cocktail hour by his chairs and their parents. In college, he was known as One-Can Cunningham. As prom adviser, he discovered he liked good Scotch.

The Pennsbury teachers were more fraternal then. On Fridays the social studies teachers would get together after school at a place called Augie's Tavern, smoky and dark and far from the school. They had a rule: Anybody who mentioned Pennsbury had to put a quarter in an ashtray, a contribution toward the next round. Even if you began a sentence with "I have a kid who is such a moron," you pulled out your change.

In the late 1980s, when the last factories closed and the Yardley and Newtown kids became more prominent at Pennsbury, the student-teacher relationship became carefully monitored, tighter and stricter. A wall was put up between school life and home life. There were many more after-school faculty meetings, and the teachers lost their desire to get together out of school. Teachers, Mr. Cunningham felt, now taught by a checklist.

"Years ago, if a kid was being obnoxious and disruptive, I'd flick his ear," Mr. Cunningham said. "Kid might wheel around and say, 'You son of a bitch!' And I'd say, 'Don't you *ever* talk about my mother that way.' You'd defuse the situation. Right now I've got a terribly obnoxious kid in one of my classes. I want to deck him every time I see him. All you can do is bite your hand. The way the courts are now, one swing and you could lose everything." So he was getting out, the sooner the better.

His greatest memories of his thirty-three teaching years were from the prom. Not just the old ones but the recent ones: when Matt came through in '95; when his daughter, Tracy, came through four years later. The prom had always been a labor of love for Mr. Cunningham. At his peak, he earned $1,500 for his role as prom adviser. In his final year, with Tracy as his overall Prom Committee co-chair for Paradise Lagoon, he calculated that his pay worked out to $1.37 an hour. He never would have done it for free in the beginning. But by his final years, in the late 1990s, he was working only for the glory, not a paycheck. After Tracy's prom, he turned the reins over to Mr. Mahoney and attended the next three proms as the unpaid, unofficial consultant. Whether he would return again in 2003, whether he would go to a prom as a retired teacher, he hadn't decided.

Out of all his years and all his proms, his fondest moment was watching his daughter come down the steps of the family's home, not far from the school. Tracy had worn a flowing, full-length off-white gown. Her hair was up. She was carrying an orchid-and-lily arrangement her father had made.

Wow, the father thought. *That's my little girl? When did she get so pretty? When did she get so grown up?*

They were words that have been expressed, one way or another, forever: Where did the time go?

Chapter Four

Expecting

November

I.

From the principal on down, Pennsbury was dominated by men. It had always been that way.

Mr. Katz set the tone for his school, and his view of the world was distinctly male: two divorces, two boys, weekends watching football and basketball. Many of the prominent jobs at his school were filled by men. The athletic director was a man with a doctorate. The coach of the girls' softball team—the most successful team in the Pennsbury sports program—was a man. Rich Lefferts had been the yearbook adviser forever. The director of the superb Pennsbury marching band had always been a man. Most department heads were men.

The career Pennsbury teachers were nearly all male, Jim Cunningham, the former prom adviser, and Al Wilson, the PHS-TV producer, most prominent among them. Steve Medoff, an English teacher and the forensics team adviser, was so entrenched at Pennsbury that he had a classroom with windows.

The teachers whom the kids talked about were usually men. Frank Sciolla, an English teacher and the boys' basketball coach, had reached a sizable but mostly ignored segment of the school population, the rappers, by organizing an occasional after-school freestyle rap competition called Sciolla's Old-School Supa-Flo. There were kids who attended Pennsbury in a zombie state but sang Mr. Sciolla's praises. Among them was Shawn Ledger, a white kid from Levittown who did very little schoolwork but had a nimble mind for rhymes. He thought Mr. Sciolla was all right. About the only other teacher he acknowledged was Miss Snyder. The in-school suspension detention center was Ledger's home base. Miss Snyder had been the first woman assigned to run ISS.

Many positions—the chairman of the science department, for instance—were men's jobs when Mr. Katz was a student at Pennsbury, and continued to be. There was nothing in the culture of the school that suggested change would be coming soon. There were female jobs, but they tended to be less glamorous and less visible. The librarians were all women, as they had always been at Pennsbury. The secretaries were all women, too. As were the cafeteria ladies, who were called exactly that. The nurses, the teachers' aides, the hall monitors—all women. The guidance department, regarded as inept by many of the kids I talked to, was run by women.

There were many female teachers at Pennsbury, but in general, they were young and hadn't made a mark on the school. Lynn Blakesley, who taught family education, was beloved by her students—the pregnant ones in particular—but her sphere of influence was small. Many of the female teachers had their noses buried earnestly in their lesson plans. Among the few veteran women teachers was Debbie Weston, a German teacher who helped with the prom. Teachers and students alike called her Frau Weston with affection. She'd joke about whom she'd have to shake down to get herself a room with a view. She had a good sense of humor, and it served her well. It made her seem like one of the boys.

Mr. Katz was grateful to the teachers who could endure the degrading bureaucratic requirements of their profession with humor. Mr. Mahoney, the prom faculty co-adviser, objected to the form that teachers were required to fill out when they wanted to take a personal day. Under the terms of their union-negotiated contract, Pennsbury teachers were entitled to three paid personal days a year. (Under that same contract, starting teachers made $36,000 a year; teachers with a decade of experience and a master's degree made $59,000 a year; and a few teachers, with thirty or more years of experience, made over $90,000 a year.) On the form, teachers had to complete a sentence that began, *I request to use this personal day to.* Then there were two blank lines. Mr. Mahoney believed if you were taking a personal day, then the reason you were taking the day was personal and should not have to be announced on a form. When he first encountered the form, he filled it out this way: *I request to use this personal day to* "find the meaning of life and get in touch with my inner self."

In the approval box, Mr. Katz wrote, "I doubt this can be accomplished in one day but give it a try." The white copy went to a file, the yellow to Mr. Mahoney. It pleased Mr. Katz to realize that being prom adviser, a time-consuming and sometimes stressful job, had not robbed Mr. Mahoney of his humor.

Mr. Katz's own job consumed an unhealthy amount of time, which had contributed to his two divorces. He was often the first person at school in the morning. He began the day by removing the surveillance tapes from the cameras that served as the school's night watchmen. His evenings were filled with school-board and PTO meetings, football games, concert recitals, and school plays. Every year he found his way to the school's fall drama and the spring musical. The autumn play in 2002 was Thornton Wilder's *Our Town.* For a couple of evenings, a group of kids from the suburban sprawl of greater Levittown served as the villagers of Grover's Corners, New Hampshire.

During the performance, a student actor planted in the audience asked Editor Webb, "Do you have much drinking in Grover's Corners?"

There was snickering from some of the student theatergoers. The play was hitting close to home, as it had for generations.

"Well, ma'am," the country editor responded, "I wouldn't know what you call *much.*"

Mr. Katz had once been in high school. He knew why the students were laughing. He also knew the other side of the joke. He spent many hours worrying about the drinking habits of Pennsbury kids. He took every precaution he could think of. At the Pennsbury prom, if there was any hint that a kid had been drinking beforehand, he or she was driven directly home. Once the kids entered the building for the night, they

could not go back to their cars. This was done to block the old custom
of loading up on liquor stashed under front seats. Mr. Katz would knock
on wood whenever he said that Pennsbury had never had a fatality related to prom-night drinking. He could control prom night to some
degree. The rest of the year, he knew, he could not. He wanted Pennsbury
to be a school where kids understood how lethal the combination of cars
and alcohol could be. He wanted Pennsbury to be different. But he knew
it was a school like any other.

Whenever the phone rang at odd hours, he worried that it was one
of his kids: one of his two sons at college in Boston, or one of the fifteen
hundred kids under his watch at school. He was Pennsbury's mayor,
police chief, and patriarch.

II.

Mr. Mahoney was always on the prowl for capable juniors. If your Prom
Committee consisted of no one but seniors, you were doomed the following year. It took more than a year to understand the intricacies of
staging the Pennsbury prom. In the first marking period, as the juniors
made their way into the building for eleventh- and twelfth-graders, the
two prom advisers listened for newly prominent names. One name was
coming up daily: Bob Costa. Costa was everywhere. Mr. Mahoney first
heard him, a confident voice over the PA system, making morning announcements with Matt Fox. Later, he saw Costa on PHS-TV, reading
play-off baseball scores. He read Costa's stories about high school life in
the *Bucks County Courier Times*. He heard Steve Medoff, the forensics
coach, talk about how Costa read, understood, and enjoyed *The Econo-
mist*, and how it helped him in his extemporaneous-speaking competitions. Mr. Mahoney sent out word that he wanted to meet this
wunderkind. If Costa passed muster and if he was willing to do it, Mr.
Mahoney wanted to put him in charge of the most audacious prom assignment he had ever given: convincing John Mayer, the fledgling pop
star, to play the 2003 Pennsbury prom.

By November, the end of the first marking period, Mayer's single
"No Such Thing" was all over FM radio. The success of the song defied
marketing logic, because its excellence was rooted in superior guitar

playing and clever lyrics, qualities absent in most modern mainstream rock. Costa came to an EOP Prom Committee meeting for a tête-à-tête with Mr. Mahoney. He knew John Mayer, his new musical hero, was on the agenda.

"I don't know if you've heard, Bob, but we're trying to get John Mayer to play the prom," Mr. Mahoney said.

Costa nodded and said nothing.

"We've written him a letter."

Costa continued to nod. He knew about the letter, too.

"But that was three weeks ago, and we still haven't heard back from him."

Costa pursed his lips and cocked his head in sympathy, but he knew three weeks was nothing.

"He seems to have several different agents, and we don't know who's in charge of what, but I wondered if you'd be interested in following up with him."

"That sounds good."

Mr. Mahoney looked pleased. Costa took over.

"Could I have a copy of the letter?"

Mr. Mahoney produced the letter for Costa, who read it.

"Good letter," he said. "You know what I could do, if you think this is a good idea?"

He was unusually sophisticated. In a brief conversation, he had already shown mastery of two grown-up dictums: Don't share everything you know; let your superiors feel superior.

"I could try to give the letter to Mayer myself," Costa said. Now who was being audacious? "He has a concert coming up at Temple." Costa was referring to the Philadelphia university from which many of the Pennsbury faculty members had received their graduate degrees. "I'm reviewing it for the *Courier Times*. I don't know if this will happen, but if I meet him, maybe I could just give him the letter."

Costa had recently turned seventeen. He had down a third art, too, one few adults master: Never promise more than you can deliver.

Mr. Mahoney was impressed. Right under his nose was a kid who would hand-deliver the Prom Committee's letter directly to John Mayer himself. Or at least try.

III.

As the date approached, the junior dinner dance was rising in importance. The kids—the juniors, anyway—were calling it the junior prom. Bob Costa, president of the junior class, managed to get a date for it. His classmate Mike Kosmin didn't even try. He figured he (and his beloved Acura) would be ready by May of his senior year for the prom, but no formal dances for him yet. Dan Bucci, of course, was going. Everybody knew Bucci was going, including, eventually, his father. Before he left his house on the night of the dance, Bucci told his father that his date was the homecoming queen, that he was taking a knockout senior to his junior dance. His father was pleased. "Good job," he said.

Bucci's mother drove him to the Bergmans' house in Fairless Hills. Alyssa's boyfriend, it turned out, was not there to inspect her date for the night. When Alyssa emerged from a room, Bucci was thunderstruck. She was wearing a black dress, cut low in the back, with a scoop neck and spaghetti straps. He had never seen anybody so beautiful, not in real life. He had tried to dress like a celebrity, in a black suit with a dark blue shirt, but he wasn't feeling like a star. He felt like an accessory. Mike Hug, the Bergmans' shutterbug neighbor, came over to take pictures. He encouraged Bucci to pose with his arm around Alyssa's shoulder. Bucci could feel the smile plastered on his face, frozen with nervousness. He wondered if his face could get stuck that way. His arm felt like a tree limb, it was so stiff. The rest of his body was shaking like the last November leaf.

When they arrived at King's Caterers in Bristol, near the school, Bucci's mouth was still dry. Alyssa was easy to talk to, good on football and cars, but Bucci knew he was in over his head. He was at the junior dinner dance with the homecoming queen only because of the happy accident of alphabetical seating. He had received a yes from her before she became a sensation. He was not worthy.

The music was supplied by a DJ, and by the middle of the night, the air above the dance floor was damp with perspiration. A long, narrow serving table was placed on the floor. Late in the night, Bucci wandered off and returned to find Alyssa on the table, dancing seductively first with one boy, then two. She was, in the term for it at Pennsbury and elsewhere, *grinding,* a dance maneuver in which a dancer, usually female, shakes her posterior in the general direction of her partner's pelvic area, with her hands in the air or on her knees. The partner, typically, makes a thrusting motion. In other words, it's simulated public sex, with clothes on.

It was too much for Bucci. In the second moment of boldness in his life (the first was asking Alyssa to the dance), Bucci jumped up on the platform. The other boys, overwhelmed by Bergman's sexuality and paying deference to Bucci's rightful move, cleared out, and suddenly it was Bucci and Bergman, alphabetical neighbors in Mr. Mahoney's modern media class, grinding away. There were boys on the floor yelling, "Boo-CHEE, Boo-CHEE, Boo-CHEE."

And then the dancing stopped, and Bucci and Bergman assumed their pre-dance roles. There was a final slow dance, during which Bucci kept a respectable distance. Alyssa drove him home in her Corvette. That was it—the best night of his life. If Costa or anybody asked about it, that's all he'd say, out of respect for Alyssa. She was no longer a cult figure for a little group of junior Pennsbury boys. She was a celebrity, and Bucci had made a vow to himself to show her the appropriate courtesies, which she would appreciate. And she would reciprocate, Bucci hoped, by saying hello to him in the hallways and the cafeteria.

In the next issue of the Pennsbury student newspaper, *The PHS Voice,* the lead news story was about the dinner dance at King's. The mashed potatoes were noted for being unusually good. The dance floor was described as "hot and congested." Bucci knew it to be an uncannily accurate report. He did not say a thing.

IV.

Mike Kosmin was making headway of his own. On weekends, after he'd wash his Acura, he went skateboarding and dirt-biking or did jobs for his stepfather, who paid him generously, in cash. He had his first time-clock job, too, bagging groceries and stocking shelves at a fancy supermarket in Yardley. He didn't want his parents buying things for him all the time. He wanted to carry a wad of cash, as his stepfather did. The jobs at McCaffrey's, a family-owned store in the spiffy Edgewood Village Shopping Center, were coveted. The working conditions were excellent (there was ample time to chat with friends), and the pay started at $7 an hour, with guaranteed raises based on longevity. The manager liked to hire Pennsbury kids. They tended to be hardworking and personable, and there was a nice camaraderie among them. There was a girl at work that Mike had his eye on. He was thinking of asking her out on a real date. He was already playing out the night in his head: picking her up in his shiny car, showing her the car's new sound system (for which he was still saving), taking her to a movie. He was getting close. He was working on his cool.

V.

Stephanie Coyle was discovering what every expecting mother learns, that an embryonic child has a mind of its own, that it arrives in the world when it is good and ready, that the things it does are not always in its own best interests.

The baby was late, but Stephanie continued to drag herself to school. She felt the kids staring at her as she waddled down the halls. It was that time in a pregnancy when all conversations, against the expecting mother's wishes, quickly head to the due date. At school Stephanie was wretchedly hot, because the building was often overheated, even on the coldest days. (Pennsbury girls used the saunalike conditions as an excuse for dressing scantily; they'd leave home in the morning with sweaters and scarves and ditch them in their lockers or stuff them in their backpacks and spend the rest of the day in midwaist T-shirts.) When Stephanie finally made it to a classroom and into a chair, her smooth, snowy skin was often red with exertion, and little wisps of her fine brown hair would fall onto her broad, pleasant forehead.

The kids she passed in the hallway stared at her belly, not in a mean way, but because they were unaccustomed to seeing a girl *that* pregnant still in school. In the weeks before their due dates, the pregnant girls were usually well into homeschooling. A private tutor, paid by the district, would come by their homes daily in the mostly futile hope of helping the girls keep up with their classes. Stephanie was intent on staying in school as long as possible, getting back to school after delivery as quickly as possible, and not quitting school, as so many teenage mothers did.

She was smart. Her written English was excellent (she had to tone herself down when she wrote papers for her boyfriend, Rob). She took honors history and honors math. Getting pregnant in high school meant she would not be going away to college. That dream had died with the baby's conception. She knew she would need the baby-sitting services her family and Rob's family could provide. She replaced lofty collegiate dreams with a more pedestrian hope: to go part-time to Bucks County Community. But first she needed a high school diploma. She was determined to get it right on time, as Rob's mother had managed to do. At Pennsbury, as elsewhere, attendance was a critical element in getting a diploma. So she kept showing up.

One fall day, during Mrs. Blakesley's teen-parenting EOP meeting, Rob surreptitiously stuck seventeen skinny birthday candles in a cake and lit them. Mrs. Blakesley turned out the lights, and the whole class, five teenagers in various states of pregnancy plus one boyfriend, sang "Happy Birthday" to Stephanie. One candle for each year of her life, without an extra for good luck. Stephanie sat on a small plastic school chair, her face, flush with pregnancy, glowing in the reflection of the candlelight.

"People say to you, 'Was it a mistake?'" Stephanie said. "They have no idea. You get so mad." She didn't have to explain herself, not in Mrs. Blakesley's room. *Of course* getting pregnant had not been intentional. If the kids wanted to ask her something profound, they could have asked about her decision to *have* the baby. But nobody did.

Rob sat behind his girlfriend, rubbing her back. He was wearing boots, jeans, and a T-shirt. Stephanie regarded this as a huge wardrobe improvement for Rob. Before she was an expecting mother, Rob's uniform by day was sweatpants and a hooded sweatshirt, about what he wore when he climbed into bed at night.

When he and Stephanie shared a bed now, it was just to nap or be together, but they were closer than ever, even if they did argue often and over tiny things. (Who has better french fries, McDonald's or Burger

King?) Their arguments would sometimes end with Stephanie saying, "Could you grow up? You're going to be a father soon." It was a line that left Rob red and silent, but he never felt tempted to pack it all in. He felt responsibility to his unborn child, and love for the unborn child's mother.

Like a lot of husbands (even though he was not one), Rob found he could not tell his better half everything. He wanted to give the appearance that things were under control. Stephanie did not know that Rob's job at Babies "R" Us was in jeopardy (he was calling in "sick" too often). She didn't know he was thinking about taking a job selling Kirby vacuum cleaners. Rob knew that at $1,700 each, they would be a tough sale. But he was enticed by the salesman's commission, $225 per vacuum, with a free one after four sales. He could imagine Stephanie's shocked and happy face when he triumphantly marched through the door with one.

They were debating baby names, first, middle, and last. In the final category, they eventually settled on Coyle-Stephens. If Rob and Stephanie ever got officially married—nobody in either family was putting pressure on them—they would drop the hyphen. Until then, the baby would have the most British-sounding surname in all of Levittown: Coyle-Stephens. That is, if the baby ever came.

Then, the week before Thanksgiving, Stephanie finally went into labor. There were complications. She had done everything by the book, but there were problems.

VI.

Bob Costa found himself enjoying a sudden popularity, although he was sometimes dubious about its roots. Word was out across the school that Costa had two press passes for the John Mayer concert. A dozen or more kids made unvarnished pleas to be his assistant for the night. Bob needed a senior who drove (as he did not), ideally a girl who could potentially blossom into a prom date in a half-year's time. Blair Maloney, far less directly than the others, let Bob know she would be willing to go with him. She met all the criteria. Bob asked her, and she said yes. His junior year was coming together.

VII.

Lisa Stephens, mother of the expecting father, was thirty-four years old and anxious. She understood better than anybody what Stephanie was going through. She, too, had been a junior at Pennsbury when she went into the delivery room, seventeen years earlier.

She was a Levittowner. She had grown up in the Elderberry section, on Ember Street, in a quiet house. Her mother had been in a wheel-chair since the age of seven, when a spinal injury from a fall left her paralyzed from the waist down. Lisa's father had polio as a child and could walk only with crutches. They were able to have children, but their impairments defined them. Lisa grew up embarrassed by the apparati of their lives. It was a time, in Lisa Stephens's memory, when people with handicaps did not live in the mainstream, not in Levittown.

She had known Harry Stymiest, Rob's classmate with cerebral palsy, since Harry and Rob were in kindergarten together. She knew Bobby Speer's kid brother with spina bifida, Danny. There was nobody like Harry or Danny around when Lisa Wynn was growing up: children with obvious differences, but still in the mix of everyday life.

Lisa's parents were stigmatized, even though they had gone to college, even though her father was a member of the workaday world, with a job in the accounting department of the New Jersey Board of Education, in Trenton. But her family was not part of Elderberry's social life. Lisa did not invite friends to her house. Her parents wanted things quiet and tidy. They *needed* things that way.

When Lisa reached high school, she started to rebel against the quiet and the rules. She stayed out late. She drank. She hung out with five or six Levittown boys a year or two older than she. She made herself available. The attention she received for that was intoxicating.

Spliff was the one she liked best. He lived in the Lakeside section, on Linden Lane. As a senior at Pennsbury, Robert James Stephens, Jr., was short, wiry, working on a mustache. He had a leather jacket and excelled at Pac Man, the video game. His sport was Hacky Sack. He and his buddies would stand in a circle for an hour or more, kicking a little sack filled with sand, listening to Rush and Pink Floyd. It was the mid-1980s.

Lisa thought she was in love. She never deluded herself about his attitude toward her: She was good-looking and willing.

One day Lisa's mother said to her, "You look pregnant." Lisa took a test. She was. She was barely seventeen. She was pleased. She knew she'd have the baby. There was no question who the father was.

She went to find Spliff. He was playing Hacky Sack at a Levittown elementary school named for Walt Disney. She pulled him aside. "I'm pregnant."

He took in the news and asked, "What are we going to do now?"

"We'll figure it out."

He returned to his game, she returned home. The baby—Robert James Stephens III—was born on May 5, 1985. While the rest of the school was preparing for the prom, Lisa was preparing formula. By September she was back at Pennsbury for her senior year. Seventeen years later, that infant was about to become a father himself.

Spliff had graduated from Pennsbury on time; a year later, Lisa graduated, and two years after that, they got married. In two more years, they had another child. There were years when their marriage was less than a joyride, but they kept at it. The father gave up pot and cigarettes and Hacky Sack until all there was left was beer. His work, building loading docks, paid $17 an hour and he worked sixty hours a week when he could get it. Lisa managed the Learning World section at the Babies "R" Us near the Oxford Valley Mall, thirty-seven hours a week at $13 an hour. Together, in good years, they earned $60,000. It went quickly. There were weeks when they worked opposite schedules and barely saw each other. As one waited up for the other, the TV was always on, filling the room with voices and light.

Lisa saw her son as she once saw herself, a person who needed attention. For a while Rob got it from sports. Then from girls (his mother gave him condoms). Then from Stephanie (his mother made them sit outside, forestalling the inevitable). Most recently, he got his attention fix from being the boy who stood by his pregnant girlfriend, the only expecting father to show up at Mrs. Blakesley's teen-parenting EOP class. Now the attention was about to shift. Rob knew the baby was supposed to become the center of his world, but all he really wanted to do was play his Madden Football video game.

"Rob lives in a fantasy world," Lisa Stephens said. "He has no idea what is coming."

And then the baby came.

VIII.

Mr. Wilson, more than any other teacher, heard things quickly, and it wasn't because he had a daughter who was a junior at Pennsbury. She told him nothing. It was because the kids felt comfortable talking in front of him.

"So let me see if I have this straight," he said to Bob Costa one day. "You're taking Blair Maloncy to the John Mayer concert, but it's not a date, because you're on assignment for the *Courier Times?*"

"That's right."

"And even though it's your gig, she's driving."

"Right."

"And you're not driving because—"

"I don't have a license."

"You don't have a license. And you don't have a license because you're, what, Amish?"

In fact, Costa, trying to read too much into the questions, had failed the written portion of the frighteningly easy Pennsylvania test for a learner's permit. His failure embarrassed him, but he turned it into an effective joke. He knew being certified a failure by a state bureaucracy could only help his hallway credibility.

On the night of the concert, Blair and Bob left hours early, worried about parking and traffic. With Mayer's hit on the radio, suddenly even parents knew who he was. The night he had played for the Pennsbury crowd and a few hundred others at the little club on Philadelphia's South Street, that might as well have been in an earlier life for Mayer. Ten thousand were coming this night, gathering at the major performing arts center at Temple University, in the heart of North Philadelphia. On the way there in the Maloney family's Jeep Cherokee, Blair and Bob talked about Mr. Wilson, PHS-TV, Eagles football, her brother at Cornell, and her applications to Brown and Penn State. They listened to John Mayer and Dave Matthews and CDs mixed by Blair. Bob made most of the effort. The truth was that even though Blair had known Bob for years, and their parents knew each other, she didn't particularly like him. Blair felt that Bob was one of those juniors who acted like a senior, who didn't know his place. *God*, Blair thought, *I hope he doesn't think this is a date*.

Bob had no such illusions. Anyway, he was worried about other things that night, like whether he had the Prom Committee letter for Mayer and whether their press passes would get them backstage. He patted his front left pocket. He had the letter. When the young woman at the will-call window asked Bob for his driver's license, he produced the only thing he had, his Pennsbury ID card. The woman looked at Bob dubiously, but she slid the passes under the glass anyhow, and he and Blair were in. Bob inspected the passes and realized they would not get them backstage, but he did not panic. Bob was fast on his feet, the feet that had plagued him so as a child.

The warm-up act, a Los Angeles band called Maroon 5, came on. Bob had never heard of them. The young man sitting next to Bob asked how he liked the band. Bob gave an enthusiastic response. The man introduced himself. He was Ben Berkman, manager of Maroon 5. Costa introduced himself: Bob Costa, music writer, *Bucks Country Courier Times*. He introduced his colleague, Blair Maloney. He was there, he said, to write up John Mayer—and Maroon 5. He said he'd love to get some quotes from the guys in Maroon 5. Berkman, naturally, was all for it. He got Bob and Blair backstage. The Maroon 5 fivesome was there. And so was John Mayer. Bob had done it again. He had talked his way in.

Mayer was hanging out with his people and eating potato chips. A. J. Feeley, a backup quarterback for the Eagles, was there, too. To Blair, Feeley was a god, young and unshaven and unmarried, someone who occupied the same lofty terrain as Mayer. She struggled to breathe. Costa was focused on his assignment. He approached Mayer and said, "I enjoyed your show." He stated his purpose, got off a few genial questions, and then, realizing that his time with the guitarist would be brief, blurted out, "I go to Pennsbury High. We'd love for you to play our prom. Here's a letter about it."

Mayer took the letter from Bob. *He took the letter*. He didn't laugh or make a face or anything. He shook Bob's hand and said, "So that's where all the lawsuits are coming from."

Bob had no idea what that meant, but, like any good reporter, he wrote it down in his notebook so he could sort it out later.

In his first-person review for the *Courier Times*, Costa described Mayer's faded jeans, his "slightly hunched shoulders," his black T-shirt embroidered with the words *Macho Man*. He wrote that Mayer had a "humble persona."

Costa, feeling like the schoolboy music critic in the movie *Almost Famous*, concluded his review with these thoughts:

"As his album *Room for Squares* continues to skyrocket in sales and popularity, John Mayer remains the same. Mayer is a musician who has gone through the trials and tribulations of playing clubs and gradually worked his way out of the Atlanta club scene by building a loyal fan base. His concert was a fantastic experience and from my first-row seat I could see by his facial expressions that he was enjoying himself right along with the audience."

When the review ran, with an equally effusive sidebar about Maroon 5, Costa read his copy carefully, picking up on the newspaper's style for the use of commas, when to spell out numbers, how to use abbreviations. As he reread his Mayer review, he realized there was one false note in the piece. Mayer did not have a "humble persona." He was something, but it wasn't humble.

Still, it had been a hugely successful night. Mayer had taken the letter from him, and there was every reason to think he'd read it and this time respond to it.

Blair would not admit that Bob's handling of the night was impressive, except to say it was *unBoblike*. Nothing more.

IX.

By November, Harry Stymiest, the PHS-TV stalwart, was already deep into his planning for the prom. He remained determined to get the DeLorean from *Back to the Future* for the night. After an extensive search of the Internet—other kids spoke of getting *Googled-out*, but Harry's computer virility was boundless—Harry found a specialty car shop in Myrtle Beach that had just about what he was looking for. It was not the car from the movie but its body double. The fee to rent it for one night was $2,000. It came with a driver and included transport from South Carolina. A good deal, Harry thought, even if it was $1,900 beyond his car budget. Harry saw not an obstacle but an opportunity (and this revealed his underlying approach to life). He sought out Mr. Minton and Mr. Mahoney, the prom faculty advisers, to share the pictures and his newest big idea.

The prom theme is Hollywood, right? This is the car from a movie every kid at Pennsbury has seen. We could have the Prom Committee pay the $2,000 rental fee for the car, but earn it back, and a lot more, by making it available for pictures. For $5, a prom couple could pose in an exact-model replica of the DeLorean from the movie!

The two teachers knew it did not matter what they said. They knew they'd be hearing from him again. Harry was an unstoppable force at Pennsbury. Every teacher at Pennsbury knew that.

Harry could not participate in ordinary gym class. Instead, he attended a special class for kids with disabilities, but nothing really was accomplished in it. With his poor eating habits and limited exercise, Harry was at least forty pounds overweight. His case was not unusual. Weight control was a widespread problem among Pennsbury students, but the school paid little attention to it. Bowling was offered as a gym class, the vending machines offered twenty-ounce bottles of soda, and supersized candy bars were sold by kids in hallway fundraisers. Harry made no apology for how he ate. He felt it was part of his character.

He didn't apologize for any of his enthusiasms. He would talk with particular relish about his goal of becoming an Eagle Scout: something achieved, he would tell the kids in school, by only 4 percent of all Boy Scouts. Harry's interests—church, electronics, Scouts—were not things most Pennsbury kids had a stake in. Still, his classmates were nice to him. Seeking to find common ground, a girl once recalled for Harry how old she was when she quit Brownies.

Sometimes PHS-TV kids would ask him technical questions, but they generally found the answers unintelligible. The only person in the entire school who really got Harry technologically was a certain English teacher. Harry would seek him out in the hallway, and the two would talk in their private language, oblivious to the world passing by in the between-periods human tide.

Harry's acceptance in school was widespread in part because he had been in the district all his life. The kids were used to him. They had grown up with more understanding of the dissimilar than their parents had. If tolerance did not come naturally to a kid, it was foisted upon him by classmates. There seemed to be a contest among Pennsbury students to see who could show the most kindness to Harry. Even Lindsey Milroy took part. One day the Prom Committee co-chair said, apropos of nothing, "I just love that Harry so much. He's the best." Of course it was patronizing. But it beat the alternative.

The most significant reason Harry was so broadly welcomed was because he did not see himself as a victim. He didn't really see himself at all. One day in his senior year, Harry and his mother, Linda, were meeting with an academic adviser at Bucks County Community, where Harry was planning to enroll after he graduated from Pennsbury. Bucks had a program in video production, Harry's chosen field. After two years at Bucks, the plan was for Harry to go to Temple. From there, he planned to begin a career that would have him soon working—according to a pre-résumé being written by a devoted relative—as Steven Spielberg's film editor. There was no shortage of people with faith in Harry.

At the meeting the academic adviser at Bucks had said, "We have a lot of disability services here that you should make yourself familiar with." While driving home, Harry asked his mother, "Did you write down anywhere that I was disabled?" There were names for the conditions that afflicted Harry. The kids at Pennsbury didn't know or care about them. Harry's parents knew them well.

"No," Harry's mother said. She was a receptionist in a New Jersey medical practice and was knowledgeable about medical things.

"Then how could he know?"

"Oh, Harry," she said. "He could just tell."

Harry, an only child, lived with his mother and father—Linda and Harry Stymiest, Sr.—in a vast trailer park, Pennwood Crossing, near Levittown. The family's trailer was a double-wide with two small, low-ceilinged bedrooms and a third for the computer. Harry's mother often burned scented apple-cinnamon candles in the house, which was cozy and fragrant, but cramped. The family owned their trailer outright, but they rented the small lot it was on for $500 a month. Electricity and oil cost another $250 per month.

Harry's parents grew up in framed houses, not modular homes, but as adults, they were afraid of overextending themselves financially, so they stayed put.

"We never thought we'd live in a trailer all these years," Harry's mother said. "But you get used to it. With the pool and the community center programs, the Marvelous Mondays and the Terrific Tuesdays and all that, it's like living in *Pleasantville*." Linda Stymiest was referring to the movie and its perfect make-believe town. Harry's life view was from the other side of the camera. Events didn't really exist for him unless he had videotaped them and could replay the scenes and the dialogue over and over and edit the whole thing down to something manageable.

Harry's parents were always adding to a nest egg they had for unexpected medical expenses. One of the driving forces in their lives, even more so after twenty-five years of marriage than on their wedding day, was for one or both of them to have a job that came with full health benefits.

Harry's father, a tall man with a buzz cut like his son's, a drooping mustache, and a kindly manner, had grown up in Levittown, on Cobalt Ridge in the Canoe Birch section. He dropped out of Neshaminy High, a Pennsbury rival, in the tenth grade. Soon after, he was working at U.S. Steel. He was born in 1955 and avoided the draft under the last-surviving son rule. His older brother, Alfred, died while serving in the navy during the Vietnam War. A day from 1972 was part of the family's collective memory: Harry and his buddies were playing football on Cobalt Ridge when two uniformed naval officers showed up at the family home to announce Alfred's death. Thirty years of trying to learn the exact circumstances had produced no conclusive answer. They know it was in a helicopter crash and not much more.

Since the birth of young Harry in 1984, his father had worked a variety of factory jobs. He'd work a job, get laid off when production slowed, and go get another job, making certain it came with health benefits. In recent years, he had been running a printing press. When his son received a congratulatory letter from George W. Bush regarding this or that Scouting achievement, Harry's father could tell whether the signature was handwritten or generated by a machine.

Linda had miscarried three times before Harry came along. He was born with cerebral palsy and scoliosis. Harry had been a regular at Shriners Hospital for Children in Philadelphia all his life, and in the seventh grade, he missed four months of school to have two foot-long rods inserted in an effort to straighten his spine.

From his birth, Linda had accepted that her son was never going to be, in the phrase people sometimes used with her, *like other kids.* Harry's father did not. He had always anticipated having a son who would someday play for the Eagles, or at least aspire to that. Over time—it took years—he came not only to accept Harry's limitations but also to embrace his interests, even when they meant little to him.

They were exceptional parents. Linda Stymiest, who had never been a religious person prior to becoming a mother, found emotional strength and guidance and a dependable community at Emilie United Methodist. Her son had grown up at Emilie. He was a true believer, a phrase mostly unused at Pennsbury, where religion played a muted role in the lives of most kids. Harry Sr. wasn't much for church, either. In Scouts, an organization foreign to him in his own boyhood, he found a place where he and his namesake could meet. The family's shelf of videos in the tight computer room was filled with tapes from one muddy camping trip after another.

The parents were always making an effort to enrich their child's life. The day Linda brought Harry to see *Bozo the Clown* being taped left a mark on both of them. Harry was six, sitting on the floor with all the other kids, except that he had a brace on his left foot. The kids were divided into teams and asked to put their shoes on their hands and lodge a balloon between their knees. Harry's balloon kept shooting out of his jiggling knees, and his team lost by whatever peculiar rules were in place that day. Bozo, intending to be encouraging, kept insisting that Harry could do it, but the exercise required more muscle control than Harry had. Harry's mother remembers the experience negatively: Linda remembers Harry being singled out. Harry's own memory is different. He knew his team lost because he couldn't keep the balloon in place. He also knew it didn't matter.

What thrilled him was seeing, for the first time, what happened on the other side of a TV set, seeing the cameramen on their dollies, zooming in and out on Bozo. A life was born for Harry that day.

It was a literal and concrete life. When Harry read *The Catcher in the Rye* in Mr. Medoff's American literature class, he could not grasp Holden Caulfield. Harry had no use for irony or for anyone, like Holden, who could use *goddam* so casually. That made Harry an enigma to most of his classmates, who had grown up under the canopy of irony. It also made him strangely respected. Harry operated under rules from another era. When a girl in Pennwood Crossing wanted to take her relationship with Harry "to another level," as his mother called it, he got out.

The Stymiests made no attempt to be modern. Linda bumped into Rob Stephens one day. She knew all about Stephanie's pregnancy.

Rob said, "Do you remember when we used to go camping in Cub Scouts?"

"Of course, Robert," Linda said.

"It seems like yesterday."

His childhood was ending fast and he knew it.

"It *was* yesterday, Robert," she said. "Now stay in school!"

When Harry presented Mr. Minton his scheme—no, his idea—to get his DeLorean for the prom paid for by others, Mr. Minton, a robustly direct man, said to him, "What makes you think anybody would pay five bucks for that?"

"You're kidding, right?" Harry responded. "To have your picture taken with the DeLorean from *Back to the Future*? You wouldn't pay five dollars for *that*?"

Chapter Five

Candlelight

December

I.

Luke Joseph Coyle-Stephens arrived three weeks late and at nearly four in the morning. A mother's instinct is close to unerring. When Luke came, Stephanie was drugged, exhausted, shivering, and perspiring, but her brand-new maternal security system was already at work. The baby was born, and Stephanie's first thought was *Why haven't I heard him cry?* Rob cut the umbilical chord and snapped a picture. The mother saw the baby for an instant. And then he was gone.

She heard a doctor or nurse say, "We're taking the baby to intensive care. He's not breathing right." Stephanie's heart raced, and her stomach dropped. She hadn't even held her son. She prepared herself to hear somebody say, "This could be fatal." She thought: *If we lose this baby, it'll kill us both*.

The baby had inhaled amniotic fluid into his lungs. To make matters worse, the fluid was contaminated by a mysterious infection Stephanie had. For five nerve-racking days, doctors worked to regulate the baby's breathing. They did, and the young mother and her baby were sent home to their small, crowded house. It was December. The Christmas tree was up. There were candles on shelves and in the windowsills.

But there was little peace. Luke was not sleeping and was barely eating. One night he began shrieking hysterically.

"Rob, something's wrong," Stephanie said.

"Nothing's wrong."

Summer had extended deep into the school year, fall had lasted about three days, and now the cusp of winter was on hand. Skies were gray and low, day after day. It had already snowed. Rob had planned to spend the day Christmas shopping.

"He's just being a little punk."

"Rob, we're taking the baby to the hospital."

They returned to the hospital where Luke was born. A group of doctors and nurses, unable to mask their worry, ordered a spinal tap for Luke. A long needle was inserted into his tiny body, drawing a sample of spinal fluid to test for meningitis and other diseases, but it came back with what the doctor called a *bloody show*, a blood-clogged result the doctors could not interpret. Stephanie was alarmed. A doctor said, "This baby needs to see a specialist."

An ambulance took Stephanie, Rob, and Luke to St. Christopher's Hospital for Children in Philadelphia to see a pediatric respiratory specialist. The baby was coughing like a chain-smoker. Rob's parents and Stephanie's mother and stepfather and father all came to the hospital. In a scary and tender time, with the baby suffering, stepfather and stepdaughter started talking again. Stephanie and Luke stayed in the hospital for four days, while the vicious virus ran its course. By the time mother and child headed home, more than the baby had been healed.

The birth of Luke was not having the desired effect on Rob's behavior in school. He was markedly inconsistent. He was taking a short-story class with Mr. Mahoney, and there were times when he showed himself to be a capable student, even when the subject matter had nothing to do with his life. One day Mr. Mahoney called on Rob to identify the voice in which an author was writing. There was no reason to think Rob had been paying attention. "Third person, limited omniscient," Rob answered correctly. But more regularly, Rob was acting out in class and calling attention to himself. More than once Mr. Mahoney heard a kid call out, "Wasn't me, Mr. Mi-HOE-nee, sweartagod." The kid was saying, of course, that it wasn't *only* him. The instigator was often Rob, talking, singing, throwing things, goofing off, encouraging those he was sitting with to do the same. Eventually, Mr. Mahoney said he had no choice—no choice!—but to move Rob to the front of the classroom, in a corner, off by himself.

Most school nights Rob would sleep in his house and get up early, go to Stephanie's house, and help with the baby while she got dressed and cleaned her parents' house. Neither Stephanie nor Rob was getting much sleep. A month into it—mostly spent in hospitals and waiting rooms—the young couple was discovering that parenting was way more work than they ever could have guessed. They continued to bicker about things large and small. Stephanie felt Rob's job selling Kirby vacuum cleaners was a waste of time and money. That should have been obvious to him, she felt, based on gas bills alone. But it wasn't. At night Rob would drive his '89 Camaro north to the development homes in Yardley and Newtown to make personal demonstrations of his $1,700 vacuum cleaners. An hour or two or three later, he'd make the deflating drive home, his sales slips untouched. When one of their disagreements settled down, another would begin: whose turn was it to change the diaper, control the remote, take out the garbage. They could quibble about anything.

II.

Lindsey Milroy's house in the Heather Ridge development, in Newtown, was a suburban dreamland. There were sofas and TVs at every turn, an alarm system, a two-car garage with an electric garage-door opener, a landscaped yard. The father of the Prom Committee co-chair, Kevin Milroy, worked in the successful plumbing-supply business he had married into. They were leading the good life, the life money can buy.

Still, cost was the most important factor in choosing Lindsey's college. Her first choice was the University of Vermont. It had outstanding snowboarding, a good field-hockey team and nursing program, and when Lindsey went there to visit a friend, a softball player, she had an *excellent* time. To Lindsey, UVM was a great party school. To her parents, it was $30,000 a year, far more money than they were willing or able to spend. If Lindsey did not get an athletic scholarship to cover at least half the UVM tuition, she wasn't going there.

Lindsey's mother, Mary, exchanged e-mails regularly with the UVM field-hockey coach. For out-of-state students, especially, admission to Vermont was difficult. But the coach seemed certain Lindsey could get in, despite her SAT score, 980, more than 200 points below the average of an incoming freshman. Whether Milroy was in a position to receive scholarship money, the coach could not say. Lindsey clearly wasn't the coach's highest recruiting priority. Lindsey wished she hadn't checked off the box for the school's nursing program on her application. Someone had told her, too late, that serious athletes didn't have time for nursing labs.

Lindsey's type of intelligence didn't show up in standardized testing. But anybody who had spent time with her knew she was insightful. She had an intuitive understanding of social dynamics. One day during lunch, she sat down and drew a social seating chart of the Pennsbury cafeteria. It took her several minutes and was deadly accurate. She marked one table for the "dazed and confused" and two for "football players." She reserved half of one table for "punks" and the other half for "thug hard-asses." She gave a table to "Goth kids," a half-table to "hippies," and a whole table to "dorks." She devoted another table to the "pretty people," which was where she sat and was a term she used with considerable sarcasm. She had her school, and herself, down cold.

The first three months of her senior year had been a disaster. The field-hockey team was mediocre, and so was she. There was something about her heart that wasn't right, and it wasn't just because of Win, although that wasn't helping any. Win—booked to be her prom date way back in September—had broken up with her in October and again in November. "He dumped me for surfing," Lindsey told her friends. It was true. He surfed the beaches of the Jersey Shore daily. But everyone knew there had to be more to it than that.

Mary and Kevin Milroy blamed Win for their daughter's poor field-hockey season. They said she was distracted. But Lindsey was not one to make excuses. She would admit to being pissed at Win. She would not admit to being hurt by him. She was adamant that the breakup had not hung over her field hockey. That sounded right; she wasn't one to let things fester. At the conclusion of one of their many breakup fights in the driveway of her parents' home, Lindsey yelled at Win, "I hope you get an STD!" (All of Pennsbury used that shorthand for *sexually transmitted disease*.) The breakup left a gaping hole in her social life and destroyed her vision for what her senior prom would be. Her friends were making lists of potential prom dates and deciding whether they would have sex on prom weekend. Lindsey was supposed to be all set, those questions already answered. Now they weren't. But all of that had nothing to do with her field hockey. Her parents' theory, she said, was "a bunch of crap."

She blamed her anemic season on burnout. On Sundays, Lindsey made a 140-mile round-trip drive to Hoboken, New Jersey, to play on a club field-hockey team. She took an annual trip to California or Florida to play in field-hockey talent showcases called HockeyFests. "I don't love field hockey," she said. "I'm playing for money." By which she meant a scholarship. A generation earlier, Kevin Milroy had played football at Pennsbury for the same reason. Football got him to tiny William Penn College, in Iowa, and out of Fairless Hills.

Lindsey figured if she didn't get an athletic scholarship to Vermont, she wouldn't play college field hockey at all. Her parents were pushing a state school, West Chester University, where the coach wanted her and where tuition, room, and board were $12,000 a year. (Even for West Chester, the Milroys would have to borrow $3,000 a year.) Lindsey was dismissive. She was interested only in UVM. And *maybe* Monmouth University, near the surfing beaches of the Jersey Shore, *if* she and Win got back together.

III.

Nobody said anything. Nobody had to. Bobby Speer's all-important senior-year football season had been nothing more than ordinary. The team had finished with six wins and four losses, and Bobby hadn't done anything to interest the big-time programs. He was a nice schoolboy quarterback. Nothing more. Kirk continued to refer to a game from Bobby's junior year, when he was sent in late in the second half as an emergency quarterback, and threw for 162 yards in eighteen minutes. But nobody gets a full ride to a Division I school on the basis of eighteen minutes.

When the season started, Kirk was dreaming big: Florida or Miami would come calling, or at least Rutgers or UConn. By the end of the season, there was only one semi-big school showing even a modest interest in Bobby, the University of Delaware. And Kirk was doing most of the work there. There were five schools at which Bobby seemed to have a shot. They were all small, and they were all in Pennsylvania: Widener, Moravian, Millersville, King's College, and West Chester.

The head coaches at those schools were serious men with staffs. All the schools had weight trainers and nutrition experts, and all the coaches bragged about their field's turf and facilities. But these were not football schools. At the University of Florida and its ilk, the populations of small cities congregated for games. The football atmosphere at the five schools showing an interest in Bobby was nothing like intense. Kirk and Bobby both knew the path to the NFL did not go through those schools. Bobby didn't care. All he wanted to do was keep playing. His pro career would take care of itself. He knew he wouldn't be having a grand send-off at the airport to some faraway place. Wherever he went, it would be only a drive from Levittown. For good or for bad, he wouldn't be far from Danny.

The family was now facing a daunting prospect they had been hoping to avoid: having to pay a good piece of Bobby's college tuition, room, and board. The five schools considering Bobby were allowed to offer grants, school jobs, low-interest loans, and scholarships based on academic performance. But they couldn't just give a kid money because he was good at a sport, as Division I schools routinely did. It turned out that Bobby's 3.2 grade-point average was more valuable than his arm. Kirk, in charge of the marketing and selling of Bobby Speer, was now a seller in a buyer's market. Like every good agent, he tried to give the appearance of having the upper hand.

"West Chester is putting too much pressure on us," he said one day, still looking for a firm offer from anybody. "The coaching staff keeps sending us decals and having kids call and ask, 'Has Bobby made up his mind yet?' And then the coach tells us that no matter who they recruit, his son is going to be competing for the quarterback job. He says, 'But don't worry, I can be fair.' But you know what? At the end of the day, blood is thicker than water."

Kirk could not see this, but it was clear to others: Bobby was barely on West Chester's list. There weren't really five small in-state schools pursuing Bobby. At best, there were four.

IV.

At the Friday-night Levittown parties, several kids told me, a weird and taboo thing was happening. They said they had seen Miss Snyder, the twenty-two-year-old ISS teacher, at occasional private-home beer bashes. Jaime Schaffer, one of Lindsey Milroy's enemies and one of Alyssa Bergman's friends, said she had seen Miss Snyder more than once and that she found it awkward. Could she drink in front of Miss Snyder? And what was she supposed to call her, Miss Snyder or Jen? Shawn Ledger, the budding rapper who had taken up residence in ISS, said he'd also seen Miss Snyder at Levittown beerfests. At first, he said, he thought it was a little bizarre, partying with his warden. But after a couple of beers, he decided that if she was cool with it, he would be, too.

Besides, he didn't mind looking at her. In ISS it was about the best thing to do, especially on cold days when she was wearing a particular tight sky-blue sweater with a high drooping collar, the kind Farrah Fawcett used to wear in her *Charlie's Angels* days. Every so often, while Ledger was doodling or writing rap lyrics and doing what he typically did in ISS, which was nothing, a thought would pop into his head: *She's pretty hot.* And quickly after it came an addendum: *For a teacher.*

V.

Mike Kosmin was having a good December. The girl from chemistry was still laughing at his jokes, he was earning $200 a week at McCaffrey's, and he was getting closer to asking out a girl from work. The Eagles were winning, and so were the Flyers, Philadelphia's hockey team. He was getting letters from Princeton, Stanford, and MIT. His scores on standardized tests, especially in math and science, placed him among the academic elite. Esteemed schools tracked such kids. They wanted his application.

For Christmas, Mike wanted to do something special for his stepfather. Since Labor Day, when Mike got his car, he and his stepfather, big Mike, had grown closer than they had ever been. On weekends they hung out together for hours. Early in their relationship, there were the expected struggles: Mike's mother and father had divorced, and the new love in his mother's life had stepped in. It took time for big Mike to learn how to be a stepfather and for little Mike to accept him. Every year they became closer. In mid-December there had been a breakthrough. Mike and his stepfather were driving home after a trip to New Jersey to buy gas; prices were cheaper there than in Pennsylvania. The younger Mike said, "I love that you take care of things." He was referring to his mother.

"You know, I love you, Michael," the stepfather said.

"I love you, too, Mike," the stepson said. He had never said that before.

Big Mike collected pocketknives, good ones. He always carried one, a handy thing to have on construction sites. Wanting to get a generous Christmas present for his stepfather, little Mike went to Herder's Cutlery, in the Oxford Valley Mall. He found a $50 knife he thought his stepfather would like. But the store manager, abiding by Pennsylvania law, wouldn't allow Mike to buy it without a parent present, so Mike called his mother and asked her to come in. The call made him feel juvenile, but he paid for the present like a man. He reached deep into the pocket of his pants and withdrew a wad of cash, just as big Mike would have done.

VI.

Winter Sundays were sacred in the lives of many Pennsbury kids, for the boys in particular, as well as their fathers and many others. On Sundays in winter, the Eagles played. Mr. Katz would sit at home, beer in hand, and watch the games while wearing the jersey of his favorite Eagle, Troy Vincent, an all-pro cornerback and Pennsbury graduate, class of '88. For the kids the routine was this: Sleep through noon, watch the game at a friend's house, watch another game, then a movie on DVD.

Think about doing some homework. Go out for pizza. Call it a day and a weekend.

On several Sundays, Mr. Wilson sent Bob Costa and another student—sometimes Blair Maloney—to Veterans Stadium to cover the Eagles for PHS-TV. There would always be a dozen or more professional TV crews on hand, but the PHS-TV crews would find a way to blend in. Mr. Wilson believed that nobody in the Eagles PR department had to know that PHS-TV was a high school cable station. On its bad days it was every bit as goofy as *Wayne's World*, but more often it was almost bizarrely adult, like the way a four-year-old looks in a tuxedo at a formal wedding. Mr. Wilson could keep the PHS-TV guise going with the Eagles as long as he sent his A-list talent. Costa was at the top of the list. Naturally, some of the PHS-TV kids resented Costa, especially since he was only a junior. One afternoon when Costa wasn't around, Mr. Wilson took the unusual step of publicly defending him and, in so doing, himself. "I know some of you guys think Bob's getting to do a lot, and he is," Mr. Wilson said. "But when I need a three-hour Thursday-night school-board meeting covered, Bob's raising his hand, and you guys are not."

There was more to it than that. Costa was an impossibly precocious on-air talent. Physically, he was nothing like mature. But when he put on a suit and a topcoat with shoulder pads and carried a microphone, he looked as though he had been conducting TV interviews all his life. He was afraid of nobody and no situation. He'd go to the games and put on what he called his Al Michaels–meets–Al Roker face and come back with one-on-one interviews with the Eagles' owner, the head coach, star players, Miss Universe, and, on one occasion, most marvelously, Patti LaBelle. Two minutes prior to the interview, Costa did not know who the soul diva was.

He had seen a woman standing near the home sideline, covered in fur on a raw day, surrounded by a little entourage of fur-wearing men. He asked a security woman in a bright yellow windbreaker to identify the furred lady.

"That's Patti LaBelle," came the reply, in a tone suggesting that anyone who didn't know Patti LaBelle should *not* have a microphone.

"Of course," Bob said. He knew the name and nothing more.

He introduced himself from a yard or two away. "Ms. LaBelle? I'm Bob Costa, PHS-TV. Would you mind stepping over here for a minute?"

In debate, he had learned the importance of moving things, inanimate or otherwise. In forensics competitions, the first thing he would do was move a chair. He felt it sent a message to the judges that before them stood a person able to move things.

"Sure, Bob," LaBelle said.

Bob asked her what she was doing at the stadium, and LaBelle answered that she was there to sing the National Anthem. *Okay,* Costa thought, *that's why I know the name—she's a singer.* He raced through the considerable musical library shelved in his mind. Nothing was coming up under LaBelle.

He asked her if she was warm underneath her furs.

"Yes," she said, "I'm wearing my long johns."

"I am, too!" Bob answered.

He was connecting with her. They discussed undergarments for a moment more. Then Bob asked her how she liked Philadelphia.

"Well, you know, Bob, I'm from Philadelphia."

Bob had no idea.

"Of course you are," he said.

You may call it lying, you may call it acting, but Costa knew what he was doing: making his subject feel comfortable.

And then something clicked for him. He *did* know one of her songs, in a manner of speaking. He knew that Christina Aguilera and Pink had both done cover versions of an old LaBelle song, "Lady Marmalade." He asked what she thought of the covers.

"Oh, I think they're wonderful," LaBelle said.

Bob suggested that the original could not be improved upon.

"Now, Bob, don't *playa* hate," LaBelle said to him, but not in a scolding way. The moment she said those three words, another thought occurred to Bob: *I've got PHS-TV gold!*

On another Sunday, Bob outdid himself. The Eagles had a large defensive end, Hugh Douglas, who had played a stellar game. Afterward, he was surrounded by reporters and TV crews. Bob nudged his way into the pack. He was a man-boy standing alongside a bunch of grown-ups—

newspaper columnists and TV sports reporters—whose work he had been reading or watching all his life.

The pros were pushing the kid out. Douglas was about to end his session, and Bob had not asked a single question. Mr. Wilson would not be impressed.

"All right, boys. I want to get home and watch *The Sopranos*," Douglas said, ending the powwow. "Get out of my way." He weighed nearly three hundred pounds.

As Douglas, in his XXXL sweatsuit, took a step, Costa, in desperation, made his move. He shouted out, "Mr. Douglas—do you think you're like Tony Soprano?"

Douglas stopped and stared at the boy reporter. Everyone fell silent for a long second or two. Bob immediately felt beads of perspiration on his neck.

"Wha'?" the giant football player asked. He turned to the other reporters and said, "Who is this guy?"

Bob beat them to it: "Bob Costa—PHS-TV!"

Douglas shook his large head.

"Rookie reporter, right?"

"Yes."

"How long you been a reporter?"

"About a year," Bob said, without shame.

"How old are you?"

"Seventeen."

Somebody said, "He could be your son." Everybody laughed except Costa and his subject. Bob had his game face on. Douglas continued to shake his head.

"Okay, what's your question, little man?"

Costa cleared his throat and said, "Do you feel like Tony Soprano on the field?"

Douglas paused before answering the question, seemingly bewildered by some of the requirements of his profession. "No, I'm not Tony Soprano! I'm Shaft, okay? Not Tony Soprano." And with that, he took off.

A writer approached Bob, gave him a sort of modified high five, and said, "Welcome to the club."

Bob could not tell if the comment was sarcastic or sincere. All he knew was that he got his question in, and he got it answered. More PHS-TV gold.

VII.

Costa often saw his forensics coach, Mr. Medoff, at the games. Whenever the Phillies or Eagles had home dates, Mr. Medoff was there, standing outside the main concourse, with a stack of programs under his arms. It was a way to make $100 on a good day. He used to stay and watch the games when he was more of a fan. Mr. Medoff grew up in Philadelphia, and for years he lived and died with the Eagles and Phillies. He no longer had that kind of attachment to professional sports. Money in his pocket, however, was always useful. It was common for a teacher to have a side income. Teachers coached sports teams, worked as camp counselors, managed extracurricular activities like proms and debate teams, sold programs. They found something. Mr. Medoff had found two things.

VIII.

Kevin Milroy, father of Lindsey, was watching an Eagles game at home, in the safety of the Heather Ridge development, in prosperous Newtown. He knew all about life on the other side of Route 1. Now he had central air-conditioning, a finished basement, new furniture, new art, new everything. No musty old anything. The money some people put into college funds or savings accounts, the Milroys spent on cars and cell phones and top-shelf liquor and clothes. The Milroys and their credit cards were keeping the American economy alive. They made and they spent. Tomorrow they would make more.

In the early 1970s, Kevin Milroy was a schoolboy football player. Thirty years later, he found himself still watching the game, but only out of habit.

"Football was a job," he said one Sunday in December, his eyes glued to the screen. "It was a way out." In high school, he ran the hundred-yard dash in 10.2 seconds, but his dashes now were shorter, from the sofa to the refrigerator. "Field hockey for Lindsey is the same thing. Vermont is thirty thousand a year. We're not paying that. She wants to go there so bad, then she's got to get the money. She's not that into it anymore, but I say to her, 'Look what you've put into it. Don't throw it all away.'"

As his daughter marched through her senior year, her mood changing from day to day, Kevin Milroy found himself reliving his own senior year. He blamed Win for the times Lindsey was sulky. "He was always so quiet, you never knew what he was thinking," Kevin Milroy said. When Win picked up Lindsey for his prom, Kevin took him aside and told him, "You be a good boy."

The father knew how prom night went—both in his day and three decades later. "You're trying to get lucky. You probably won't, but you're hoping you will."

The particulars of Win's prom weekend, that was a subject strictly for Lindsey and her mother. But Kevin Milroy knew one thing about his daughter, and it was good enough for him: Nobody could *make* her do *anything*.

IX.

One December day, Matt Cunningham had his mother and father and sister join him at Kennedy Airport for the arrival of Katie, his girlfriend from Vermont. There was a period—all of Matt's Pennsbury years, essentially—when he and his father were not close. The father was forever pushing his son, more than he realized. He wanted Matt to do more in the classroom, in sports, in extracurricular activities. Jim Cunningham wanted his son to have all the things that had come to him because he had applied his superior intellect in gainful ways. As a highly paid teacher, Mr. Cunningham was enjoying a level of comfort that his own father never knew. Mr. Cunningham took his family and Katie out to lunch at Tavern on the Green, the legendary Central Park restaurant. It was expensive, but he could afford a grand lunch.

Matt had attended his prom with the first love of his life, a Jewish girl named Jamie who was a year ahead of Matt at Pennsbury. The relationship continued through Matt's first year of college. His parents had dinner with Jamie's parents several times. Mr. Cunningham was knowledgeable about Jewish traditions. The parents were all comfortable with one another.

One night Matt came home alone after a date with Jamie with an ashen face. His father—and this day had marked a turning point in their relationship—asked his son what was wrong.

"Jamie ended it," Matt said. He was wailing. "She said she couldn't be with somebody who wasn't Jewish." He blamed the breakup on her parents' convictions. They had only one objection to Matt: He wasn't Jewish.

It hurt the father to see his son in such pain. Jamie and Matt had made a gorgeous couple on prom night. Jim Cunningham had married his prom date, and they had lived happily ever after, with an allowance for life's unexpected bounces. Mr. Cunningham had half-guessed his son would do the same.

He tried to explain Judaism to his son, that it was more than a religion; that it was a culture, and there was an ancient ancestral dictum at work that had nothing to do with Matt.

Eventually, the wounds healed, and now Matt, at age twenty-five, was about to propose to Katie on the day after Christmas. Matt and Katie left the restaurant and walked over to the skating rink at Rockefeller Center. He asked her to marry him, got a yes, and soon after, Mr. Cunningham was pouring champagne. They celebrated an impending marriage and an impending retirement, too. One was giving up his freedom to be part of something larger. The other was hoping to find a freedom he had not known in years.

X.

In December the first news of a confirmed prom date made the rounds. Harry Stymiest had asked a tenth-grader named Kelly Heich. She was considered a nice girl, smart, a promising member of the forensics team. The first person Harry told was Mr. Wilson. The second was Costa. Then third was . . . everyone. Harry knew Kelly from Emilie United's Sunday-afternoon youth Bible-study sessions. He knew she had a boyfriend who lived in central Pennsylvania, but Harry and Kelly would be attending the prom as friends, and the boyfriend did not object.

"Mr. Wilson, I've got news," Harry said. He was returning to Studio 230 with a double order of cafeteria fries.

"What's that, Harry?"

"I got a date for El Promo," Harry said.

"Oh yeah? Who's the lucky girl?"

Harry told him.

"She said, 'I would be honored to go with you, Harry.'"

"That's great, Harry," Mr. Wilson said. "Honest to God."

"You know I've *got* to get that DeLorean now."

Harry loaded up on his fries.

"Harry," Mr. Wilson said with admiration, "you've got balls."

XI.

Alyssa Bergman joined Michael Castor and his family on a Christmas-break trip to the Virgin Islands. For Christmas, the young couple decided to buy rings for each other. Alyssa designed the one she wanted: a yellow gold band with a half-carat diamond on top and a quarter-carat diamond on either side. Michael paid $1,200 for the ring. His was a band of yellow gold with five small diamonds across the top, adding up to a half-carat. Alyssa paid $900 for his. They talked about how her ring could be upgraded, if it were ever to become an engagement ring. The rings were expensive, but they regarded them as an investment. They were pleased when an appraiser told them Alyssa's ring was worth more than double what Michael had paid for it.

Alyssa was well versed in jewelry and ring-wearing customs. She wore her new diamond ring on the ring finger of her right hand. He wore his on his left pinkie. She knew what people would think if she wore it on her left hand. She didn't want anyone to get the wrong impression, even though the whole thing did seem like a pre-engagement engagement. Alyssa had never felt so secure in all her life.

XII.

Mr. Katz spent New Year's Eve at home, watching TV by himself. One son was back at MIT with his girlfriend. The younger son was downstairs, watching a different channel. As midnight approached, Mr. Katz opened a bottle of champagne for himself. His younger son was not of legal drinking age yet. Some years ago, Mr. Katz had joined the Pennsbury marching band on some Christmas-break junket. Once he went to Paris with the band. Another year he went to Hawaii. But there was no trip this year. There were no invitations of any kind. A quiet evening at home suited him fine. He watched the ball drop in Times Square, hit the clicker, and went to sleep. A calendar year was done. The school year was at halftime.

Chapter Six

Florida

January

I.

On Friday afternoons, and on the afternoons before vacation began, there was a moment when time slowed and the kids paired and merged and meshed. It was a serene time, in its way. The final bell rang, and the hallways flooded with kids, but there was no mad rush. The kids lingered and discussed party plans and holiday itineraries and wrote cellphone numbers in blue ink across their palms. The kids sat in the parking lots for a moment behind the wheels of their cars, which were filled with music and maybe the lingering aroma from the half-joint smoked in the Burger King lot just before A period. Not in Alyssa Bergman's Corvette or Mike Kosmin's triple-black Acura RSX or Bobby Speer's fifteen-year-old Integra, but in other cars, certainly. The after-school air was filled with the music of Eminem and John Mayer and the new Foo Fighters. In backseats there were backpacks stuffed with textbooks that would not see daylight until school resumed.

And so it was on the December day when Pennsbury began its winter break and the kids said, as kids always have, *See you next year.* Mike Kosmin dawdled in his car as he got the right track from the right CD at the right volume. He waited, in accordance with his custom, for Alyssa

Bergman to get in her Corvette, and after she did, he drove home with his buddy and neighbor Mikey Coluzzi, the son of a local police chief.

"Sometime we should drive this car to Florida," Mike Kosmin said. He was the older and more confident of the two. Mikey was just a tenth-grader. Mike had befriended him when Mikey was new and didn't know anyone. That was Mike's way. He always included the slow kid from down the street in the driveway basketball games. Nobody else would think to do that.

They weren't worldly kids, Mikey and Mike, and didn't pretend to be. A big hoot to them was to eat dinner twice, macaroni and cheese with meatballs at the Coluzzi house, then a second meal with big Mike and Cyndi. Or dinner at the Coluzzis', followed by a run to Steve's Steaks, in northeast Philadelphia, one of his stepfather's old hangouts, for a cheesesteak. Things in the classroom that came easily to Mike did not come so readily for the police chief's son, and Mike took it upon himself to be his buddy's tutor. Some nights they liked to drive to Tweeter, a stereo shop at the mall, to listen to car sound systems. Mike was still saving for one. They were always home by eleven, because both had curfews. Mike's junior license required him to be off the road by then, anyhow.

Mike Kosmin couldn't wait to begin his vacation. He was excited to give his stepfather the expensive knife and to give his mother, who collected nutcrackers, a special wooden one, handmade in Germany. Their plan was to open Christmas gifts on December 22, because the following day, Mike was flying to Florida to spend the rest of the break with his father, Scott Kosmin, and to celebrate a delayed Hanukkah with him. Mike was looking forward to seeing his Florida friends, going to the beach, maybe trying out his new assuredness on a girl he liked who lived amid the stucco palaces of his father's development, called Boca West, near Boca Raton.

Scott Kosmin owned a luggage company that he had moved to South Florida after he and Cyndi divorced. They separated when Mike, their only child, was in fourth grade. When they told him, Mike made an angry face, burst into tears, and said, "I knew this was coming." He marched out the front door. But as he got older, he came to realize that his parents were happier apart. His father had moved a thousand miles away, but in the right direction; Mike liked visiting his father in Florida. He didn't have as playful a relationship with Scott as he did with his step-father, but he knew his father was a good provider and respected him. Mike spent ten or more weeks with him a year, all of it vacation time. It was easy.

His mother's maternal grandfather was Pete Palangio, the oldest living retired NHL hockey player, a former Chicago Blackhawk and Montreal Canadien. Mike knew his great-grandfather well and treasured the bloodline. His interest in hockey was fanatical. He had worked hard to become a good player. He had an unusual appreciation of a fine thing done well. In football he was more interested in the perfectly run pass pattern than seeing a linebacker take off a quarterback's head. He hated violence. When he watched hockey, he looked for superior footwork, while other kids wanted to see one player squash another against the glass.

Big Mike saw his stepson's commitment to hockey. It impressed him. In their first years together, the stepfather, eager to prove his devotion, would get up before five to take Mike to practice. They were both silent and groggy on the pre-dawn drives to the rink, but in the silence, a closeness was developing. On the drives home, after big Mike had his morning coffee and cigarettes and little Mike a workout, they were garrulous.

While riding together, they often talked about cars. The stepson would admire a Fiat, and big Mike would say, "Please. Don't you know what Fiat stands for? *Fix it again, Tony.*" And they would laugh. A yellow Porsche would pass by, and the younger Mike would say, "Whaddya think?" The stepfather would say dismissively, "A frickin' taxi." They talked while returning home from hockey, from Steve's Steaks, from the synagogue where Mike had gone for bar mitzvah lessons. What they were talking about, indirectly, was manliness.

Cyndi never converted to Judaism, but Scott Kosmin was insistent that their son be raised as a Jew. Mike considered himself Jewish, but there was no wall between him and his non-Jewish friends. Cultural changes—the popularity of *Seinfeld*, for example—had done a great deal to make Jewishness part of life in the Pennsbury school district. It wasn't a hard place to be Jewish, especially if you were a Jew who celebrated Christmas.

Mike saw that his mother's religion was important to her, and his father's religion was important to him. The effect on Mike—trying to split things down the middle as his parents fought—was that religion did not play a powerful role in his life. But having both Hanukkah and Christmas, that was fine with him. He didn't believe in Jesus, but he'd held on to Santa Claus for as long as he could.

His stepfather realized that Mike was getting all the religion he needed, so he exerted his influence in other places. He gave Mike the religion of the city, the rules he had learned growing up in Philadelphia. He often said to Mike, "Always be aware of everything within thirty feet of you."

Big Mike knew there were parents who believed in introducing their children to alcohol. Or fathers who simply drank beer with their sixteen-year-old sons while watching football games. He didn't believe in that. He'd never seen anything good come out of underage drinking. He and Cyndi believed that the legal drinking age was there for a reason. But it wasn't much of an issue in their house. For one thing, they weren't big drinkers. They'd have a glass of wine or two with dinner and little more than that. Their son seldom expressed interest in alcohol. Once, while Cyndi was making chicken cacciatore and having a glass of white wine, Mike had asked for a sip and promptly spat it out.

They opened their Christmas gifts on December 22. Big Mike was thrilled with his knife. He was touched. He had never felt closer to his stepson. The next day Cyndi drove her son to the airport.

"You got your cell?" she asked.

"Yeah." It was early.

"Call us."

Cyndi had wanted Mike to come home on January 1, because school resumed on January 2, a Thursday. But Mike convinced his mother to let him skip school on Thursday and Friday and fly home on Saturday, January 4. Reluctantly, she signed off on the plan. She knew to pick her battles.

Cyndi thought about sharing with Mike the career decision she had made. For eighteen years, she had been selling houses like the one she lived in. As she sold houses, she also sold school districts, divorce lawyers, plumbers, peewee hockey leagues. She was selling her life experiences. She liked her work, and she was good at it. She wasn't merely a real estate agent. She was an adviser. Her clients appreciated her candor.

A buyer would ask, "Do I want to be in the Council Rock school district or in the Pennsbury district?"

"We chose Pennsbury for our son."

"Really. Why?"

"Council Rock kids are spoiled. Pennsbury has a little of everything. It's the real world. School is supposed to prepare you for the real world, isn't it?"

But after eighteen years of selling five-over-four with a door, her intensity fueled by cigarettes and coffee, Cyndi needed a break. She realized she wasn't being the wife she wanted to be, and she especially wasn't being the mother she wanted to be. She wanted to fulfill her idealized vision of the mother from the 1950s: wife first, mother second, homemaker third—and to hell with career.

Cyndi figured Mike had about eighteen months until he left for college. She wanted him to have more home-cooked meals. She didn't want to say *maybe tomorrow* anymore. When he wanted to wear his favorite cargo pants and faded hooded sweatshirt, she didn't want to say they were in a pile on the basement floor. She wanted to see him off to his senior prom and move him into his freshman-year dorm. Maybe she'd go back to work once he was away at school.

The Philadelphia airport was busy and noisy, and Cyndi decided not to tell him about her decision just then. It could wait until after he got home, after Cyndi had talked to her boss, after it was official.

With the new airport security measures, Cyndi was not allowed to walk her son to the gate. Mother and son hugged good-bye amid the security people and the metal detectors and the southbound kids wearing shorts on a cold winter day.

On December 30, Cyndi went to her office at Prudential Fox & Roach and told her manager she was going to put her real estate license in escrow for eighteen months. Her manager tried to talk her out of it, to no avail. Her mind was made up.

With Mike in Florida, the final days of 2002 were quiet for Cyndi and her husband. A quiet Christmas was followed by a quiet New Year's Eve, which was big Mike's birthday. He was forty-five years old. They celebrated in their usual way, with dinner at home. Mike called from Florida. He was having a quiet New Year's Eve, too, playing Scrabble with his father. His stepmother was the arbiter. On New Year's Day, Mike and Cyndi stormed the mall for the post-Christmas sales. They had dinner at Olive Garden and went to sleep a little after ten. Mike would be leaving for work the next morning shortly after six. At 2:30 A.M. the phone rang. A screechy voice came on and said, "Happy New Year!" Cyndi knew who it was—those bratty teenagers from down the street, a year or two behind Mike in school. Damn kids. Then the next night, at 2:09 A.M., the phone rang again.

II.

A principal's office phone rings often, a thousand or more times over the course of a school year, in Mr. Katz's case. Any phone call could bring good news, or bad. One year three kids died. *Wham, wham, wham.* The school had tried to recover, but the impact of the deaths was too great. It could not get out of mourning.

Mr. Katz tried to do everything he could to make the kids safe, but there were inherent limits. Sometimes kids made bad decisions, sometimes they had bad luck. A football player goes swimming in the Delaware River and gets caught in a current and panics and drowns. The tragic news comes and you think of the things you could have done, but the only thing you can do is grieve with the parents, knowing all the while it could have been one of your own. What is sadder than the death of a student? Nothing. One year a Pennsbury boy drove his car into a train trestle in Yardley, an apparent suicide, though nobody ever knew for sure. A year later, the boy's girlfriend, a Pennsbury girl, drove her car into the same spot, a conspicuous suicide.

And now Cyndi Mackrides, mother of a Pennsbury junior, Mike Kosmin, was on the phone, the first call of Mr. Katz's day. It was Friday morning, January 3, the second school day of the new year, not much past six-thirty.

My son was killed this morning. The mother was rushed and emotional but coherent. She apologized for being so brief, but she was about to board a plane. She wanted Mike's principal to know right away.

Mr. Katz was raised in a military home, and at such moments that upbringing served him well. The army acronyms so familiar to his sergeant father were part of his language, too. Mr. Katz had a standard operating procedure for handling the death of a Pennsbury student. The first thing to do was attempt to bring comfort to the grieving family. The second thing was to get the news out as quickly as possible. He didn't want one of his teachers cracking a joke about Mike's extended vacation, a line the teacher would never be able to retrieve. The third thing was to follow up on the first.

In his brief conversation with Cyndi, Mr. Katz said that next year's yearbook would, if the family wanted, include a page dedicated to Mike. The suggestion came out of his manual. He knew from experience that it was a meaningful gesture to aching families, even in the hysterical first hours after a death. For a few minutes, it gave a family something concrete to think about.

The morning announcements were fast approaching. Mr. Katz asked his secretary, Mary Ellen Rickerl, with her advanced degree in efficiency, to get out Mike's file and yearbook picture. In his academic transcript, Mike Kosmin came to life for the principal. He saw that Mike was one of the school's outstanding students, particularly strong in math, science, and computers. As Matt Fox made his announcements and Bob Costa his, Mr. Katz gave no hint that anything was wrong. He took the microphone with his trembling hands. While Costa and Fox were walking to their classes, Mr. Katz delivered the horrible news in a measured voice. The announcement left Bob and Matt reeling. Mr. Katz said Mike had died while visiting his father in Florida. He asked for a moment of silent meditation. He told the students that grief counselors were available.

Mr. Katz went to the viewing. He hated funerals, and he was nervous and uncomfortable, unsure of what to say. But he went. *Of course* he went. It was part of his job and his SOP. He met the Pennsylvania mother and stepfather and the Florida stepmother and father. He mentioned the yearbook again. He said that a group of kids wanted to conduct an in-school memorial service, if that was something the family would like. He said the graduation program for the class of '04 would make a special mention of Mike, if the family wanted. "There are things the school would like to do," he told them. "When you're ready." He had no idea the deep impression he was making on them.

Mr. Katz had a son at MIT; Mike Kosmin had been planing to apply there. Death is random. Mr. Katz knew that. A phone rings at an odd hour of the day or night, an unfamiliar voice comes on. *Is this . . .* The caller wants to know exactly with whom he is speaking. Your mind flashes through the possibilities before settling on the worst.

III.

Mike Kosmin's death was covered in the *Courier Times* and embellished in the Pennsbury hallways. The newspaper's first story, published on Sunday, January 5, was about what a good student Mike was, how he was funny and smart and skilled at computers. The story noted that he had taken every computer class offered in the district and that he had hoped to attend either Stanford or MIT.

The article also cited a report from the Palm Beach County sheriff's office, which stated that Michael, as the story referred to him, was struck by a 2002 Dodge Ram truck driven by a twenty-seven-year-old woman as he attempted to cross, on foot, busy Powerline Road in Boca Raton around one in the morning on Friday, January 3. The sheriff's report said the woman had swerved to avoid Mike and that she was not driving under the influence of alcohol.

On Monday, January 6, the paper ran a brief obituary that announced the funeral service on the following day. It mentioned two sets of parents, Mike and Cyndi Mackrides and Scott and Lisa Kosmin. Among the three dozen surviving family members listed, the first, after the four parents, was Pete Palangio, the old hockey player.

Rumors swirled through the school. One had Mike talking to his mother on his cell phone when he was struck. Another had Mike drunk. To Costa and Fox and Mikey Coluzzi and others who knew Mike well, that seemed unlikely. They didn't think of Mike as a drinker.

On Tuesday, the day of Mike's funeral—or his life celebration service, as his family preferred to call it—the *Courier Times* ran another story. The headline read POLICE: TEEN KILLED IN CRASH HAD BEEN DRINKING. The story quoted a spokesman from the Palm Beach County sheriff's office who said the police report would not have referred to alcohol "if it wasn't verified." The spokesman said, "We're not saying he was drunk, but he was drinking."

The newspaper story also said, "Reports that Kosmin was talking on a cell phone as he was hit could not be verified." Now he was *Kosmin*. The story pointed out that no cell phone was noted in the sheriff's report.

Three days later, the paper ran a letter to the editor from a man named Austin Thornton. The letter read:

I think the follow-up story on the accidental death of Michael Kosmin was ill-timed and insensitive for an accident that is still under investigation in Florida. Whether alcohol was involved or not, now is not the time to add speculation to this profound tragedy.

Think of the parents of this only child who must now try to cope with intense grief, anger, and sadness. This is a nightmare they will not soon awake from.

Instead, focus on a bright and friendly young man whose flame was extinguished much too soon. He was very well thought of at school and at work, where his energy and talent were just starting to emerge. There has been a tremendous outpouring of emotion for Michael and that only happens when there is a good life to celebrate.

I hope and pray the parents of Michael Kosmin can find comfort and strength during this time of bereavement and personal loss.

Cyndi called directory information to see if Austin Thornton was listed. He was. She called him, identified herself, and said she was moved and gratified by his letter. She asked him why he wrote it.

"My daughter works with your son at McCaffrey's," Austin Thornton said, using the present tense. "One night after work she couldn't get her car to start. Mike and others tried to help her. One by one, everybody left, except Mike. He stayed and continued to try to get the car started. I came to pick her up. He stayed with her until I got there. He wasn't going to leave her alone."

IV.

The funeral service was attended by scores of Pennsbury students, teachers, and employees. The casket was ornate and open. That surprised those who thought Mike was Jewish and knew the Jewish burial custom called for a simple wood coffin, always closed. Mike had a yarmulke on his head and rosary beads in his hands.

Bob Costa didn't want to look at Mike, but he couldn't turn away. The face he saw! It looked just like Mike, with his familiar half-smile, except it wasn't really Mike, because the Mike he knew was either pressing buttons on his car stereo or cracking a joke or watching Alyssa Bergman parade across the student parking lot. Bob could not accept that his friend was dead or how his friend had died.

Between the morning announcements and being on PHS-TV, Bob had become about as famous as any nonathlete could be at Pennsbury. With his increased fame, he found himself invited to more and bigger parties. He went to some. He occasionally found it amusing to see kids drunk and stoned, but maybe a little pathetic, too. He was still in a position to collect the $1,000 reward from his father. He didn't know if he would be through graduation, but nothing had tempted him yet. At parties, joints and beers would pass by him, and Bob would say, "I'm cool." He felt no need to follow the crowd.

He wondered if drinking had actually played a role in Mike's death. He looked at Mike's parents, all four of them, gasping for air in their grief. He had never been so sad. The things that normally defined him—the forensics team, school politics, PHS-TV, trying to get himself and John Mayer to the prom—went into some dark space. All Bob could think about was the parking spot he had and how he should have given it to Mike; how Mike's car should have been smack-dab in the middle of student parking, not off in Siberia, at Marcelli's.

V.

There had been no hint, no foreshadowing. Is there ever when a healthy student dies? The first day of school in the new year—Thursday, January 2, 2003—began like any other day at Pennsbury, with Matt Fox and Bob Costa reading the morning announcements. No one was expecting it to be what it became, the last full day of Mike Kosmin's life. The absentee list was long; lots of kids were stretching the holiday. For those at school, the day was sluggish. The kids did not come out of winter break at the sound of a bell.

At Cyndi and big Mike's house, it was quiet, with Mike in Florida and nobody there to wrestle the dog. Mike and Cyndi knew that would change soon enough. In the meantime, they did their customary things. After dinner, they smoked their final cigarettes of the day. Little Mike hated their smoking, and more than once, Cyndi and big Mike had resolved to quit, but it wasn't on their list of resolutions for 2003. They watched some TV. They went to bed.

At 2:09 that Friday morning, the phone rang. Cyndi looked at the phone and thought about picking it up and hanging it straight back down. *Two nights in a row!* When she finally took the phone off its cradle, she was ready to read those kids the riot act. But the voice on the other end belonged to a man.

"Michael's dead, Michael's dead, Michael's dead," the voice wailed.

"What? What are you saying!" She could not identify her caller or comprehend what he was saying.

"Michael's dead, Michael's dead."

"Scott?"

A police officer took the phone.

"Is this the mother of Michael H. Kosmin?"

"Who is this!"

"I'm very sorry to tell you . . ."

What do you do when your life as you know it has ended? For six years, the life of Cyndi Mackrides had been her two Michaels. She shrieked, she cried, she vomited. She held her husband. She called her family, funeral homes, and US Airways. There was an early flight to Fort Lauderdale, and she booked two tickets.

Cyndi and Mike were on the road to the airport as the weak January sun started to rise. Cyndi took a Xanax, not only for the trauma of her son's death but to get her on the plane. She was a nervous flier. She called Mr. Katz from the Philadelphia airport. In Florida, Cyndi and Mike picked up a rental car and drove to Cyndi's ex-husband's house. Scott Kosmin was heavily sedated. He couldn't talk.

Cyndi and Mike went to the funeral home to see their son. All Cyndi could think about was getting Mike back to Pennsylvania. He had brought nothing but shorts and T-shirts and jeans to Florida. Cyndi wanted him in a suit for his funeral. She made arrangements to get him one.

They met with police officers, who were gentle but vague. They told Cyndi and her husband that Mike's death was part of a criminal investigation, which was why an autopsy had been done immediately and why a blood sample was taken. They said that the initial test indicated that Mike had been drinking. How much and where they did not know. A group of kids, all juveniles, had gone to a club on a teen night, with the bottles of alcohol put away for the night. The police said that Mike, for reasons they did not know, had left the group to walk home. It was not an area where anybody walked. He was struck by a truck driven by a woman who was not impaired in any way, who stopped and called the police immediately from her cell phone. The police said they would be interviewing the other kids, the last people to see Mike alive.

"But Mike didn't drink!" Cyndi said.

"It's just a preliminary report," the officer said.

"Who were the others?"

"We're working on that."

The stepfather's bullshit detector went off. He thought, *Mike wasn't trying to walk home. There was a fight, probably over a girl.*

He thought, *Mike was an innocent, a baby. He didn't know shit. He was threatened and went running right into the goddamn traffic.*

He thought: *Fuck you, God—fuck you!*

By two P.M. Mike and Cyndi were flying back to Philadelphia. Their son's body, in a suit and laid out in a carved casket, was underneath them in cargo. It was Saturday, January 4, the day Mike was supposed to be flying home from his extended winter break.

VI.

Mikey Coluzzi's father got word early, as police chiefs do. He heard about the death of his son's best friend early on Friday morning, January 3. He was a former Philadelphia cop. He had seen more than his share of violent deaths. But this one reached into his own home.

The police chief went into his son's room. Mikey was getting dressed for school. Usually, the two boys drove to school together.

The father sat down on the bed and asked his son to come near. He held him as he told his son the awful news, held him tight as his son sobbed and sobbed and sobbed.

Chapter Seven

Early Graduation

February

I.

Bob Costa could not believe how hard it was to reach John Mayer's agents, let alone John Mayer. Over the course of the school year, Mayer had gone from cult figure to pop star. (Alyssa Bergman had done about the same.) Mayer had been nominated for a Grammy for Best New Artist, and his song "Your Body Is a Wonderland" was nominated for Best Male Pop Vocal Performance. The song had become the background music to a thousand mundane activities—eating in an airport T.G.I. Friday's, riding an elevator, sitting in a traffic jam—as well as some more inter-esting activities. In college dorm rooms, the song was a staple, like Van Morrison's "Moondance" had once been, and it was used about the same way, with the lights low. At Pennsbury you heard "Wonderland" while the volleyball team was practicing, in the student parking lot, and in the faculty rooms. You heard:

Take all your big plans
And break 'em
This is bound to be a while

Followed by the song's ubiquitous refrain:

Your body is a wonderland

As far as Costa could tell, Mayer had three agents in New York and one in Nashville who did nothing but book concert dates. Costa managed to get street and e-mail addresses and telephone numbers for all of them and wrote and called at irregular intervals. Harry Stymiest went to the PHS-TV studio and made a video clip of proms past, and the school sent it to Mayer's people. But no one was responding, and the prom was only four months away. "He has your message," the secretaries would tell Costa. Or sometimes, "He has your messages, Bob."

The Maroon 5 manager, Ben Berkman, always responded to Bob. When Bob had sent a copy of his review of the Maroon 5 performance at Temple, Berkman wrote back, "What a brilliant and heartfelt piece! You are a very promising reporter. Keep up the fine work!" Costa again felt like the kid music writer in *Almost Famous*, that he was starting to count. Berkman was cool. The others Costa could not figure out.

Bob had been particularly surprised by one of the people ignoring him, Michael McDonald. While doing Internet research, Costa had discovered that McDonald worked not only with Mayer but also with Dave Matthews, Costa's favorite musician. During the summer after his sophomore year, Costa had gone on a youth-group tour through Europe. In Assisi, Italy, where the tomb of Saint Francis lies, Costa had stumbled into Matthews and his wife and child. They were all touring the Basilica, viewing the Giotto frescoes. In that holy setting, Matthews, who had been selling out stadiums for years, was almost anonymous. Costa approached him and chatted genially with him for a minute or two. As Costa was leaving, Matthews said, "See ya later, Bob." That was Matthews. How could he have a blow-off artist like McDonald working for him?

Costa changed tactics. He called the assistant to Mayer's Nashville booking agent. Bob did not identify himself as a high school junior. He asked for Mayer's concert fee and whether the singer was available on the third Saturday in May.

"The booking fee depends on the size of the venue, but it's generally between a hundred and fifty thousand and three hundred thousand," the assistant said.

"Right." Bob knew about the $3,000 in the prom budget. *A lot of car washes*, he thought.

"May seventeenth, the Saturday? No, John doesn't have anything booked for that night."

And in a moment of clarity, Costa understood why nobody was getting back to him. Suddenly, it was so obvious. John (Bob could use his first name, too) *did* want to play the Pennsbury prom. He must have been telling his people to work it into his schedule. You could tell by what they weren't saying. Why else would the date be open? Costa was optimistic. He was always optimistic.

II.

The Republican congressman had been coming to Pennsbury for years, and the visits had always been worthwhile. Even though there was a strong Democratic tradition at Pennsbury because of Levittown—once populated largely by union factory workers who pulled Democratic levers—Jim Greenwood, in his sixth term in Washington, was a liberal Republican, and Levittowners and their neighbors in Fairless Hills were conservative Democrats. Greenwood and Pennsbury were an easy fit.

Greenwood came to the school again on an icy Wednesday afternoon in February, when the national conversation was about going to war. He was the guest of Donna Danielewski, a government teacher who kept a picture of the congressman on a wall in her classroom. He went to the Pennsbury cafeteria, where the distinct smell of boiled hot dogs still lingered in the air, and spoke of the looming war in Iraq. He reminded his audience that he had kids, and that a congressman could vote on no issue more grave than war. He asked for hands, to see who favored and who opposed military action. Arms went up limply all the way around. By a slim margin, there were more against armed intervention than for it.

The congressman, a 1969 graduate of Council Rock, didn't look like somebody you'd see at Pennsbury. In his sensible winter boots, heavy khaki pants, blue blazer, tie, and button-down shirt, he looked like one of those folksy middle-aged L. L. Bean catalog models. His tie was neatly knotted. His hair, longish and white, was all in place. There was a forced casualness about him, and the Pennsbury kids picked up on it. His title impressed very few of them. Politics was not a high-status profession at Pennsbury.

Fifty or sixty students marched down to the cafeteria to hear Greenwood, seniors taking AP American history or U.S. government. In the Vietnam years Pennsbury was not notably political and it was not now either. There were maybe a dozen seniors who, looking for a job and free schooling, had enlisted in a branch of the military before the threat of war had become so real. There were a few more who had signed on amid war's drumbeat, teenagers high on testosterone and looking for action. There were scores of kids who had parents or relatives in the military reserves. But the possibility of war did not galvanize the school. There were no bumper stickers, no signs, no petitions, no protests. When teachers brought up the topic, the kids who rejected the idea of war were more outspoken than the supporters. The general view was that war did not solve problems. Many kids had fathers who had served in Vietnam or, through either luck or deferment, missed it. They had seen war movies. They weren't believers.

And now Jim Greenwood, Republican of Bucks County, declared supporter of the proposed war, was in their school. PHS-TV was present, of course, represented by Harry Stymiest, sent out of Studio 230 and down to the cafeteria by Mr. Wilson. As Greenwood talked and took student questions, Harry worked the room, a bulky video camera lodged in his fleshy neck. He circled the cafeteria as if he were working one of those CNN afternoon-discussion-group shows. A half hour into his taping, there was a red mark on Harry's neck, above the collar of his T-shirt.

"What are the chances of there being a draft?" Greenwood asked, repeating a question posed to him. "Zero."

Harry honed in on the congressman. He was nailing the thing. He was in his element.

Greenwood, a verbal Houdini, looked comfortable even when he was being challenged. He had clearly thought extensively about the prospect of war. He had traveled in the Middle East. He had met with President Bush. He was knowledgeable about his subject. He was a true believer. In his assuredness, there was arrogance.

A senior, Jeff Heinbach, posed a rambling question in a barely audible voice. The congressman asked the kid to rise from his cafeteria seat. He did, all one hundred pounds of him quivering. He was wearing jeans, a T-shirt, and a leather jacket. Resting atop his schoolbooks was sample artwork for his band, Jeff Says No. "Bush would be a nice guy to talk to at a bar, but maybe not at the UN," Heinbach said. He said that Bush was "whitewashing everything" and that the public couldn't believe what it was hearing from a "corporate-controlled media." He said there were no humanitarian reasons for going to war in Iraq and that if Bush wanted to do something humanitarian, he should help the poor living in Washington, D.C. He said the U.S. wanted war to steal Iraqi oil. Heinbach went on for the better part of a minute, reducing the probable war to a fight over oil. "I don't think going to war and having Americans and other people die is the right answer," he said.

The cafeteria was suddenly tense. There was nothing original in what Jeff Heinbach was saying, but a kid was standing up to a six-term congressman, and that was enough to make the other kids stop doodling. Harry's focus went from Heinbach to Greenwood and back.

As the congressman started to answer, his voice was controlled, even when he accused Heinbach of calling the president of the United States a liar. Greenwood said American troops would not be going to Iraq "to steal their oil," belittling Heinbach with his own words. His tone was even as he praised Jeff for having the courage to voice his opinions. He said skepticism was healthy.

But then the veteran congressman talking at a high school filled with the children of his constituents did an unexpected thing. He got oddly personal. He verbally confronted a kid who obviously did not come out of the mainstream. Heinbach said he didn't ever expect to become a congressman, and Greenwood responded by saying, "No, I don't think that's going to happen, either." Then he lectured him directly. He said, "It's not good for you or anybody around you to be cynical, and that is what you are." There was a reporter from *The Philadelphia Inquirer* there, and she was speed-writing. "To me, you sound like someone whose opinions might exceed your knowledge base."

It didn't matter whether Greenwood was correct. The only thing the Pennsbury kids heard was an attack on one of their own, a hundred-pound

kid whose father was a local dentist. They saw a trembling kid in retro
Chuck Taylor Converse high-top sneakers and a thrift-shop shirt who had
the nerve to stand up to a congressman—to the *man*—even if he was
saying nutty things. Before, Heinbach had been a social recluse at
Pennsbury. At that moment his status changed. There was a murmuring
of support for Heinbach. One kid asked his neighbor, "Did Greenwood
just insult Jeff?" A dozen hands shot up like missile silos, straight toward
the low acoustic-tiled ceiling. They were the hands of defenders. The highest of them belonged to Bob Costa.

Costa was the only junior in attendance. (He had simply talked his
way out of class.) He had introduced himself to Greenwood before the
talk began. But Greenwood wasn't calling on him, so Costa ripped a piece
of paper out of a spiral notebook and, getting down the words as fast as he
could, wrote, "You spoke of a rocky road to peace. Don't you believe that
if we truly want peace, we must work with our allies, and wait for our
allies, *before* we attack? Your voting record as a congressman is steadfast
in Bush's corner. As *our* representative, don't you need to have some res-
ervations?" When a friend had the floor, Costa thrust the piece of paper
in his hand. But his question never got read, and the 2:10 P.M. final school
bell rang, with nothing resolved in the cafeteria.

There was, at the request of Mrs. Danielewski, a round of applause
for Greenwood. It was lukewarm. A half-dozen or so students surrounded
the congressman when he was through, trying to continue the discussion. Many more kids were high-fiving Jeff Heinbach on their way out.

III.

The next day, buried on page four of the B section of the *Inquirer*, there
was a short news story about Congressman Greenwood's hour-long visit
to the big public high school in Fairless Hills. The headline read: TEEN
GETS AN EARFUL ON IRAQ AT PENNSBURY HIGH. The reporter, Kellie Patrick,
had all the salient quotes, including several from Costa, naturally, and
from the protagonists. "I thought it was an important lesson for him and
everyone in the room," Greenwood told the reporter. "Words matter.
There are consequences to speech. If you make an accusation, you have
to expect to be challenged." The story gave the final word to Heinbach,

who acknowledged that his opinions did exceed his knowledge, but that his beliefs stemmed more from feelings than information. His final quote was brilliant: "I'm just a . . . teenager." What defense is there to that?

Evidently, people read stories buried on page four of *The Philadelphia Inquirer*'s B section on a weekday in February. That day Greenwood's office fielded calls from constituents who wanted to know why the congressman was beating up on a kid. In Pennsbury's hallways, Heinbach was being greeted with raised fists. *Right on.* The night after their lives first crossed paths, Heinbach and Greenwood went on a Philadelphia talk radio show, each reciting lines that already sounded scripted. The next morning there was a follow-up in the *Inquirer*, this one buried even further, on page nine of the B section. The first quote was from Greenwood, who said, "This is a little bit of a tempest in a teapot." The last quote was from Heinbach. "He's a congressman, and I'm just some kid." A variation on a theme.

Then there was a hilarious anti-Greenwood column in the *Courier Times*. The columnist, J. D. Mullane, recounted his telephone interview with Greenwood regarding the Heinbach affair. The writer had asked the congressman, "Why'd ya call the kid stupid in front of his friends?" The interview ended with Greenwood hanging up on the writer.

The *Courier Times* also ran an editorial, befriending Heinbach. "The congressman could have challenged the student without getting nasty about it," it read. The editorial reminded readers that when Greenwood first won a seat in Congress in 1992, he had promised to limit his time in the House to six terms. "If words truly matter, then he should expect some challenges should he decide to run for a seventh term in 2004. Or will those challengers be dismissed as cynics, too?"

There was a follow-up column in the *Inquirer* as well, where Bob Martin wrote, "This was not *The O'Reilly Factor.* This was not a congressional inquiry into Enron, which Greenwood has led. This was not a partisan assault on his worthiness for office. This was an eighteen-year-old mustering up all his nerve at a school forum to raise concerns about a possible war." Martin said that Greenwood should apologize for his remarks.

The two papers published two dozen letters on the Heinbach-Greenwood affair, more supporting Heinbach than Greenwood. One letter chastised Greenwood for deflating the tiff to "just a little tempest in a teapot." That was not what Greenwood had said, but the whole little tempest now had a life of its own. When Greenwood called the incident "a media echo chamber over nothing," he got hammered on talk radio all over again.

Back at Studio 230, Mr. Wilson was receiving urgent calls from news organizations and a press guy from Greenwood's office. The word was out that somebody—*Harry Stymiest!*—had taped the whole session. They all wanted to know the same thing: Could they get a copy of the tape?

Harry was in the story now. He had shot the whole episode beautifully, panning left and panning right, zooming in, shooting *B roll*, the professional term, favored by Harry, for cutaway footage. Mr. Wilson discovered only one problem when he went to play the tape. There was no sound. Harry had forgotten to press the audio button.

For about a day Harry was ill with embarrassment, but Mr. Wilson covered for his cameraman. He told all the callers that he wasn't going to let the tape out. But he made an offer to Greenwood that the congressman could not refuse: a session, taped by PHS-TV for broadcast to sixty thousand homes in Lower Bucks County, that would allow Greenwood and Heinbach to clarify their positions. Greenwood seized the chance. Heinbach's mother, now following the lead of the *Inquirer* columnist and looking for an apology, said yes, as long as she could veto the airing of the interview if she was unhappy with it. Mr. Wilson agreed.

Mr. Wilson assembled his A team. Costa would be the host. Blair Maloney, Costa's "colleague" at the John Mayer concert, would be the director. Mr. Wilson, not wanting to put Harry back in the fray but not wanting to exclude him, put him in charge of graphics. The morning interview took place in Studio 230. Greenwood, who had a meeting scheduled with President Bush that afternoon, was wearing a suit. Costa, sitting in the center, wore jeans and a cotton sweater with a T-shirt underneath. Heinbach sat on Costa's left, wearing a checkered flannel shirt and jeans. He was noticeably nervous, absentmindedly scratching his right palm on his armrest.

But Heinbach was never at a loss for words. He told Greenwood, "I'm willing to forgive you for the comment you made," although the congressman never offered anything like an apology. The closest he came to it was when he said, "The point I was trying to make, however

clumsily," and then continued his civics lesson about the difference between cynicism and skepticism. When Greenwood paused for a breath,
Heinbach jumped in, beginning a long soliloquy with "Permit me to rant
a little bit. You have to understand my sense of humor. It's dark."

Costa was left trying to put some sort of positive face on a weird
and uncomfortable cable encounter. He closed the discussion by saying, "It's great that we are able to come together as congressman and
constituent."

It was a woefully lopsided debate among unequals, and it was painful to watch. "We don't want the interview aired," Jeff's mother told
Mr. Wilson when it was over. She did not need to. Mr. Wilson had made
his decision long before Costa had signed off. This was *not* PHS-TV gold.
PHS-TV didn't do weird and uncomfortable.

When Heinbach departed, Costa did a one-on-one interview with
Greenwood, a special edition, Costa reminded his viewers, of PHS-TV's
The Voice. Costa asked the veteran congressman about the SEC and the
IRS, medical malpractice abuse, campaign finance reform, term limits.
He asked what Bush was really like. "He's smarter than people think,
I'll tell you that," Greenwood answered. With considerable help from
Costa, Greenwood did a brilliant job of reminding voters that he did more
than beat up on hundred-pound teenagers. At the end of the interview,
Costa asked Greenwood whether he planned to run for a seventh term,
despite what he had said in 1992. The congressman was vague. In
Pennsylvania's Eighth District, the Democrats had been running weak
candidates, and it was an easy seat to keep. "I have the sense I'll be
there until you run against me," Greenwood said, reaching to shake the
interviewer's hand.

"I don't think I'll have to run against you," Costa said. "You'll be in
the Senate by then."

IV.

In the first Heinbach-Greenwood *Inquirer* story Costa was described,
while introducing himself to the congressman, as "a happy-to-see-him
young Republican." It must have been a message Costa sent inadvertently. Costa's own parents, who were Republicans, assumed their

politics fell to their firstborn son. Maybe they were fooled by Bob's deep interest in the Republican National Convention, held in Philadelphia in the summer of 2000. But the thing Bob loved about the convention was being near the action, not the politics being preached. One night Bob got swept into a busload of conventioneers on a midnight tour of Philadelphia and wound up separated from his father until three A.M. Bob was never worried.

He did have a wide conservative streak. As a matter of law, he believed in a woman's right to abortion. But as a matter of personal conduct, he did not believe teenagers should have sex unless they were ready to raise an unwanted, unexpected child. In the winter of his junior year, that was his thinking, and that was his practice. (It was a practice that had gone unchallenged, because he had never been in a relationship where both parties were ready to have sex.) Bob knew Stephanie and Rob, the young Pennsbury parents. He knew what happened weekly in Mrs. Blakesley's fall EOP class, how only one expecting father—Rob—showed up. "I'd like to tell those others to shape up, get a job, and be the best father you can be," Costa said. He respected Stephanie and Rob for having a baby and carrying on with their changed lives.

But Bob was a Democrat. On the freezing January day when Ed Rendell, the former Philadelphia mayor, was sworn in as Pennsylvania governor, Costa skipped school, hitched a ride to the state capital with a busload of Revolutionary War reenactors, and watched. The ride to Harrisburg was long and the bus was crowded. Bob, dressed in modern garb, was wedged into a group of Continental soldiers wearing musty period costumes. But when he saw Governor Rendell up close, when he shook the governor's hand and looked up at him and said, "Make us proud, Ed," he knew the trip had been worthwhile.

He thought of the moment, captured on film and seen by the world decades later, when Bill Clinton, Arkansas schoolboy, had shaken hands with President John F. Kennedy. "Nobody knew then that a sitting president was meeting a future president, except Clinton," Bob said. "Kennedy was looking him right in the eye. Rendell was the mayor, now he's the governor. Someday he could be president. You don't know. Would I want to be president someday? Yeah, sure, of course. But I hope I would want to be president for the right reasons. I wouldn't want to be Newt Gingrich, ruling by ego. I'd want to be Rendell. I'd want to be Clinton. I'd want to help people."

Costa dismissed Clinton's Oval Office hanky-panky as a sideshow. His hero was the Clinton who cared about ordinary people, who had been elected president because he felt people's pain.

The congressman had Costa pegged. Greenwood had found the Democrat in Lower Bucks County who would be able to unseat him.

V.

Sometime later, there was a competition at Pennsbury called Wing Bowl. Costa was master of ceremonies. The idea was to eat as many wings as you could without throwing up. But if you did vomit, that was okay. The event was staged in Studio 230 and carried by PHS-TV. Going into the event, Harry Stymiest was one of the favorites. He told a PHS-TV interviewer, "I'm a wing-eating machine—I kill at the buffet line."

His effort was gallant. He assumed what appeared to be the classic position for high-speed wing-eating: elbows on the table, mouth by the plate, lips loaded with grease to reduce friction. It wasn't good enough. He lost in the quarterfinals.

"What do I do now, Mr. Wilson?" Harry asked. "Eat more wings or go to the cafeteria?" Harry was often looking for direction.

Blair Maloney was sitting at a nearby table, eating her lunch: fat-free key-lime-pie yogurt, water, peanut butter on whole wheat.

Mr. Wilson looked at Blair and then at Harry and said, "Let your conscience be your guide, Harry."

VI.

Jim Minton was one of Pennsbury's beloved teachers. The Prom Committee members appreciated his artistry, but it was the Levittown kids who really gravitated to him. He had lived in Levittown all his life. His age was a mystery. (He was fifty-five.) His ponytail was long but gray. He had artful tattoos up and down his arms. His approach to teaching was simple: *You bring me the kids, I'll size them up and teach them accordingly.* Because he taught art and photography, and because he was an artist himself, academic prowess in the upstairs classrooms—math and science in particular—was unimportant to him. He saw skills and possibilities in kids that other teachers did not.

He had a son, Nick, who had graduated from Pennsbury in 1999 and was now a teacher's assistant at the school. His actual title was *mentor*, and his job was to tutor kids who struggled to function in a regular classroom. In high school, Nick had been a wild child. As a senior, he and a buddy had a yearlong contest to see how many girls they could get to flash their breasts in the school's hallways. (Nick won, with a high two-digit score.) The prediction back then was that Nick would someday move from Levittown to the Bucks County Prison. But three years after graduating from Pennsbury, he had an associate's degree, a job, and a purpose.

Mr. Minton believed in giving kids, his students and his own, ample room to figure things out for themselves. But he knew there had to be limits.

One Sunday morning he sent an e-mail to a group of his photography students about an upcoming art show. Late that afternoon one of them wrote back to him: "What a fucking loser you are, you old lady. It's Super Bowl Sunday. You should be out partying, getting high and drinking, like I am now."

Mr. Minton's correspondent was one of his favorite students, a Levittown girl who was funny and pretty but difficult to figure out. She had a strong artistic bent, but she was also often in fights, verbal and physical. She was hard to reach.

There was a snide joke in her e-mail that made Mr. Minton laugh. Her class had been looking at a group picture from a trip. Mr. Minton had pointed to a figure with long gray hair and innocently asked, "Who is this old lady?"

But as soon as read the letter, he knew what he'd be doing with it: forwarding it to the girl's guidance counselor. Pennsbury teachers were obligated to report to a counselor—though not an administrator—*any* suspected drug use.

Mr. Minton knew that his ponytail and tattoos sent out a mixed message. Kids felts they could tell him anything, that he was one of them. He wasn't. He was a teacher, an authority figure. He was obligated to be cautious. He knew the girl came from a troubled family. She craved attention. She wore tiny T-shirts and low pants, and periodically she was sent to the main office for dress-code violations. Whenever she dressed with relative modesty, Mr. Minton would lavish praise on her, but his efforts at positive reinforcement invariably failed. The next day her navel would again be on public display.

Shortly after Super Bowl Sunday, the girl was sitting in Mr. Minton's classroom and describing for a friend how she had been shepherded into her guidance counselor's office. Her parents had been called in, too. She was being forced to join a drug-abuse counseling program.

"Somebody turned me in," she said to her friend. "It was probably *you*," she said, pointing to Mr. Minton. She was joking.

"Actually, it was," Mr. Minton said.

"What?" The girl was flabbergasted. "No way."

"You sent me that e-mail. I don't know if you do drugs or not," Mr. Minton said. "But if you overdosed and I had that e-mail and never did anything about it, I couldn't live with that." He would have been fired, too.

Mr. Minton's relationship with the girl had changed. The playfulness was gone. Mr. Minton had no problem with that. He was the girl's teacher, not her friend. One day the girl told him some good was coming from her counseling sessions. It confirmed for him the soundness of one of his operating principles, as a father and as a teacher: *You're responsible for what you know.*

VII.

The Pennsbury kids used e-mail and instant messaging to reveal their real selves or to be the people, hiding behind LCD screens, they wished to be. Sometimes it was hard to know which person was more real, the one online or the one in the hallways. In her online profile, one popular Pennsbury student described herself in her own words and with grammar and spelling borrowed from rap culture:

Im a princess I live in the clouds if ya wanna kick it you betta bow down so get on ur knees and call me ur hiness so baby believe me

im Pennsburys finest Party hardy, rock n roll drink beer smoke a bowl
life is great sex galore we r the class of 2004.

And when you passed her in the hallways, she seemed like such a
nice girl.

VIII.

Shortly before Valentine's Day, another popular girl wrote a poem and
taped it to a school wall:

This Valentine's Day
Everything's kinda crazy

If Osama has his way
We'll all be pushing up daisies

Codes Orange & Red
Won't get US down

He gets satisfaction
When we worry and frown

So in the spirit of love
I'll give you this

I'll put my heart on your hand
With one last request . . .

USE PROTECTION!

IX.

As a young father, Rob Stephens was motivated to make money, but
the job with Kirby Vacuums had not worked out for him, as Stephanie
Coyle had predicted. In school he was doing okay. He defined the word

epitome on command one day in Mr. Mahoney's short-story class. Still, even with the prodding of the mother of his child, there was no saying what his report card would look like. He needed to pass every class for the rest of the year if he was going to graduate in June. He needed to have nearly perfect attendance. (He could miss the Monday after the prom, but that was about it.) Mr. Mahoney said something often of kids, and in Rob's case, it was particularly true: He was a smart kid, he just didn't apply himself. But that didn't stop him from having grand dreams. He planned to graduate and enroll in a local technical school to learn computer programming, where graduates could expect to find jobs starting at $30,000 or more. The school cost $24,000 for an eighteen-month program. Where that money would come from, Rob did not know.

Away from school, pushing Luke in the stroller at the mall, Rob and Stephanie seemed to be twice their actual age. Not in appearance but in manner. They were each other's best friend, even when they squabbled. Rob never tired of listening to Stephanie's dreams: to one day own a home away from Levittown, a house with a basement and a full second floor. She hoped to have enough money to send Luke away to college. They talked about getting married, far in the future. Rob's parents had worked things out, despite the odds. Rob and Stephanie figured they could, too.

In February, Stephanie returned to school as a full-time student. She was in first lunch, and Rob was in fourth. The scheduling annoyed Stephanie. How hard would it have been to put her in the same lunch as the father of her child? She realized then that there would be no breaks for her just because she was a teenage mom.

One day Stephanie and Rob brought the baby—the ultimate show-and-tell item—to Mrs. Blakesley's teen-parenting EOP class, where Rob and Stephanie were held up as model teen parents. They carried Luke through Pennsbury's halls. Rob's mother had never taken him as an infant to school, but these were different days.

As they left Mrs. Blakesley's class, one of the first people they saw was Harry Stymiest, the first friend Rob had told about Stephanie's pregnancy. "Nice little baby," Harry said. "Give him an earring and a red goatee, and you'd think it was Rob!"

Most of the school knew Harry was working on getting the DeLorean
for prom night. Prom transportation was a big subject at Pennsbury, and
Stephanie—even with everything else going on in her life—was swept
up in it. She knew Rob had a dream about going to his prom in the Oscar
Mayer Wienermobile, a real and sizable van shaped like a hot dog but
many times longer. Stephanie began to wonder if there was a way to
make that happen.

X.

Jim Cunningham's final day of teaching came in February. The father
of the Pennsbury prom had known the day was coming for a long time,
since his return from his nine-week leave of absence in 2000. He was
ready to leave the building that had been a second home to him for over
thirty years. He was ready to say good-bye to people who had known
him all his adult life. He was ready to call it a day on a career that had
transformed a working-class kid into a secure member of the upper
middle class. It was a career that had provided him with an outlet for
his love of American history, and for his creative streak. He was leaving
behind a legacy: the Pennsbury prom. He wondered what his emotion
would be as he walked out of Pennsbury for the final time.

As a farewell gift, Mr. Katz gave Mr. Cunningham *The Writer's Hand-
book*. The principal hoped the reference book would help his longtime
history teacher find a publisher for the historical novels he had been writing about the slaves who built the White House and the curses they put
on it. Mr. Cunningham had been unable to work on the books since the
September 11 attacks. In retirement, he thought he would be able to return to his writing.

There was no champagne on his final day, just a lot of people shaking his hand. There was no rousing final lecture, no last walk through
the classroom door amid raucous applause. There was no teaching at
all. Another teacher was in Mr. Cunningham's classroom on his final
day. The only reason Mr. Cunningham was in the building at all was
because some district bureaucrat required him to be. Mr. Cunningham
spent most of the day sitting in the department faculty room, one eye
on the clock, counting down the minutes until 2:10 P.M.

He waited for some feeling to hit him as he walked out of the building. But there was nothing.

He woke up early on the first morning of his retirement, a Thursday. He got dressed, had breakfast, and . . . didn't go to school. It felt normal. Emotionally, he had been retired for years.

The prom, his baby, was three months away. He had heard there was a problem with the prom hypnotist, who wanted a legal release in his contract. Once, such talk would have kept Jim Cunningham stirring through the night. Not anymore.

XI.

Soon after Mr. Cunningham's last day, Alyssa Bergman had her final day. Her mother had questioned the wisdom of graduating early, and now, when it was too late, Alyssa felt conflicting emotions. Suddenly, she couldn't understand why she had ever been in such a rush. When she had first asked about graduating early, she never imagined becoming homecoming queen. Now she was more attached to the school than she had ever been. She enjoyed her status. She liked knowing that people were watching her. She knew her friendships in school, with Danielle Nutt and Jaime Schaffer and a very few others, depended on the daily exchange of gossip and observation. She knew those friendships would suffer when she left Pennsbury.

But when her final day came, what she felt most was excitement. She was ready for bigger and better things. As she walked out the front door, she felt she was having her own private graduation ceremony. She was certain she was the only person in the world marking the occasion.

She was wrong. Costa and his buddies were watching as Alyssa made her final departure. They stood in the parking lot and beheld the sight of Alyssa Bergman slipping into her sleek black Corvette and driving off one last time.

XII.

For Bobby Speer, football season ran into wrestling season, and wrestling season ran into baseball season. There was no time to breathe. There was homework and helping with Danny and nightly visits from his girl-friend, Lauren. Sports Nite was coming up, and Bobby was a team captain for that. He had college forms to fill out and coaches to talk to on the phone, and now he was volunteering to work on the stage crew for the spring musical, *Camelot*. He had no sudden dramatic urge, but he felt there were whole areas of the school and whole parts of the student body he knew nothing about. He wanted to fix that before it was too late. He was overbooked. His every moment seemed accounted for.

His every meal, too. He weighed 190 pounds during the football season and wanted to drop twenty pounds before his first wrestling match, so he could wrestle in the 171-pound weight class.

Extensive guidelines in Pennsylvania—one of the few states where high school wrestling continued to be a prominent winter sport—stipulated what a wrestler was allowed to do to make weight. The policy emphasized healthy eating and banned the use of rubber suits, saunas, fasting, and diet drugs. Violations were rampant, at Pennsbury and elsewhere. Bobby Speer lost twenty pounds in a month in a way that would never get the stamp of approval from any pediatrician, nutritionist, or trainer. He slept as late as he could so he would be forced to run out the door without eating. During his half-hour school lunch, he'd move from table to table, flirting with girls while drinking water. After school he went straight to practice. Then he'd have dinner either at home or at Burger King. He felt fast at 171. Wrestling is all about feeling fast.

Bobby had been written up in the *Courier Times* as a member of a dying breed, the three-sport athlete, for years the mark of athletic excellence in high school. But by Bobby's era, high school athletes were configuring their bodies with athletic scholarships in mind, seeking excellence not just in a single sport but in a specific position. The three-letter athlete was heading for extinction, just like the prom in the school gym. Bobby didn't see why people made such a fuss about his playing three sports. He wrestled and played football and baseball because he could, and because competing was in his blood.

At the start of football season, Bobby had wondered how he would get along with his new head coach. Kirk Safee had known immediately that Coach Snyder's reliance on the running game would be costly to Bobby. But Bobby couldn't help himself: Coach Snyder treated him like a man, and Bobby liked him. He asked Bobby, a team captain, his opinion of plays and players. Only once did he go into a full-blown screaming tirade at Bobby, when he handed the ball to the wrong back in summer camp.

Bobby's relationship with his coach had been a pleasant surprise, but the season was dismal, and the Falcons had failed to make the play-offs. They lost to lesser teams. No college recruiters were knocking down Bobby's door. It had been an exhausting four months.

And now here was wrestling season, which was every bit as demanding as football. Pennsbury excelled at wrestling year after year—the wrestling room was crowded with banners—and in Bobby's senior year, the Falcons were considered contenders for the state championship. Bobby's teammates were telling him that at 171, he'd have a chance to wrestle for the individual state title. The wrestlers were a bunch of guys in a room. They were like fraternity brothers; they hung out together on Saturday nights. Bobby, of course, was welcome to join them. But he never did.

At one big meet in Bobby's freshman year, the Pennsbury wrestling room was packed with parents and wrestling fans and even cheerleaders. A Pennsbury wrestler was pinned. While he was stretched out on the mat, it became obvious that he had an erection. One of the cheerleaders pointed at it, and then others did, and in the time it takes for a referee to slap his hand on a rubber mat, the wrestlers, cheerleaders, and spectators had broken into fits of laughter. The boy might have survived the moment, but his mother, horrified, threw her coat on top of her son. Afterward, the boy got the silent treatment from his teammates. He quit the team. The next year he switched schools. The story became a team joke.

But not for Bobby. There was something different about him. He didn't go to certain parties, he didn't laugh at certain jokes, he didn't *need* to be one of the boys. It made him even more of an icon.

XIII.

In February the police investigators in Florida completed their toxicology report on Mike Kosmin. At the time of his death, Mike's blood alcohol level was .16, twice the level that could get a person convicted for drunk driving in Florida. He had been drinking cranberry juice mixed with vodka. Cranberry chasers, the police called it.

Cyndi and Mike were astounded. They wanted to know where Mike was served alcohol. But a criminal investigation was still under way, and the police were limited in what they could say.

Cyndi and Mike could only imagine what effect so much alcohol had on a boy who was not, as far as they knew, a drinker. For weeks, they tortured themselves with questions. Why had they let Mike extend his Florida stay? Why hadn't they asked who he was hanging out with there? Why hadn't they introduced him to the mysteries and dangers of alcohol themselves? But all the while, they refused to assign any blame to Mike's father. They knew how he was suffering, too.

A full night of sleep had become a distant memory to Mike and Cyndi. Every night at 2:09 A.M., they woke up in horror and struggled to get back to sleep.

XIV.

One freezing weekday night in the dead of winter, when the roads were icy and slush mountains towered over the Pennsbury parking lots, Mr. Minton and Mr. Mahoney held the first parents' meeting of the prom season. Eighty or ninety people, mostly mothers, assembled in the school cafeteria. The rest of the building was still and silent. A janitor ran a wide broom down the hallways, collecting candy wrappers and leaving luster in his wake. The parents sat on the plastic cafeteria chairs and enthusiastically signed up for inherently dull jobs. They volunteered to serve dinner on prom night, to check coats, and to monitor the restrooms, among other mundane tasks. "The kids want to outdo last year's prom," Mr. Mahoney said, reciting a practiced speech. "And I think we have a real chance to do that." While he talked, a TV in the cafeteria played a videotape of the previous year's prom. The dancing was indecent and thrilling, hair flying and bodies exposed. The mothers were once those kids, but now they were forty- and fifty-somethings, many of them with stiff hair and wide waists and baggy sweatshirts that hid their bodies. They were moms. Their lives and anatomies and priorities had changed.

Mary Milroy, Lindsey's mother, was at the meeting, front and center. Her daughter was an overall Prom Committee co-chair and Mary wanted to be part of the action, too. When she graduated from Pennsbury in 1972, she was Mary Thiel, of the plumbing-supply Thiels. She wasn't a glamorous member of her class, but she had a date for the prom, and she had friends. As a senior she spent her Saturday nights driving around the farms beyond Newtown and Yardley, before the developments had sprung up, drinking beer in cans and throwing the emptics into cornfields. They didn't wear seat belts. They didn't have a designated driver. All they had was good luck.

As a mother in her thirties and forties, her good genes, spending money, and athletic life kicked in. She was closing in on fifty, but she had a young woman's slim body, maintained by skiing and an overworked nervous system. She and her daughter shared a skillful hairdresser, Norma at Innovations IV in Yardley. Mary Milroy looked young and acted young.

But the key to her youthfulness was her children, Lindsey and her brother, Kevin Jr., two years younger. Mary was in their lives. She kept their secrets. An enemy of Lindsey's was Mary's enemy, too. Mary pushed field hockey, dresses, hairdos, and boyfriends on her daughter. The daughter, in return, could say, "Shut up, Mom," as if she were talking to one of her friends. Lindsey said those words often. It didn't faze her mother one bit.

With young Kevin, the same: The mother wasn't afraid to be involved. When she and her husband came home one night and found that Kevin and a friend had polished off a bottle of Crown Royal whiskey, they made a midnight run to the emergency room. Somehow she managed to push two drunk teenage boys across a driveway and into her car. Mary's mother, who lived with the Milroys, was worried about what the neighbors would think. Mary was not. "I don't care who knows," she said. "I'm not going to have them choke on their own vomit!" Kids drink, get drunk, do stupid things. Everybody knows that. The crime would be to ignore it.

Chapter Eight

Unplugged

March

I.

Mr. Mahoney and Mr. Minton, as Mr. Cunningham once had, waited eagerly for the conclusion of Sports Nite, held each year on a Friday and Saturday night in mid-March. For Sports Nite, the juniors and seniors were divided into two teams, Orange and Black. The teams competed in line dancing, tug-of-war, piggyback races, something called Izzy Dizzy, another event called Grab Ball, and other competitions not likely to become Olympic sports. Each year a Sports Nite queen was named, and the 2003 winner was Alyssa Bergman's friend Danielle Nutt, dressed in a gown and looking like a lounge singer, circa 1955. Sports Nite, like the prom, was another long-standing Pennsbury tradition with roots in a vanished era. It had ardent support from Mr. Katz and was extremely popular. Well over a thousand kids took part. In the weeks leading up to it, the Pennsbury gym was turned over to cheerleaders and dance troupes and various musical ensembles. After Sports Nite, the Prom Committee owned the gym in a two-month dead run to the prom.

Bobby Speer was the captain of the Orange team. Costa was the master of ceremonies. Harry Stymiest taped hours and hours of the action, with instructions from Mr. Wilson to edit it all down to three hours for a $20 souvenir PHS-TV tape. Jeff Heinbach, enjoying sudden fame after the Greenwood debate, was a Sports Nite subcaptain for the Black team, a role he approached with the same kind of manic energy the late Keith Moon once played drums for The Who.

The audience for Jeff Says No was expanding with Jeff's new fame, and more people were aware of his band's occasional Friday-night coffee-house gigs in the basement of the Sacred Ground Quaker Meetinghouse. A Jeff Says No CD was making the rounds at the school. Kids were urging Jeff to have the band play at Spring Breakout, an after-school jam session on a Friday in May. People who had never noticed Heinbach were now starting conversations with him.

You going to college?
Yeah.
Where?
Temple.
Prelaw?
Film.
Film?
To be a director.
Like Spiegelberg or something?
Maybe more like Wes Anderson.
Oh. The guy from those Elm Street movies?
That's Wes Craven . . .

Sports Nite was a coming-out party for Heinbach.

Sports Nite started late and ran late and gave kids an excuse to come home late. After it was over, kids piled into the Pennsbury haunts on Route 1, the boundary that would have separated Levittown and Fairless Hills from Newtown and Yardley, if Pennsbury didn't exist to bring them all together. They filled up booths at the Great American Pub and Diner and the Blue Fountain Diner. They went late-night bowling at the Levittown Lanes. Some tried to get into Da Pub. They hung out in front of the 7-Eleven by the school. They drove by the places where their parents ate and shopped and drank: Olive Garden, Reedman's Auto Mall, a bar called the Red Raven. Lindsey Milroy, driving her silver '99 Mercury Tracer, stopped for a passing train, and the girl riding shotgun, a senior with a notable wild streak, got out and started dancing in the road while idling men honked. In the frigid late-winter air, and under the moonlight, an off-duty cement mixer sat in the driveway of a tired suburban home, its gloomy, massive keg brightened by brilliant jagged stripes of red and green and blue. The cement mixer might have been a startling sight, its beauty so unexpected. But not to the Pennsbury kids. They drove right by it. They'd seen it plenty of times before.

II.

Bobby Speer's stint on the stage crew for *Camelot* opened up new worlds to him: actors, musicians, painters, stagehands. And many of them were girls! His girlfriend, Lauren Cognigni, was not pleased. She knew Bobby loved to flirt, and it bothered her. She was a star in her own right, the ace pitcher of the Pennsbury softball team, which was predicted to be among the best high school softball teams in the Philadelphia suburbs. But in her relationship with Bobby, Lauren, a junior, was in the passenger seat. And she knew that the more she complained about Bobby's flirting the worse it would become. It was a vicious cycle. By March it was what they talked about most.

Not that Bobby was much of a talker. Coaches and teachers found it perplexing that someone who was so quiet could become such a magnet for girls, but that's how it was for Bobby. When Lauren came to Bobby's house, as she often did, they sat on the living room sofa, with Danny nearby in his wheelchair, watching TV, all three of them comfortable in the quiet. Sometimes they played board games. Between turns, there was no adolescent chitchat about what they would do with their lives, the places they would go, the people they would meet.

For Bobby and Lauren, their most substantive discussions were conducted by computer, through e-mails or by instant messaging. IM exchanges had the impermanence of talking on the phone, which was good, but they provided more of a mask than a telephone conversation or— please, no—a face-to-face discussion.

Even in their electronic conversations, Lauren did most of the talking. Bobby wasn't much for technology. He didn't like computers or telephones. He felt videotape was valuable for studying opposing defenses and not much else. He didn't like to overanalyze anything. Sometimes in his IM conversations with Lauren, Bobby would have his step-sister represent him while he hung out with his brother-in-law. On the March day that Bobby decided to break up with Lauren, he had his step-sister do the heavy lifting. He felt that IM would be the best way to deliver the news, and that Chrissy could express his views better than he could. Poor Lauren never knew what had happened: that after a year and three months of loyalty, she had been given her unconditional release by her boyfriend's stepsister.

They had been Pennsbury's biggest celebrity couple for a long time, and their breakup, among the many Pennsbury girls who cared about such things, was a major event. News of it swept across the cafeteria tables with incredible speed and reasonable accuracy. There were girls making lists of Bobby's potential prom dates. There were girls volunteering to be on that list. There were girls who argued that Bobby would still take Lauren, out of respect for the fifteen months they'd been together.

Everybody assumed Lauren would still want to go with him. Juniors always wanted to get to the prom. (*Costa!*) Also, she already had her prom dress, which she had acquired over Christmas vacation in an elaborate trade with a friend in college. It was salmon-colored, beaded and sleeveless, with a V-neck and an exposed back. Lauren had bought matching high-heeled shoes.

The breakup was unpopular in some circles, but Bobby was an untouchable. He remained Pennsbury's prince.

At a school function one night, a woman approached Karen Speer.

"Are you Bobby Speer's mother?"

"Yes."

"I just want to thank you."

"What on earth for?"

"Your son talks to my son."

"Well, why wouldn't he? I'm sure your son—"

"You don't understand. Your son *talks* to my son. Your son is a star. My son is in the marching band. Football stars don't talk to kids in marching band."

With the *Camelot* kids, Bobby did more than talk. He tossed a football with them. He smudged the line between athlete and thespian. The football star who routinely said no to the Brew Crew keg parties attended the *Camelot* cast party. He asked out one of the drama girls. An impulsive and excited yes spilled forth from her.

Later, when she returned to earth, she cited a house rule: Her mother had to meet any boy taking out her daughter.

Bobby was not happy. "I just met you—I've got to meet your mother already?" But as soon as he said those words, he regretted them. He realized he was taking advantage of his celebrity status, and that was a violation of his code. "That's fine," he said. "Yeah. I'll meet her."

Only athletically, and only among the few people paying close attention, was Bobby's reputation taking a hit. The wrestling season, like the football season before it, had been a disappointment for Bobby. Twelve Falcons were named as Suburban One League, National Conference, Patriot Division, all-league wrestlers, but Bobby was not among them. He hadn't wrestled well in the state championship and was uneven in the regular season. His best moment was a close defeat against a kid who was supposed to dismantle him. Bobby found a positive in that, as athletes do. His friends and teammates and supporters spun it for him.

They were providing Bobby with damage control. He needed it. In the offices of some of the Pennsbury coaches, there was murmuring about him. He had once been the obvious front-runner for the Falcon Award, given to Pennsbury's athlete of the year, but the race was suddenly murky. To restore his name, he needed a good baseball season—and he needed people to notice. It was a tall task. It would be hard to shine on a team that was weak on pitching and power. Anyway, the spring sport at Pennsbury was girls' softball, a team that would go as far as Bobby's former girlfriend would take it.

III.

With the first day of spring came the first day of war. For two senior boys from the Pinewood section of Levittown, Nick Gasinski and Rick Swinnerton, close friends who had already enlisted, war was still too distant to be terrifying. They talked excitedly about meeting up on the other side of the world from Peachtree Street.

The war remained far away to most Pennsbury kids. The Jim Greenwood debacle in the Pennsbury cafeteria made the war more personal for some of them, but not many. Mr. Katz was nervous. On the day the U.S. and British tanks rolled through Iraq and U.S. bombs started to fall, the principal felt the way he had after the September 11 attacks. Bad news—the death of a pilot who had children in the distict—had come quickly that day. Mr. Katz was prepared for the same thing to happen again. He delivered the morning announcements ashen-faced and trembling more than usual. He said there was a plan in case the country—or Pennsbury itself—was attacked. He sought to be reassuring, but everybody could tell he was a wreck.

At first Mr. Katz planned to have the cafeteria TVs turned to CNN so the kids could see for themselves what was happening. Then he reversed himself, worried that war coverage, live and unedited, might be too graphic and too disruptive. It was not like Mr. Katz to waffle like that. Instead of carrying CNN, the cafeteria TVs showed Harry Stymiest's unedited tape from Sports Nite.

In the cafeteria and in the hallways on spring's opening day, many of the kids carried daffodils bought at a cancer-awareness fund-raiser. After school, scores of kids lined up for free ices at Rita's Water Ice, next to Marcelli's, the pizza place where Mike Kosmin used to park. It was a day of teeming cold rain, raw and awful. But Rita's gave free ices on the first day of spring, and the kids always lined up for them. Bad weather and a distant war weren't going to change that.

IV.

Shortly after the accident, Cyndi Mackrides received a phone call from the woman who drove the truck that struck Mike. By March the calls were coming more regularly. They were intended to comfort Cyndi, but before long, she realized that the driver was also in pain and looking for peace. The police weren't telling Mike and Cyndi much, but they did say the driver was blameless, and Mike and Cyndi didn't doubt that. The driver was twenty-seven, with a husband and an infant, and she had been driving home on a rainy night when the accident occurred. No alcohol, no drugs. Just a young mother driving home from work after finishing her eight P.M.-to-midnight shift, entering data in a computer. She was crossing Powerline Road west of Boca Raton, with its busy four lanes, eager to get home to her husband and baby when a boy darted into traffic and the path of her new Dodge Ram truck.

Cyndi wanted to know what had happened. The woman, Melissa Nermesan, from the Florida town of Coconut Creek, told her. Mike's body hit the front fender and he went flying high in the air. He landed on his face. Nermesan stopped her truck instantly and leaned down to a body she realized immediately was lifeless. Despite her shock and horror, she was thinking clearly. She called 911 on her cell phone and stopped traffic in both directions by raising her hands. While she was on the phone with the police, a group of teenagers, maybe four or five, came from the parking lot and kicked Mike's body to see if there was life in it.

The moment Cyndi heard that, she decided to hire a private investigator. She wanted to know *exactly* who these kids were and what they had been doing with her son.

V.

Bob Costa was writing regularly now for the *Courier Times*, and some of his pieces were creating a stir. He wrote a long story, using anonymous sources, about the prevalence of marijuana in high schools in Lower Bucks County. It ran under the headline STRAIGHT FROM THE SMOKER'S MOUTH. He quoted, without attribution, many kids who smoked pot and some who did not. One was a girl who said, "Even though a lot of smokers say they're friends with nonusers and talk about how they're so welcoming and Bob Marley-ish, pot still is a wall from really connecting with a lot of people at our school."

Bob's parents were fine with the story, just as they had been when Bob wrote an opinion piece objecting to the use of search dogs to find illegal drugs stashed in school lockers. (The dogs came up empty.) Costa maintained that the search was unconstitutional because the school did not have probable cause to send a sniffing dog to each kid's locker.

Free speech was important to Bob's lawyer parents. They applauded him for exploring his rights to it, even when his subjects left his school's administrators, and his parents, wriggling. They were raising a child who could think for himself.

Bob found himself thinking about Mike Kosmin daily. He tried to piece together the weird confluence of events, as he knew them, that had resulted in Mike's death. He began to accept that Mike had been drinking on the night he died, and possibly on no other night of his life. During a school memorial service at which Bob spoke, there was a video tribute to Mike, accompanied by The Who's "Teenage Wasteland." Bob knew there was no commentary in the selection, that it was just a place where Cyndi's musical tastes and her son's overlapped.

Bob's hatred—his *hatred*—for peer pressure (the rare meaningful buzz phrase) was intensifying with each marking period. He was determined to be, as the football player Hugh Douglas had called him, his own little man.

VI.

Costa continued to send John Mayer's agents e-mails, but they went unreturned. The musician was no longer Pennsbury's secret. He had won the Grammy for Best Male Pop Vocal for "Wonderland." At the awards show, Mayer clutched his award, leaned in to a microphone and millions of living rooms, and said, "I pride myself in being bigger than the moment. And this moment is kicking my ass." It sounded sort of humble.

Costa was certain that Maroon 5 would be the next big thing. He had been sending e-mails to the Maroon 5 manager, Ben Berkman, trying to get the band to play Pennsbury. One Sunday night Berkman wrote back with good news. The band had a gig that Thursday night at Princeton and could play a free concert that afternoon at Pennsbury. Bob immediately called Mr. Katz at home.

"I don't know, Bob," Mr. Katz said. "Let's meet tomorrow morning. Bring me some of their music."

Monday morning the principal found himself reviewing the band's lyrics.

"I don't know, Bob," Mr. Katz repeated. "They're talking about sleeping with an awful lot of women."

Bob did not know if Mr. Katz was being serious. He had a wry sense of humor. Bob kept his mouth closed.

"Okay, Bob, you can have them come."

As soon as Bob was out the door, Mr. Katz realized he had done something out of character. He had said yes without any logical basis for doing so. Nothing positive could come of this free concert, not in a tangible way. And much could go wrong.

Before the afternoon concert began, Mr. Katz was filled with regret. The band showed up late, with the kids already assembled in the auditorium. Upon arrival, the band kicked everybody out, to conduct a sound check. Mr. Katz had lost control of his own house. He wondered what fresh hell he was in.

But the chaos was short-lived, and before long, the doors were reopened and the kids streamed in. Mr. Katz's youngest son, visiting from Boston University, was a Maroon 5 fan and attended the concert. He liked seeing his father in the role of concert promoter, even if he did mistakenly write *Moody Blues* instead of *Maroon 5* on one concert pass. Harry Stymiest worked the entire room, onstage and off, with laminated PHS-TV/Maroon 5 credentials hanging from his neck, as if he were a cameraman for the MTV concert series, *Unplugged*. Mr. Wilson tapped his loafered, sockless right foot to the music. Mr. Katz and his son held up the back wall. The music was mellow, rhythmic, wholly original. The frontman, Adam Levine, thanked "Mr. Bob" for getting them there. Applause and whistling filled Mr. Bob's ears. The kids clapped in time with the music and rushed the stage in midconcert. For a moment Harry and his Canon GL2 got swallowed up in the crowd. Before it was over, Mr. Katz realized that something good was coming out of the concert, something intangible. The Maroon 5 gig had helped make the school year more interesting. It was an event the kids would not forget. It brought them—several hundred of them, anyway—together.

Costa was in his glory. And then his afternoon improved. A high, airy voice reached him amid the hum.

Hey, Bob.

Costa turned his head and took in the amazing sight of Alyssa Bergman. She was on her first visit back to the school since her final day of classes. "Great concert," she said. There was a smile across her perfectly made-up face. Bob was elated. She knew his name.

Somebody else called for him. He turned for a moment, and when he turned back, Alyssa was gone and the moment was over.

VII.

One day in March, Alyssa came home with news for her parents. She and her boyfriend were moving to Florida. They would be getting jobs at a T.G.I. Friday's in Tampa, where Michael's grandfather lived. They would use the grandfather's address to establish residency in Florida, where life, they felt, was tropical and easy. Alyssa would take classes at the University of Central Florida and pay in-state tutition, and Michael would enroll there, too, with the hope of making the basketball team and getting an athletic scholarship. She would have her Corvette there, and Michael would have his Camaro. (How good would those two cars look, side by side in a driveway, basking in the Florida sun?) They had it all figured out.

"I'm disappointed that you're telling us what you've decided to do instead of asking for our advice," her father said. He was under control, as always.

Frank Bergman knew his daughter well. Ever since Nick Driscoll, her first boyfriend, Alyssa had sought to avoid disappointing her father. He was playing his highest card first. But Alyssa was ready for him.

"Well, Dad, if it were up to you, I'd spend the rest of my life in this house," Alyssa said. She sought a playful tone.

"That's right. We have plenty of room." He didn't say, as he typically did, *For you and Michael.* That was how he conveyed his annoyance that Alyssa's boyfriend was not there to help explain the couple's decision.

He carried on, therapist-style: "Maybe a better thing would have been for you and Michael to come here and tell us what it is that you wish to do." No response was forthcoming. What could he say next? Stalling, he asked his daughter what the rush was, but he knew the answer. She was always in a rush for the next thing. That's why she'd left Pennsbury in the middle of her senior year.

Her father reiterated his great game plan, that she go to Bucks for two years, live at home, and save her money. He would pay for the community college, and she would live rent-free. But there was nothing new in his offer, and it made no impression. He upped the stakes.

"If you want to go, I think you and Michael should save ten thousand dollars together first, so you have something to fall back on," he said.

"Ten thousand! You just don't want me to leave!"

"How much do you really want it? If you really want it, you have to work for it. You both have jobs. You should be able to save. If you can't save here, how are you going to make ends meet in Florida?"

"What if we save five thousand?"

"Ten thousand, and you'll have my blessing."

Alyssa was ready to get on with her life, and nobody could see that—except Michael.

"We're moving to Florida!" she said. She stormed out.

VIII.

Over the course of the year, ISS was becoming more and more untamed. When the kids were out of control, Miss Snyder would yell, "Shut up! Shut up!" It was not effective. She was a rookie teacher with problem kids in a lousy space—a windowless, walled-off section of the auditorium—where they spent the entire school day. They all had too much time on their hands. One ISS inmate hung a sign that read:

ISS Prison
Protected by
Officer Snyder
Badge # 69 69 69

In March, Shawn Ledger, the senior rapper who held the record for most days in ISS, started telling people he was spending more time with Miss Snyder away from school than in it, which was saying something. Three other kids told me that they had seen Ledger and Miss Synder, the ISS teacher, with each other at parties or at the mall. Ledger, a handsome, impish kid, was wearing a $179 retro Chicago Cubs jersey to school regularly, which he said Miss Snyder had bought for him. Other students were present when Miss Snyder flipped Ledger the keys to her car, parked in front of her house in Levittown. She said that she had something—the jersey—for Ledger in the trunk. Ledger also said Miss Snyder drove him to Street Road Tattooz in Bensalem, ten minutes by car from Levittown, and paid for a tattoo he wanted. *Irish*, it read, across his upper back. Another student told me he was with Ledger and Miss Snyder when Ledger got the tattoo. He described how Miss Snyder had to leave the tattoo parlor and get more money from a cash machine to pay for it.

On a cold weekend night in February, Ledger said that he and a friend, Steve McIntyre, attended a raucous party for Miss Snyder's twenty-third birthday at her house. McIntyre, a Pennsbury basketball player, told me separately that he and Ledger arrived at the party together and that he took off before midnight, leaving Ledger there. Miss Snyder encouraged Ledger to stay, Ledger said. Steve drove home and Ledger remained, drinking one can of Miller Lite after another until he had knocked off two six-packs, by his counting. Most of the other people at the party were much older than Ledger. He barely talked to them. For a while, he played solitaire.

Ledger said he was reclining in a chair in the Snyder home when somebody said to him, "Look at these young bucks, already wasted."

"Hey, I'm eighteen and you're twenty-five," Ledger said he responded. "How do you feel about yourself now?"

One by one, as Ledger recounted the night, all the other party people left until the only ones remaining were the ISS star and the ISS warden. The party ended when Miss Snyder drove Ledger home.

"Don't tell anybody about this," Ledger said Miss Snyder told him.

Right then, he said, he was thinking the exact same thing.

IX.

By March it became clear that the University of Vermont wasn't going to come up with money for Lindsey Milroy to play field hockey, which meant that she was not going to go there. Nor was she going to Monmouth, near the New Jersey beaches that Win surfed, because she wasn't *ever* doing *anything* with Win again. That left West Chester University as her only real option. She was often cranky. She despised the subject of her college "decision," along with almost any other subject her mother raised.

"Fine, West Chester, whatever," she told her mother one spring day. "But I'm not playing field hockey there."

"What do you mean you're not playing field hockey? After all this?"

"I'm not playing anymore."

Lindsey's mother retrieved a newsletter from Lindsey's field-hockey club. On it was a list of every high school player on the team and where they would be playing in college. Lindsey's name was the only one without a college next to it.

"Would you shut up, Mom? I'm not playing field hockey anymore, okay? I hate field hockey, okay? Do you understand that, Mom? I hate field hockey."

She wasn't having the senior year she had dreamed of. Something was wrong with her, and she knew it.

Chapter Nine

Showers

April

I.

Every so often Dave Driscoll would hear something about his son Nick's first girlfriend, Alyssa Bergman. Mr. Driscoll was the head custodian at Pennsbury's athletic center, where there was a gleaming pool. Mr. Driscoll knew that Alyssa had been voted homecoming queen. He knew she had graduated early. Nick had dropped out of school after his sophomore year. Now he was twenty, living at home, looking for work. His father looked tired. He had worked at Pennsbury all his son's life.

"He could have done the work," Mr. Driscoll told me one April day. He was on his break. It was windy and cool, and he was wearing a flannel shirt and a sweatshirt over it. He had exited the building and gone to the bottom of an outdoor stairwell, out of the wind and out of view, to have a cigarette. Old leaves swirled in the corners of the stairwell like undying memories. "All he had to do was buckle down and do the work. But we took him to the school psychologist and to the doctor, and they said he had attention deficit disorder. ADD, they call it. And that became his excuse for why he didn't do the work. My wife and I would scream and yell: 'You're going to school.' But at some point, it's not worth the yelling anymore."

He had seen the pictures of the nominees for homecoming queen in the fall and thought Alyssa was the star among them. He had rooted for her. He remembered how nice she had once been to his son.

"They were a young couple, they were a nice couple, she was a nice girl, very pretty girl," Mr. Driscoll said. "But she was Nick's first girlfriend, and Nick was her first boyfriend, so the chances of it all working out weren't all that good. It's a shame. She came from nice people. The father was a chiropractor."

A gym class assembled on the track a short distance away. Mr. Driscoll rubbed out his cigarette against a cement wall and put the stub in his pocket.

"Nick's just home. No steady work. He thought he had a job at Lowe's, in the gardening department or something, but that didn't work out, what with all the bad weather we've had and all."

He shrugged his tired shoulders. There were shrieks from the playing fields, muffled by the wind. His break was over. He went back to work.

II.

April was all showers. The Pennsbury baseball season was off to a slow start, and the weather didn't help. Some days the team had to practice indoors. Only the most devoted fans were attending the games. Bobby's mother, Karen Speer, came, unless she was doing something with Danny. Her father, Vernon Bullock, never missed one. He had been an army soldier during World War II, and when he returned home, he began a small business, ThurO Exterminating. (*If it's exterminating, it's got to be ThurO!*) He was long since retired, and baseball was one of his hobbies. He was a member of the generation that had grown up on the pastime. The game's hooks were still deep in him.

Kirk came too. He got wrapped up in every pitch, at least when Bobby was at bat or on the mound. The family brought peanuts, umbrellas, blankets, and folding chairs. Sometimes Danny came, if he didn't have anything going on himself and if the ground was dry enough so that Bobby or Kirk could push his wheelchair across the clumpy grass field that separated the parking lot from the baseball diamond.

The girls' softball team and the boys' baseball team often played at the same time, and there were days that Bobby's former girlfriend, Lauren Cognigni, and Bobby pitched simultaneously. Lauren, in her junior year, was establishing herself as *the* best pitcher in Bucks County. The day after Lauren pitched, her name was routinely in headlines. Her season was a pitcher's dream, with one shutout after another, including a no-hitter and a perfect game. One game she pitched seventeen innings and gave up one run. She routinely struck out two or three batters per inning.

Bobby found himself missing her, and their breakup turned out to be brief. Bobby had only one date with the girl from *Camelot*. Soon after, baseball and softball season were under way, and Bobby was asking Lauren to forgive and forget and to come by the house again.

Danny was as pleased as anybody. He thought the world of Lauren—she treated him so nicely. He knew what it was like for her to have so much of her identity entangled with Bobby's high status. Despite Kirk's best efforts to make Danny a wheelchair baseball and basketball star, Danny was always known as Bobby's kid brother. He was either that or "the kid in the wheelchair." Danny found the idea of Bobby leaving for college both scary and oddly exciting.

But by late April, long past the height of the signing season, only one small-school coach was committed to even the idea of someday making Bobby the starting quarterback of his football team. That coach was from King's College, a small Catholic school in upstate Pennsylvania, with an enrollment of twenty-four hundred and a football stadium no bigger than Pennsbury's. Bobby thought King's would be a good fit for him. The football coach would allow him to try to play baseball, too. The school had a good academic reputation and a lovely, leafy campus. Most importantly, the financial-aid office would provide $20,000 a year in scholarships and grants, leaving the family responsible for $8,000. Bobby could manage that with a student loan (which his grandfather would cosign) and with a part-time job. Bobby had a school.

Meanwhile, Lauren's softball coach was preparing her family for a rush from recruiters. Coaches from Division I softball programs from across the country—from North Carolina, from Ohio, from Wisconsin—were already saying they wanted her. They were talking about a full scholarship, tournaments in warm places, private tutors, travel by plane, big parties. They were wasting their time. Lauren's father, Lou, a landscaper, didn't want his daughter going to an out-of-state school. He wanted her where he could watch her pitch, and keep an eye on her.

The athlete herself was unmoved by the attention. Lauren told friends she'd be just as happy going to the Levittown Beauty Academy and getting certified as a hairdresser. Hair was one of her abiding interests. Her own was shiny and magnificent. (She already had intricate plans for it for prom night.) In games, when she was mowing down batters, longish strands would sometimes fall over her lean face. She'd brush them away absentmindedly with her glove, stare into her catcher, and reel off another strikeout.

Bobby's season had been a struggle from the start, in the field and in the batter's box. The head coach, Steve Nielsen, and his assistant, Mike Barnes, both members of Pennsbury's class of '73, were accomplished baseball people. Coach Nielsen had gone to Penn State and Coach Barnes to William Penn College in Iowa, the same school that Kevin Milroy had attended. Both had played high-level minor-league ball. They knew the game. They felt Bobby looked tense in the batter's box. They were trying to show him a stance that would relax him.

Their stance and his personality were not a good fit. "I'm a tense kid," Bobby said one day, but not to his coaches. He wasn't one to confide in coaches. He kept it all in and went hitless, or close to it, game after game. He started to resent the men who were trying to change him. In his summer leagues, he had always pounded the ball.

There were other things going on in his life. The modest scale of his college football future was hitting him. Bobby was grateful to Kirk, but there were moments when he heard his stepfather talk about his life—*Bobby's own life*—and he didn't recognize it. Lauren was great, but sometimes he felt married. Then there were the travails in the life of his brother, who would soon be undergoing a series of delicate operations, including the surgical construction of a bladder, with the hope that he might someday be able to use a bathroom unassisted. (Bobby and everybody else worried about how Danny would respond if the surgeries failed to give him greater independence. Once, Danny had stopped eating for weeks and had lost forty-four pounds, hell-bent on showing everybody the control he had over his own life.) Mother's Day was coming up, not a day of celebration in Bobby's household. On Mother's Day, in 1982, Karen had told her mother she would be marrying a man her mother detested, Leo Speer; later that day, her mother died of a heart attack. And then there was the case of Leo Speer, whose unknown fate was always somewhere in Bobby's mind, deep in a vault where he chose not to go. There were things in his life, all right.

In an April game at Central Bucks West, Bobby, wearing the same number 1 he wore for football, was playing center field. The game was tied in the bottom of the eighth, in extra innings. (High school games are seven innings.) There was one out and no runners on base and a powerful C. B. West hitter was up. When the Pennsbury pitcher went into his windup, Bobby was standing in a slouchy, nonchalant way, with his hands at his sides. The batter smashed one in the gap between Bobby and the left fielder. Bobby got a late jump. The ball got past Bobby and kept on bounding, on a field with no outfield fence. It turned into a game-winning home run.

Coach Nielsen was pissed. Bobby had played the outfield all his life. He knew the correct way to stand when a pitch was delivered: knees bent, weight on your toes, shoulders forward, hands in front of you, ready to bound in any direction at the ping of a batted ball.

On the bus ride home, Coach Nielsen and Coach Barnes decided to bring Bobby into the baseball office when they returned.

"What do you think he'll say when we ask him what the ready position is?" Coach Nielsen asked his assistant.

"He's gonna say he doesn't know," Coach Barnes answered.

Coach Nielsen hoped his assistant was wrong.

The coaches sat Bobby down. They asked him to define the ready position. Bobby said he didn't know.

Now Coach Nielsen was more than pissed. He was disappointed. He said to Bobby, "If baseball isn't working out for you, son, tell me. Maybe there's something else you'd like to be doing." In his mind, he had already scratched Bobby from the next game's lineup.

Bobby's face went pale. He was a three-sport athlete, a senior, written up regularly in the *Courier Times*, still the leading contender for the Falcon Award. Was his coach really asking him if he wanted to be playing baseball? This was not the way his Pennsbury career was supposed to conclude. This was not part of the script.

III.

The day after the benching, Coach Nielsen did an unusual thing. He announced that Bobby would be the starting pitcher for the next game, at home against Central Bucks East. It was a big game against an old rival, and Coach Nielsen was giving Bobby the ball. The coach's methods confounded Kirk—benching Bobby one game, making him the starting pitcher for the next—but Bobby knew what it was: another chance, possibly a last chance. Bobby pitched a complete game and pitched well, and the Falcons won, 5–3.

Afterward the star pitcher was interviewed by an old-gent radioman from a local station.

"We at WBCB have really enjoyed watching you compete in *three* sports, Bobby," the sportscaster said.

"Thank you." Bobby was unfailingly polite. There was no wiseguy in him, not that any adult ever saw.

"What did you throw today?"

"I relied on my junk." That is, second-rate pitches, not a powerful fastball, not a sharp-breaking curve.

"Do you throw a slider?"

"I try to."

"Well, Bobby, we have some nice gifts for you: a certificate for a hoagie from All-Star Hoagie, and a Joan's Cream Soda, and another certificate for a small order of french fries from the Morrisville McDonald's."

"That's awesome," Bobby said, genuinely pleased. He liked cream soda.

Later that night Bobby and Danny and Lauren watched TV in the Speer-Safee living room. Lauren had pitched a no-hitter that day. Her name would once again be in headlines the next morning. That night, on Elm Lane in Elderberry, things were quiet. Everything was back to normal.

IV.

One day when baby Luke was down for a nap, Stephanie Coyle sat down and wrote a letter to the headquarters of Kraft Foods, makers of Oscar Mayer wieners and owners of the Oscar Mayer Wienermobile.

My dream is to be escorted to my prom in the Oscar Mayer Wienermobile. For a long time I was shy about my dream, but not after I met my boyfriend. We were talking about various things when out of the blue he asked me, "If we ever go to a prom together, what would you want to arrive in?" I was hesitant to answer because I thought he would think I was silly. I finally said, "OK, OK—I want to arrive in the Oscar Mayer Wienermobile." He stopped dead in his path. I had never seen someone so shocked by what I had said.

My boyfriend and I recently had a child together. My boyfriend is always buying me little things so that I'll know he's still thinking of me, that not all the attention is going to the baby. Now I feel it is my turn to give something back, but in a bigger fashion!

Would you please help me and my boyfriend become part of our school's ongoing prom history? Thank you so much for your time. A quick response of some kind to let me know that you got this would be great, but a response to let me know it can happen would be the best of all!

V.

Shawn Ledger claimed Miss Snyder was the first person to talk to others about their time together. He figured if she wasn't honoring their code of silence, he didn't need to, either. Stories linking the two were sweeping through the school. Eventually, they reached Mr. Katz's office. One day Miss Snyder was the ISS warden; the next she was gone from the school.

Ledger continued to wear his retro Chicago Cubs jersey to school and he showed off the fancy lettering of his tattoo to friends. One day when Miss Snyder's name came up, he said, "*Man, she bugs me out.*"

But he was happy to recount in rich detail his version of their days together.

Near the end of April, of her own volition, Miss Snyder left Pennsbury. She did so, she told me, because she got a better position at another school. Shawn Ledger's stories, she said, were total fabrications. She said she never bought him a tattoo or a baseball jersey and that he was never a guest at a party at her house, not that she ever knew about.

The Pennsbury jurors—the students and teachers who followed the Ledger–Miss Snyder soap opera—didn't have much at their disposal. They had his detailed stories, and those of his friends, and her blanket denials and abrupt departure. Trying to weigh the evidence, they asked themselves a question: Did Ledger have any reason to make up such elaborate lies?

VI.

The prom was no longer months away, but weeks. Spring had been cold and wet, but prom season was approaching. Kids talked about who was going with whom. Shops renting tuxedos distributed coupons in school. There were naturally pale senior girls getting darker by the week—through the magic of tanning salons—wanting just the right contrast between their dress and skin tone.

On the first night they were available, 354 prom tickets were sold, at $115 per couple. The kids came with crumpled tip money and crisp twenties and personal checks. Nobody complained about the price. The other Bucks County schools had proms that cost $160 per couple, or more. It was far less expensive to hold a prom in the gym than in a hotel ballroom, which was one reason Mr. Katz was determined to keep it at the school. The lower the cost of the tickets, the higher the percentage of the senior class who could and would attend. (There was a special fund, discreetly run, that helped kids from indigent families buy tickets.) Mr. Cunningham's attitude was the more, the better. The prom was an experience that helped define each class because *so* many kids attended. It was a shared experience. From such things civilizations rise—or classmates have something to talk about at their reunions, anyway.

The kids buying tickets were required to bring their student IDs to prove they were seniors at Pennsbury; the school had had trouble with interlopers. One senior boy bought a pair of tickets but asked if he could get a refund if he couldn't find a date. The answer was yes, but Frau Weston, the popular German teacher, advised the boy that she was an expert at finding matches for the matchless. She also reminded him he could buy a single ticket for $60.

The line to buy tickets snaked through the cafeteria and into the gym lobby. It took forty-five minutes to get through. The kids had to fill out a form listing their name, their date's name, emergency telephone numbers for both, and their nominees for prom king and queen. One white girl who had been dating a black boy, without her parents knowing, wrote *TBA* for her date. Many girls nominated themselves for prom queen. Many boys nominated their dates. One kid nominated an effeminate senior boy. Frau Weston confiscated that ballot. Every year somebody tried to pull a stunt like that, and every year Frau Weston caught it.

VII.

Bob Costa's report card from the third marking period included three disasters: a C in French, a C in chemistry, and a B- in journalism. The journalism grade was wrought by a ruinous combination of student precociousness and young-teacher insecurity. Still, an obvious pattern was showing up in Bob's academic performance. The things that interested him, he excelled at: forensics, school politics, PHS-TV, trying to pursue John Mayer and Maroon 5, guiding his own fledgling band, 1903 (he was the manager and bongo player), writing for the *Courier Times*. His English and social studies classes, the same. However, in choosing his courses, he didn't play to his strengths. He took the same math and science classes the "brains" took, but he had little affinity for those subjects, and it showed.

There was no point in Bob explaining any of this to his father. Tom Costa was looking for results. He examined the report card late one night while eating spaghetti and meatballs by himself after work. All he said was "If you want to go to the places you want to go, you can't have this."

He tossed the report card aside and said nothing more. The words crushed Bob. He knew they were true.

Tom Costa traveled often for work, and his days in the office were long. Dillon Costa ran the house and the lives of the four Costa children, but Tom Costa was not an absentee father. He presided as a moral authority in the lives of his children. His time with them was often an occasion: going to church, to a Phillies game, to the Republican National Convention, to *something*. He was involved.

Hours after Maroon 5 played Pennsbury, Bob sent an e-mail to John Mayer's various representatives, telling them about the success of the concert. Maroon 5 had opened for Mayer many times. Now Bob was hitting close to home, and this time he got a response. Michael McDonald, Mayer's manager, called and invited Bob to his office in Manhattan. Bob knew that his parents would view such an excursion as another distraction in their son's fragile academic life. Anticipating that, Bob scheduled the meeting for late afternoon, after school. His plan was to take the train from Trenton, his first solo journey to New York. But just before the train left the Trenton station, Tom Costa hopped aboard. "You could have handled it yourself, I just thought it might be better if I came," he said. Bob did not mind. The trip was now a certified occasion.

The offices of ATO Records, where Michael McDonald worked, were on the twelfth floor of a plain building on Chambers Street, just off West Broadway, in lower Manhattan. There were platinum albums and pictures of the Grateful Dead on the walls. It had the feel of a chic, spare, and massive loft apartment, with old Oriental rugs casually thrown here and there.

There was a comfortable sofa near the elevator, and Tom Costa sat down. "I'll just wait here," he told his son. He got out *The Wall Street Journal* and began to read.

Bob was about to embark on the biggest moment of his (unpaid) professional life. His years on the Pennsbury forensics team, his voracious reading, his writing for the *Courier Times*, his work for PHS-TV— it had all been unintentional preparation for this moment: to convince John Mayer's manager that John Mayer should play the Pennsbury prom. Bob was motivated. If he could somehow land John Mayer, he'd become an important footnote in a memorable Pennsbury night. He'd be part of the Pennsbury prom legend.

"How did you come up with the name ATO Records?" Bob asked as he sat down. McDonald wasn't that much older than Bob, in his early thirties, Bob guessed. Talking to Dave Matthews was part of his job. Bob thought he had the life. He noted that McDonald was wearing a purple sweater. He thought of his father out in the lobby, in his dark suit.

"Dave came up with that name," McDonald said. "It's shorthand: 'according to our records.'"

They spoke of Dave Matthews and Bob's love for his music. Bob told his story of meeting Matthews in Italy, but he didn't prattle on. Bob monitored McDonald for antsiness, but wasn't detecting any. When his phone rang, McDonald called out to his secretary, "Take that."

McDonald asked Bob to tell him—again—what he wanted from Mayer. Bob explained the tradition of the Pennsbury prom. He told him the date of the prom, May 17, a Saturday night, six weeks away.

"That would be a lot of fun," McDonald said. "Let's check the schedule. Tell me what you really have in mind."

"Playing a song or two, or a set, whatever he wants. Being with the kids. Maybe posing for a few pictures," Bob said.

McDonald looked at a calendar. "Well, he has no tour dates after May fourth," he said. "I shouldn't be telling you this, but John is recording a new album in New York between May 10 and the beginning of June."

Bob thought McDonald was heading to: "So he's got nothing going on that Saturday night—let's see if we can work this out."

Instead, McDonald said, "The way this industry works, I really don't think this prom thing is going to happen, Bob." McDonald continued saying something about the intensity of the modern recording process, but Bob's mind was somewhere else. It was racing.

McDonald had all but shut the door, but Bob believed that Mayer himself would want to play the prom, or at least be involved in the prom in some way. Maybe Mayer would consider making a video greeting to the school that could be shown on prom night. He could try out a new song on it, if he liked. Maybe Bob could come to New York to tape it. Bob casually presented this idea to McDonald. On their way to the elevator, they had stopped at a bin from which McDonald gave Bob an armload of DVDs and CDs. Bob timed his follow-up perfectly. McDonald said he was open to the idea and that he would run it by Mayer. At the elevator, McDonald shook Tom Costa's hand and said, "You've raised one of the good ones."

McDonald had given Bob nearly forty minutes, a dozen CDs and DVDs, a warm compliment—and hope. Bob was unsatisfied. He had come looking for results.

VIII.

Cyndi and Mike Mackrides wanted to keep their son's name alive. A family member had suggested they start an annual scholarship at Pennsbury in Mike's name, and before long the parents were talking to Mr. Katz about how much money the Michael Harris Kosmin Memorial Scholarship, to be given to a Pennsbury senior planning to study computers or a related field in college, would award in its first year. The donations were coming in fast: from kids, from teachers, from strangers. By the end of April, Cyndi began reading applicant essays to decide who would get the first-year award of $1,000.

"My long-term goal is to partake in some kind of government job in computer security or military intelligence," a senior named Davis Pham wrote. "Due to recent hostile activities against our nation, I feel a need to assist toward the effort against terrorism and cyber terrorism." His plan was to attend Drexel University, in Philadelphia. "Since God has given me a talent with computers, I hope to use it to help others. As Edmund Burke said, 'The only thing necessary for the triumph of evil is for good men to do nothing.' If I don't do anything who else will?"

Cyndi read that and knew she had her winner.

IX.

When Harry Stymiest finally became an Eagle Scout—after tying the tedious requisite knots—the Stymiest family and the Troop 102 Boy Scouts turned it into an event. On a Saturday in April, more than one hundred family members, friends, and Scouts congregated in the Emilie Methodist social hall for Harry's induction. Costa was there, PHS-TV camera in hand. He came in an act of friendship, to record the event for the Stymiest family. It seemed to Costa that the ceremony lasted most of the day, but it was not even five hours. "It was like being at Harry's funeral," he reported back to Mr. Wilson. "It was Harry as God."

Within days, Harry was directing people to his write-up in the *Courier Times*. The story told how Harry was never expected to walk but did, and how he had learned to tie the Eagle Scout knots despite a nearly useless left hand. The piece was a Harry primer, and a reminder of how difficult his life had been and was. It was easy to forget that, if you saw him daily.

In a matter of weeks, Harry would be going to his prom, like any other senior. His work, and his parents' work, was paying off.

X.

While writing his first historical novel, *Within the Sandstone Walls*, about the slaves who built the White House, Mr. Cunningham would write a chapter, hand it to the secretaries in the Pennsbury office, then get to work on the next one. He told them his primary purpose in writing wasn't to get published—although that was a goal—but to see if he *could* write. The first draft of the original novel, 498 manuscript pages, was done, and he was at work on its sequel, when the September 11 attacks occurred. They extinguished his desire to write. He hoped that once he retired, he'd be able to return to the book. After six weeks away from Pennsbury, nothing had changed. He couldn't write, not about the White House.

There was a job he had once dreamed of having, as a boy dreams of playing big-league baseball: being the chief usher at the White House. On class trips there, Mr. Cunningham could not contain himself. Once he heard a tour guide identify a coffee urn in the Green Room as a legacy of the Andrew Jackson presidency. Mr. Cunningham knew the guide meant John Quincy Adams. He could not stand idly by while such misinformation was being disseminated. He had to stop watching *The West Wing* because the set designers had fabricated a space off the Oval Office they called the Mural Room, when no such place exists. He was qualified for the job. He knew he'd never get it.

Then he heard about an opening for a job with a historical bent. In Philadelphia, a few hundred yards from where the Declaration of Independence was signed, a building called the National Constitution Center was under construction. It was to open on Independence Day, at the height of the Philadelphia tourist season. The center was hiring "interpreters," glorified tour guides, who would answer constitutional questions both obvious and arcane. Mr. Cunningham filled out his application slowly and carefully.

XI.

Things were not going well for Alyssa Bergman and her boyfriend, Michael Castor, and their plan to move to Florida. It had nothing to do with her father's savings plan, although that was gnawing at them. The problems went to the logic behind the move. They discovered that establishing Florida residency would take at least a year, and the University of Central Florida basketball coaches weren't showing *any* interest in Michael, let alone offering him a scholarship.

"Maybe we should wait," Michael said. His parents, unlike Alyssa's, had been supportive of the move.

"Maybe we should," Alyssa said. Her disappointment was profound.

Alyssa went home. Her parents were in the living room.

"Well, we're not going," she said. "I hope you're happy!" She stormed off to her bedroom, closing her door quickly behind her.

XII.

Mr. Katz replaced Miss Snyder with another woman, Peggy Mitchell. Their styles were far different. From her first day, Mrs. Mitchell ran in-school suspension with a firm hand.

The ISS holding tank was a sealed-off, windowless quadrant in the back of the auditorium, separated from the rest of the performance hall by a sliding, folding wall. Normally, the ISS inmates couldn't see the stage, but one day early in Mrs. Mitchell's regime, the sliding wall was inadvertently left open. The Pennsbury school orchestra was practicing for the National Honor Society induction ceremony. They were playing Vivaldi.

"This music sucks," one of the detainees said. "Can we put on our Walkmans?"

"No," Mrs. Mitchell said. "Listen to the music. Learn some culture." Nobody dared revolt.

XIII.

Even people who knew Lindsey Milroy well—her parents, Mr. Minton, friends, enemies—felt she was being unusually moody. They could see through her attempts to appear content.

Sometimes she would have her new boyfriend, Jamie Quinn, come by the Prom Committee work sessions to pick her up. He had graduated from Neshaminy and was in his first year at Bucks County Community. They had known each other for years, but only started seeing each other in the spring. Jamie was lavishing Lindsey with attention and gifts. Jamie and his family went on a spring-break trip to the Caribbean, and he returned with diamond earrings for his new girlfriend. Lindsey tugged on the earrings and asked a friend, "Are they too big for my terribly small face?"

She'd talk about how much she loved Jamie. When Lindsey was in a fender-bender and her car was in the shop getting $2,500 worth of repairs, she said, "I don't care. My boyfriend drives me everywhere I need to go." It seemed like a performance to some of the girls, proof that Lindsey was still tormented by Win's breakup with her. Everybody knew how much she loved her Tracer. But Lindsey was insistent: Jamie was the one.

Her life continued to be harried. She was sorting through her college choices (except that there weren't any, really). She was working nightly as the overall Prom Committee co-chair. She was growing her luscious hair to the ideal lengths in just the right places so that it would be perfect for the prom. She was working two after-school jobs, at the Grey Nuns home and now a second job, at Express, a clothing store at the mall. She had schoolwork. She was dealing with a speeding ticket and, separately, the expensive car repairs. She didn't feel well. And a series of unsigned messages left on her cell phone—from her old Spy Kids enemies—hadn't helped any.

One was little more than a traditional crank call. She said, "You have a small face. It's very much tinier than most. You should have a Web site, www.smallface.com."

Another caller was more vicious. She said, "I fuck Win every day of his life. Don't ever talk about Win ever again in your life."

Another caller, believing that Lindsey was dissing her behind her back, said, "You are fucking gay. You're a fucking faggot. And if you have anything to say to me, you can call my fucking cell."

One night one of the anonymous callers got a hold of Lindsey's mother on her home phone. Mary Milroy screamed at the girl, demanding that she leave her daughter alone. The caller was not remotely unnerved. "All I can say is that small faces and rudeness must run in your family," she said before hanging up.

Lindsey was starting to lose it.

There were pictures of her going up in the girls' bathrooms, with the fake Web site listed, www.smallface.com. One day, in the odd way borrowed clothes get rerouted among high school girls, Lindsey saw one of her sworn enemies wearing Lindsey's sandals. "You stupid bitch," Lindsey screamed. "Give me those sandals!" Later that day, in the main hallway, Lindsey and another girl, even slimmer than Lindsey, got into a vicious fight. For a minute or longer, they slapped and punched each other, their long hair flying in each other's faces. The fight ended when they were each dragged into an assistant principal's office. Neither girl had a record, and both girls got off with nothing more than a scolding and a warning. They were lucky. Their parents were not called in, and neither was Mr. Katz.

Lindsey remained cocky. She was always ready to take somebody on. There was a weekday in April when the kids were off but teachers were not. The Prom Committee had organized a daylong work session. Setting up was an involved process. The committee had a big walk-in slop room that held paint and brushes and dozens of murals in progress. For painting, the murals were unfurled across the gym floor. On this bonus workday, Mr. Minton arrived at the school at 9:30 A.M. with a box full of warm

Dunkin' Donuts and a large container of hot coffee, only to see the volleyball team occupying the gym. He was dismayed. Mr. Katz had just sent out a letter reminding everybody that the Prom Committee had first dibs on the gym, from the conclusion of Sports Nite through the prom.

Mr. Minton marched down to the school office, dropped his donuts in protest, and said, "Take 'em."

"What, no kids showed up?" an assistant principal asked.

"No—the volleyball team's got the gym!" He marched out.

Lindsey was on her way in. She went to the gym and saw the volleyball players. It was more than she could take. "Get the fuck out of the gym!" she yelled. She stomped down to the main office screaming, "What is the fucking volleyball team doing in the gym? *We're* supposed to be in there. I'm sick, I'm having my period, and this school can't do *anything* right." She marched out, too.

A half hour later, the volleyball team finished its practice.

Lindsey *was* sick. Very few people knew.

Worried about what a guilty plea for the speeding ticket would do to her insurance rates, she accepted a hearing date. A family friend, a lawyer, came with her. As she stood before the judge, Lindsey could feel her heart racing. It was the same sensation she had felt during field hockey. Her heart felt like it was going to pop out of her skin. Lindsey fainted, caught by others before her head hit the floor. The judge, startled, called for medical help and dismissed the ticket.

Soon after, a Philadelphia cardiologist was telling Lindsey that she needed heart surgery. When she had a racing-heart episode, her heart rate was dangerously high, 250 beats per minute, four times higher than normal. The cardiologist told Lindsey she did not need major surgery, but no heart surgery could be regarded as routine. They talked about dates for the operation.

Lindsey said it would have to wait, that first she had to go to the Pennsbury prom with her new, fabulous boyfriend.

Chapter
Ten

Primping

May

Thursday, May 1

I.

On May Day the prom was two weeks and two days away. Pennsbury was deep into its prom season. The third Saturday in May was coming way too fast for everybody. The Prom Committee was meeting nightly in the gym, painting furiously, often to a curious collection of oldies by John Denver, Neil Diamond, Queen, The Monkees. Handmade posters about drunk driving were going up. (THERE ARE 47 MORE DAYS UNTIL GRADU-ATION. WILL YOU BE THERE?) In health classes, the curriculum turned to sexually transmitted diseases, because, as Mr. Cunningham had noted many years earlier, prom night is sex night.

"I'm going to tell you how to get STDs," Mr. Nielsen began his health class on the morning of the first of May. (In the afternoons, at baseball, he turned into Coach Nielsen.) "If you want 'em, you can get 'em."

He was dressed as a mid-1970s gym teacher, one from his own era: Adidas sneakers without socks, dark blue cotton shorts, long-sleeved gray T-shirt. His nose was sunburned, even though the weather had been cold and rainy for weeks. Whatever sun there was, his nose, forehead, and graying blond hair caught. His delivery was devoid of emotion. He had perfected the coach's monotone, which was particularly effective as he discussed squeamish topics.

"What is the proper term for pus from the penis or vagina?"

"Discharge?" a girl offered quietly.

"Correct," Mr. Nielsen said. He sounded like John Wayne.

"When I was in a fraternity at Penn State, it was a fairly regular oc-currence to hear someone say, 'Stay away from Jimmy—he's got crabs.' What are crabs?"

"A genital infection that makes you really itchy."

"Correct."

He moved on to abstinence. He spoke of A. C. Green, the retired NBA basketball star who played out his entire career as an unmarried virgin. "He was smart. When you have sex with somebody, you're having sex with every person your partner has ever had sex with. Think about it."

The kids were silent. Sitting in Mr. Nielsen's health classroom, sterile and windowless, early on a weekday morning, they were ac-tually thinking about it. Late on a Saturday night, of course, all bets were off.

II.

Danielle Nutt, the Sports Nite queen, had turned eighteen. She wanted to do something special, some ungoverned thing, to celebrate. There was a nightclub in Philadelphia called the Cave, where male dancers in nomi-nal bathing suits performed for female patrons. Most nights the required minimum age was twenty-one, but Thursday was College Night, and the admission age was dropped to eighteen.

Danielle wanted two of her good-looking friends, Alyssa Bergman and Jaime Schaffer, to join her. (Jaime and Lindsey Milroy remained sworn enemies. At one Prom Committee meeting, Lindsey said of Jamie, "She thinks she's a model or something, like Heidi Klum or somebody, but she ain't shit.") When Jaime and Danielle asked Alyssa to come, they thought she might put up a fight. Jaime and Danielle were well known at Pennsbury for being uninhibited; Alyssa exuded an air of restraint.

But they were wrong. Alyssa was in her other mood, in which she liked to, as Jaime said, "get crazy." They got a quick yes. Entering the club, they looked like the threesome of hot-chick detectives from *Charlie's Angels*. The Cave dancers paid attention to them.

Jaime and Danielle returned to one of their favorite subjects with Alyssa: that she could "do better" than Michael Castor; that she was too young, too pretty, and too fun to be half of such an old married couple. Alyssa defended Michael and their relationship. While the girls talked and laughed and enjoyed their beauty and their youth, half-naked men with shaved chests came by their table again and again. They were looking for tips, and for a party.

Friday, May 2

I.

Prom-car dreams were dying. Stephanie Coyle never heard back from anybody at Kraft Foods regarding the Oscar Mayer Wienermobile, so she and Rob and another couple decided to split a limousine. Stephanie went to the Yellow Pages and found the cheapest limo, $120 for a one-way trip from her house to the school, a distance of two miles. Harry Stymiest, with great reluctance, finally decided that his quest for the DeLorean was a pipe dream. "It was only a two-seater, and the guy from Time-Car in Myrtle Beach was going to have to drive it, so where would Kelly and I actually sit?" Harry asked rhetorically while sitting in the PHS-TV studio. He gave up on the DeLorean the day he learned he had secured a substitute. His beloved Aunt Lil worked with a woman whose husband collected street-legal hot rods, and that man volunteered to chauffeur Harry and his date. Harry shared the good news in an IM conversation with Kelly while sitting with his laptop in the PHS-TV studio. They used the grammar distinct to instant messaging.

Harry: soooo I am getting so excited about the prom how about you
Kelly: definitely
Harry: I just got a car for the prom a 37 plymouth convertible

Kelly: awesome!!!

Harry: what do you think top up or down

Kelly: either or down would be cool

Harry: ok if it's nice

Kelly: good plan

Harry: prom goes to 3 am my dad will drive us home

Kelly: coolio

Harry logged off and said to me, "I'll be going strong at three A.M., because I'll be so hepped up on Mountain Dew!"

II.

The disappointment of the aborted Florida move put a strain on Alyssa Bergman's relationship with Michael Castor. Alyssa looked at her sister. Dianna was twenty-one years old, living at home, working for her father, taking classes at Bucks. Dianna's boyfriend, Tom, a mechanic at the Goodyear by the mall, continued to live in the basement, paying his monthly rent to Alyssa's parents. Dianna and Tom seemed destined to get married, but not until they'd saved a good nest egg. They were right out of the Frank Bergman school of saving. Alyssa loved her sister and Tom—she trusted him with her Corvette—but she had always thought of *them* as the old married couple. And then it dawned on her. Danielle and Jaime had it right: She and Michael weren't any different. They weren't going to Florida. There was no exciting next step on the horizon of their lives. They were bound to Lower Bucks County. They were an old married couple, too.

Alyssa and Michael had a class together at Bucks, Intro to Drama. As they left class, Alyssa began a conversation they both knew was coming but neither wanted to have.

"Maybe we should cool things off for a while," Alyssa said.

"Maybe you're right."

And with those simple words, their lives together went into a state of limbo that neither could define.

Wednesday, May 7

Word of discord in Alyssa Bergman–Michael Castor happyland spread quickly, and when it reached Bob Costa, he seized the day. She had said hi to him by name after the school's Maroon 5 concert, and that gave him all the opening he needed. With the prom ten days away, he worked his sources, got her e-mail address, and sent her a note, in the style of e. e. cummings:

> hey alyssa
> what's up? the prom is
> coming soon, and i
> hear that you may be free.
> it would be cool. let's
> talk soon.
> peace
> bob

It was either slapdash, an ultrasophisticated postmodern haiku, or a carefully considered study in nonchalance. Bob did not know. Sitting with Harry Stymiest in the PHS-TV studio, Bob shared the e-mail and said, "It just seems right, you know?" Harry knew. Of course Harry knew.

Thursday, May 8

Evidently, Costa knew what he was doing. Alyssa was taken by his e-mail, flattered by the attention and Bob's respectful tone. She responded as soon as she received it:

> Hey Bob, it's Alyssa.
> I can't believe prom is so
> close already. Me and my boyfriend
> did put things on hold for
> a little bit but for right
> now we are still going to

the prom together. If things
change though I'll definitely
let you know. Hope to
talk to you soon. Alyssa.

Bob was filled with hope.

He was still waiting for an answer from John Mayer. He thought for sure he'd get a yes on his request to videotape a Pennsbury greeting from Mayer. If he didn't, he thought it would only be because Mayer was secretly planning to show up at the prom by himself, with no advance warning. Bob imagined Mayer getting in a car and driving to Pennsbury, trying out a few new songs on a stacked audience, and driving home, much the way Bruce Springsteen, when the mood moved him, used to show up at the Stone Pony in Asbury Park, New Jersey, to get his fix of live performing.

Saturday, May 10

The baseball season never came together for Bobby or the Falcons. At times Bobby pitched well, but not consistently. He continued to hit poorly, even in the lower rungs of the batting order, where, in theory, there's less pressure.

Some rare players can be inspirational, even in times of struggle. Bobby was not one of those. "I don't know," Coach Nielsen told Coach Barnes one afternoon. "Maybe we're trying to make him something he's not." They wanted Bobby to be a leader. Quarterbacks usually are, wherever they go.

On this Saturday, Coach Nielsen was upset by how many stragglers there were, Bobby among them, showing up for the game well after the announced time. As punishment, the coach sent the latecomers to the outfield for an hour of running. The delinquent ballplayers trotted out grumpily. That was when Bobby Speer, Pennsbury's quiet, polite-to-all golden boy, said something even his teammates were stunned to hear:

"Coach can come out here and suck my dick."

As soon as the words were out of his mouth, he regretted them. But they were in his mind, and they came out.

The assistant coach, Coach Barnes, heard what Bobby said. He heard him clearly. The coach's face turned red, and the veins in his neck bulged. He sprinted toward Bobby, got his chest in his center fielder's, and screamed, "What did you say?" He was daring Bobby to say those words again.

Bobby said nothing.

"That's horseshit," Coach Barnes said. "After all Coach Nielsen's done for you? Huh, Bobby? Huh? *You are horseshit!*"

Bobby had crossed the line, and he knew it.

Saturday, May 10
Sunday, May 11
Monday, May 12

I.

The Saturday and Sunday before the prom were always critical for the Prom Committee, the last chance to go on an uninterrupted painting and decorating bender. There were kinks to be worked out; the fog machine, for instance, kept setting off the fire alarm. But Lindsey Milroy, overall Prom Committee co-chair, missed the Saturday session when she couldn't get out of her shift at Express. On Sunday, a day when many committee members worked on prom projects at home, Lindsey had her mother put highlights in her lovely hair. But something went wrong, and half her head came out orange. Monday morning, instead of going to school, Lindsey went to the home of her hairdresser, Norma from Innovations IV, for an emergency session.

On Monday night, her hair fixed, Lindsey showed up at the gym. She explained, unabashedly, why she had missed the Saturday session and why she had missed school Monday morning. She was not easily embarrassed. Her mother attended the Monday session, which was not unusual, and her father did, too, which was. Decorating was then in a state of controlled hysteria. The problems were small and large. The gigantic papier-mâché Oscar was drying in the wrestling room, but there was no workable plan to get its gold-painted self into the lobby and standing upright. People were nervous. But they kept on working.

Parents were painting movie-studio banners. They were getting the unique type styles of the old studios—Warner Bros., Paramount— exactly correct. The red carpet arrived. So did the stars for the Pennsbury Walk of Fame. If the whole thing came together, it would be wonderful. Mr. Mahoney had called it right in September: Hollywood Nights was not a cheesy prom theme, even if there was a bench with a mannequin dressed as a bizarre-looking Forrest Gump sitting on it, much ridiculed by Lindsey.

At the nightly meetings, people talked effortlessly, jumping from one topic to the next, the way people with intersecting lives do. On this mid-May night, the conversation turned to which actors could play them in the movie version of their lives. Mr. Minton wanted to be played by Ozzy Osbourne or Christopher Walken. Mr. Mahoney believed Tom Cruise could capture his inner manliness, but that the TV actor Kevin James, not a slim man, might be a better fit. (Mr. Mahoney's adorable two-year-old son was at the meeting, and the Prom Committee girls said the boy should play Mini Me to his father.) Lindsey Milroy, of course, would be played by Jennifer Aniston. She was wondering what actor could play her boyfriend.

"What about that Damon?" her father offered.

"Who?"

"You know, that Damon, from something hunting?"

"Matt Damon from *Good Will Hunting*?"

"Yeah—that guy."

"He's *blond*, Dad." Jamie Quinn was dark-haired.

"That's right. He looks like Win."

"I'm not going to the prom with Win, you loser," Lindsey said.

Kevin Milroy tried to recover, but he was in a tough spot, and he knew it. "Yeah, well, if I ever see that Win again . . ." He didn't finish his thought. Lindsey had walked away.

II.

After his meeting with Michael McDonald in New York, Bob Costa called the office or sent an e-mail weekly. The calls never went through, and the e-mails were ignored. Costa was not disturbed. He was almost impervious to rejection.

In May, Costa was seeking to become the successor to Matt Fox as school president. He needed to make his candidacy known to the sophomore voters in the West building. In between classes there was a great deal of foot traffic on the path that joined the two buildings, but during classes the path was empty and monitored. Costa needed to get there to do some rigorous campaigning while school was letting out. He talked his way into being excused from his last class of the day. He slinked his way, tree to tree, and made it without getting caught. He entered the West main office as a female assistant principal was finishing up final announcements.

Costa commandeered the bulky microphone from the bewildered woman with "There are a few announcements I'm supposed to make." (In getting what he wanted, Costa was careful not to tell bald-faced lies. Who had said he was supposed to make "a few announcements"? He had.) Costa then proceeded to tout his presidential bid. He cited a few of his accomplishments, leading with the Maroon 5 concert. Just when he was about to be cut off, he said he would be available to answer questions at the bus-loading dock, right after the final bell sounded.

He was there, handing out flyers and shaking hands, when the kids started streaming out. The group around him mushroomed to twenty-five or thirty at one point. As a sophomore Costa had run for class president and lost. The memory of that loss continued to motivate him.

He wasn't one to delude himself. One day Blair Maloney said to him, "You should know, Bob, there are a lot of people who hate you." She seemed to resent Bob; her tone was cold and matter-of-fact. The words hurt, of course, but Bob knew Blair was right. He was doing audacious things that were bound to engender some animosity. Once, during morning announcements, Costa broadcast his availability as a prom date to any senior girl who might be in the throes of dating discord. His cheeky pitch didn't go over well with everybody. But the response didn't slow him down, either.

Bob's PA trick prompted Harry Stymiest to make a get-Bob-a-date tape, which he sneaked onto the lunchtime TV feed. There were manipulated pictures of Bob on Mount Rushmore, at a presidential podium, conducting an orchestra. "Bob really wants to go to the prom with a nice young lady like you," a frame near the end of the spot read. Then came a tagline: PAID FOR BY THE COMMITTEE TO SEND BOB COSTA TO THE PROM. Bob had nothing to do with the spot, but everyone assumed he did. They figured it was Bob being Bob: brazen but good-humored.

He knew what it meant to keep at something. When Alyssa offered no updates on her prom status, he wrote again, by e-mail, five days before the prom, with a more formal tone than in his first letter, and with more conventional grammar:

hey alyssa
What's up? I hope you're well. I miss looking forward to being floored whenever I'd see you in the halls. How's the BF situation? If things are changing, I would still love to be, honored to be, your date. It's going to be a memorable night and as someone who loves a good time and our school as much as you, it would be great. Hey, ya know, I gotta tux and would love to do whatever you want to do. Anyways, we should talk sometime. Someone as cool/beautiful as you deserves a good time.
peace.
bob costa

Tuesday, May 13

Costa called Michael McDonald at ATO Records once more, and this time he got past the secretary and to the man himself.

"Bob, I've been receiving all your e-mails and phone messages," McDonald said. He didn't seem irritated. "John's been entrenched in the studio. I've flown this by him. He's not going to be able to play the prom."

"That's disappointing," Bob said. He knew the conversation would be brief. Bob also knew now there would be no surprise gig on prom night either. It was evident in McDonald's tone.

"Do you think I could come up there and shoot some sort of video?"

"No, Bob, that's not going to work out, either."

That answer surprised Bob. How long would it take to make a little video greeting to Pennsbury? McDonald was leaving no wriggle room.

"That's disappointing," Bob said again.

"You know we're playing Camden in summer," McDonald said. "Maybe we could get you on the list for a meet-and-greet?"

Bob said something with forced cheerfulness, and the conversation was over.

Meet-and-greet? Bob was embarrassed. What did McDonald think he was, some sort of pathetic John Mayer groupie whose life would be made complete if he had a signed picture of the two of them standing awkwardly together? Bob could understand Mayer not wanting to come to the prom. That was committing an entire evening. But to say no to the video greeting? That Bob could not understand. It was a chance to create so much goodwill with so little effort.

Bob thought back to when he'd met John Mayer, backstage after the Temple University concert. Mayer had taken the Prom Committee letter and said, "So that's where all the lawsuits are coming from." Bob had never figured out what that meant. Now it bothered him more.

There was something else about his "interview" with Mayer that had been gnawing at him. Upon introduction, Bob's first words to Mayer had been, "I enjoyed your show."

To which Mayer had responded, "What show?"

What show. Ha, ha, ha. Mayer, of course, didn't know Bob. Bob was nothing—*nothing*—if not earnest. But John Mayer had decided to turn Bob's little icebreaker compliment into a joke for his entourage.

Now Bob was wondering why he ever wrote in his review that Mayer had a "humble persona." Mayer didn't have a humble persona. Nothing like it.

Wednesday, May 14

I.

Three days before the prom, there was a midmorning EOP session for the entire school, held by the west entrance, the very place where fourteen hundred promgoers would be making their arrivals in three days. Local police, emergency medical technicians, and firefighters had towed in two smashed cars. They littered the ground around the cars with Miller Lite beer cans. A half-dozen kids, who had been recruited to play crash victims, were milling about or lying still, with fake blood painted on various body parts.

Everybody was there. Shawn Ledger, wearing his favorite Cubs jersey. Matt Fox and some of his pranksters. Blair Maloney, with a salon tan. Bobby and Lauren, together. Harry Stymiest, video camera on his shoulder.

The police officers, as if directing a TV movie, created different scenarios. One kid survived but was in a wheelchair for the rest of his life, with no brain function. Another was arrested on a DUI charge. A third was a Class 5. "That means he's dead," an officer said.

Some of the kids were somber as they took in the reenactments. Others paid no attention. It was a chilly spring day. Mr. Katz was there. He thought of Mike Kosmin. He wondered what more he could do.

II.

Alyssa did not respond to Bob's formal second e-mail, Mayer was not playing the prom, and Bob was resigned to the fact that he was not going to the Pennsbury prom as a junior.

And then his fate changed. Mr. Wilson decided he wanted extensive prom footage for the annual video yearbook he produced. Harry Stymiest, of course, would not be available. He was going to the prom as a participant, not as an observer. Mr. Wilson chose to send four juniors to work the prom: his daughter, another kid, Costa, and Lisa Mamzik, a high-fashion junior and a rising PHS-TV star. Bob and Lisa were assigned to work the red carpet and get interviews as the promgoers arrived,

like entertainment reporters working the entrance to the Kodak Theater on Oscar night. The assignments were gifts from Mr. Wilson.

Bob was in.

III.

Coach Nielsen decided he was not going to let a couple of bad senior-
year episodes with Bobby Speer ruin a four-year relationship. He would
be bigger than that. He decided to vote for Bobby for the Falcon Award.
Many of his fellow coaches were making the same decision. They all
followed the same thought process. It was true that Bobby did not domi-
nate any one sport. But he was graduating with ten varsity letters. Beat
that.

Coach Nielsen opted to let Bobby pitch the final game of his high
school career. It was against Malvern Prep, a private high school that
had, years earlier, recruited Bobby. Kirk often wondered how different
Bobby's athletic life would have been had he gone there. He might have
had more football success. He might have had more college offers. There
was no way to know.

On the Wednesday before the prom, and for the first time in his
Pennsbury career, Bobby was pitching without Kirk or his mother or
his grandfather watching. They were at the duPont Hospital for Children, near Wilmington, Delaware, where Danny was preparing for surgery. To ready his body for the doctors, Danny's bowels and stomach
had to be cleared, and tubes were run down his throat, resulting in a
horrid case of the dry heaves. When a nurse asked him if there was anything he needed, in a moment of humor, he said, "Yeah, a cab—I'm outta
here." But most of the time he could not mask his pain. At one point he
cried out, "When is this gonna stop?"

Karen was there often, and Kirk was right by Danny's side all the
time, night and day, getting by on sporadic naps on a cot in the room.
Kirk's commitment to Danny never failed to amaze Karen. "I was meant
to have Danny, and Kirk was meant to be his father," she said. All other
explanations of his devotion failed.

Even with the tumult in Danny's life, Bobby could not put his own
life on hold. Danny would not want that, and Bobby couldn't do that

anyhow. Bobby pitched a complete game and won. Coach Barnes was still giving Bobby the silent treatment—he felt Bobby owed Coach Nielsen an apology—but Coach Nielsen had buried the whole thing. He congratulated Bobby on a fine game and a fine career. Bobby's days as a Pennsbury athlete were over. There had been some rough spots, but by and large he left it, as sportsmen have always said, all out there. Bobby went home and worked on the float he and Lauren would ride to the prom. It was orange and black and a symbol of Falcon pride.

Friday, May 16

I.

The day before the prom was the day Mike Kosmin would have turned seventeen. Ten kids came by his mother and stepfather's house carrying yellow roses, symbols of friendship. Mikey Coluzzi came with a dozen, hugging them hard to his chest. The kids and Cyndi and big Mike drove to the Newtown Cemetery and placed the roses on Mike's grave. They sang "Happy Birthday" to him. By the time they got to the song's final *you*, all their voices were quivering.

II.

Lindsey Milroy and her parents walked the school halls Friday night, inspecting the decorating job and accepting congratulations. Lindsey looked like an obedient little girl, staying near her parents, listening as they talked about their prom experiences. She was oddly subdued. Kevin Milroy mocked his wife for how long her hair had been thirty years ago. Mary Milroy talked of all the class trips she'd gone on with Lindsey. "The thing I remember," Lindsey said, "is you saying, 'I need this to be over, and I need a beer.'"

Lindsey saw an old friend, a girl she had known since kindergarten, a former shift partner at the Grey Nuns. The two girls talked about their applesauce fights in the Grey Nuns kitchen and how the old Grey Nunners left their dentures in their teacups. It was very funny to them and nobody else. They laughed, literally, until they cried. They knew what was happening. The prom would come and go. Graduation, the same. Summer would be a blink. And then each would be heading down her own road. Their girlhoods were fast coming to an end.

III.

Friday night, Coach Barnes was showing off the school to his fiancée. She asked if he had gone to his senior prom, in 1973. "No, I didn't, I was a creep in high school," he said. She laughed, as people do in the face of unexpected candor.

Out of the corner of his eye the assistant baseball coach saw Bobby Speer. Then Bobby saw him. Coach Barnes said nothing. He wanted to see if Bobby would speak first. He did. "Hey, Barnesy," he said.

It wasn't much, but it was enough. Coach Barnes knew what Bobby was doing. In the indirect way of the proud athlete, he was apologizing. The coach decided to bury the hatchet, too. It was time to move on. He introduced Bobby to his fiancée, and for an awkward minute or two they talked about this and that, repairing their relationship with every word and gesture.

Saturday, May 17
The Day of the Prom

I.

Cyndi and Mike Mackrides knew all about the prom's traditions. Most everybody who lived in the district did. But they had never seen the transformation of the school with their own eyes. They had never done what thousands of people did on the day of the prom each year: the midday, no-charge, self-guided tour through the reconstituted school. *The walk-through.* Mr. Cunningham had come up with that name. In the year of their son's death, Cyndi and Mike felt a longing to be part of the experience that defined Pennsbury.

They stopped every few feet to inspect something, to say hello to Mr. Mahoney or Karen Speer or Lindsey Milroy. It was magnificent, what the Prom Committee had done to the school.

It was a testimony to what kids, left to their own devices, can do. The red-carpet entrance, the giant popcorn boxes, the gold-painted Oscar, the way every square foot of drab Pennsbury wall had been covered in original artwork, it was outstanding, even Forrest Gump on his bus-stop bench. There were student drawings of James Dean, Judy Garland, the Three Stooges, Clint Eastwood, Marilyn Monroe. One hallway had been converted into Beverly Hills's Rodeo Drive, with storefronts for Armani and Tiffany and Chanel. Another hallway was a replica of the Hollywood Walk of Fame, in which each senior had a star. (During the walk-through, friends and parents wrote notes to the promgoers on the stars, as if signing a yearbook.) Another hallway wall was the *Titanic*, complete with portholes. There was a student-made marquee protruding from one wall. On one side were the words *Pennsbury High School Prom 2003 presents . . .* And on the other, *Hollywood Nights*. An intimate little lounge had been created in the normally dank gym lobby, with crushed velvet sofas and chairs, the kind of lounging area once common in downtown movie palaces. Mr. Mahoney had proved prophetic, and so had Lindsey. It was spectacular, even the standing cardboard life-size pictures of Whitney Houston, Justin Timberlake, and Alyssa Bergman.

At one point, big Mike stepped away from Cyndi to get some fresh air and gather his emotions. He didn't want his wife to see him crying. *It just kills me*, he thought, gulping for air, *that he's going to miss all this shit*. He returned when he was composed. Before leaving, he inspected the picture of Alyssa.

"So this is her?" he said. "This is the hot girl in the hot car?"

He looked at Alyssa for a long moment. He curled his lips and nodded. He could see it. She was stunning.

"She doesn't do anything for me," he said coyly.

He took hold of his wife's elbow, led her to his big black BMW, and drove them home, out of Fairless Hills and through Levittown and finally into the Yardley and Newtown developments. All of it was Pennsbury.

On the drive, Cyndi and Mike talked about their own proms back in the 1970s. "Remember the lapels on the tuxedos we wore then?" Mike asked. Cyndi remembered. They didn't know each other then, but big Mike went to his prom in one state, and Cyndi went to hers in another, and across the miles there was still something to share. "Those lapels were like wings, they were so big. Man, we thought we looked sharp," Mike said. Cyndi smiled, and almost laughed.

II.

On the walk-through, Linda Stymiest's mouth was often open. "Look at all this," Harry's mother said. "Doesn't it just blow your mind?"

III.

Mr. Cunningham did not know what to do. Hollywood Nights represented the first prom of his retired life. By all rights, he could have gone. He knew that. He knew that the "Mr. Prom" certificate of appreciation given to him in 1999, the year his daughter graduated, came with a lifetime invitation to the prom. Mr. Katz had been very clear about that. Mr. Cunningham had attended in 2000, 2001, and 2002. Somebody had always urged him to go, and he went happily. The 2003 prom was different. He had had no interaction with the Prom Committee. Nobody had mentioned anything to him about attending the prom. He was retired. Since his final day, he had heard from no teacher, no student, no administrator. He wasn't hurt, not particularly. He figured they were getting on with their lives, and he needed to do the same. (Well, he might have been a *little* hurt.) He was still waiting to hear from the National Constitution Center about the job.

Around noon, he drove over to the school with a carload of flowers. He had planned to do that. Every year he designed the exotic flower arrangements that stood at the main entrance, under *The Noodle*, and on the banquet tables. He had done it again for Hollywood. And once there, he decided what the hell, he'd do the walk-through. He inspected the Prom Committee's work carefully. By nature he was critical, but he thought the work was fine. It was better than fine. It was *excellent*. He saw that his legacy was flourishing. Driving home, he made up his mind not to return. He didn't need to. His run was over. His prom—no, the prom—was in good hands.

IV.

The day had been gray and damp and cold, but in the late afternoon the skies suddenly cleared. By 4:30, the time at which the public could start staking out places in the bleachers by the prom entrance, the sky above the school—above Fairless Hills and Levittown and Newtown and Yardley—was bathed in a fine golden light, just about the color of watery beer and ideal for picture-taking. The air had no weight; there was no moisture in it at all. It was still. You felt like you could run through it all day without getting tired. The night was all promise.

Which meant that Harry Stymiest would need neither a video camera nor an umbrella. He was ready. The doors to the prom opened at 6:30, and Harry wanted to be one of the early arrivals. He looked terrific in his black Men's Wearhouse tuxedo, with a silver vest. (The tux was a rental; the shoes were his own.) He and his parents drove from his house to Aunt Lil's in Levittown, on Crescent Lane in the Crabtree section. There Harry's car and driver would meet him.

The car turned out to be not a '37 Plymouth convertible but a somewhat less special '41 Chevrolet Fat Fender, with electric windows installed by the owner and driver, Bob Goughan, who refused to accept any money for his services, not even for gas. The car switch didn't register with Harry. He was about to begin the most important social experience of his life, and he was in another world. He was excitable and nervous, perspiring in the chilly air. His mother and father and Aunt Lil were taking one picture after another, to document the start of his big night. He was wondering when, if ever, the pictures would stop and his night would begin. There was a series of reminders for Harry: Don't eat too quickly; don't overfill your mouth; remember your left arm. The final reminder was not some sort of peculiar arm joke. Harry's left arm was his dormant one. If he didn't do something with it consciously, it had a tendency to get in the way. Harry reeled off a series of affirmatives.

The chauffeur opened the door of the old Fat Fender and Harry climbed in, a prince for the night.

V.

Stephanie Coyle was a planner. She worked off of a budget. She spent $25 on a pedicure and $50 getting her hair done. She borrowed her dress. Luke's babysitting was free. (Stephanie's mother worked the first shift, Rob's mother the second.) She and Rob split the limo costs with the other couple, Joe and Katie, so the limo fee worked out to $30 per person. Everyone was pleased. They knew of couples spending $500. That gave Stephanie a laugh. How much different could one limo be from another?

The limo arrived, late, and Stephanie held Luke at arm's length. She wanted to say good night to her baby, but she didn't need Luke spitting up on her cousin's champagne-colored bridesmaid's dress.

She stepped into the limo. One armrest was broken. The overhead light was dangling from the roof. The sunroof wouldn't open, and the partition wouldn't close. A hubcap was missing. The carpet was dirty. The seats were mushy. The driver was surly and so was his girlfriend, riding in the front with him. The two couples in the back made the best of it. They turned it into a joke.

VI.

The sea-green Fat Fender arrived at Kelly Heich's house right on time, at half-past five. Harry Stymiest was smooth. He handed Kelly her corsage, posed for pictures, talked to her parents. She looked even prettier than she did when Harry saw her each Sunday at Emilie United Methodist. He got her in the car and whisked her away. Kelly was exuberant and chatty.

"See this cell phone?" Harry said to her. "The whole PHS-TV crew knows: I'm off tonight. The only way it should ring is if somebody screws up real bad or dies." They both laughed. Harry lifted his left hand, the lifeless one, and lowered it onto Kelly's left shoulder. She did not mind.

They were in front of the Burger King next to the school before six P.M. There were people in the bleachers, but no prom-ride processional. There was no traffic, no commotion, no excitement. They were way too early.

"What should we do?" Harry asked.

A tortured silence filled the car.

Harry got out his cell phone.

"I'll call Mom," he said.

Harry was about to begin dialing when Bob the driver, a round old man, experienced in the subtleties of life, said: "Maybe we could just take a nice leisurely drive?"

Slowly and indecisively, Harry put away his cell phone while Bob started driving away from the school. Before long, the backseat was filled with chitchat again. Kelly asked Harry if he knew whether John Mayer was coming to the prom. "I would freak, even though that's not lady-like, if he did," she said.

Harry's chauffeur glided the Fat Fender along the back roads of Lower Bucks County. They went past a flooded quarry and past Pennwood Crossing, the mobile-home park where Harry lived. They went past where the U.S. Steel Fairless Hills works once stood, past a defunct Rohm and Haas factory, past enormous open tracts where the 3M, Paterson parchment paper, RCA, McGraw-Hill, and Dial soap plants once teemed with life. These were the companies that had indirectly financed the building of Levittown and the "new" Pennsbury High. The views of the Delaware River were now unimpeded by industry. The Fat Fender continued south on Bristol Pike through the old factory towns of Tullytown and Bristol and Edgely.

By the time they arrived back in the vicinity of the school, it was close to seven. Now there was a traffic jam of prom vehicles. The Fat Fender, with Harry and Kelly in the backseat, was in the thick of it.

"I love to dance," Kelly said.

"So do I," said Harry.

"I can't guarantee that I'm any good," she said.

"Neither can I."

"Then we'll make fools of ourselves together," Harry's date said.

VII.

It was a traffic jam nobody minded. The promgoers came from a half-dozen different streets, all of which funneled into Hood Boulevard in front of the school. The party began in the congestion. The attendees knew that. They'd watched the pre–Academy Awards shows on TV. They were following suit.

When they arrived at the red-carpet entrance, they no longer looked like kids. They no longer resembled their everyday selves. The girls— young *ladies*—wore gowns, their hair up and cleavage exposed. There were peach gowns and sky-blue gowns and floral gowns; the girls in them looked like bridesmaids. A half-dozen or so girls wore chic black-and-white gowns that looked like chessboards. Few of the tuxedos were plain, and some were droll. Shawn Ledger was dressed like a gangster, in a big-shouldered black double-breasted tux, with black-and-white shoes—and a date from Yardley. There was a foursome of black friends who arrived carrying canes and wearing gloves and top hats and looking spiffy.

The boys—the *men*—opened the doors for their dates and offered a hand, and then sashayed toward the entrance, into the flashing lights and the cheering throng. Many of the promgoers released orange and black helium balloons into the Fairless Hills gloaming, or handed out roses to kids standing behind the barricades, or shook hands with strangers, just as movie stars do.

They came in fire trucks and police cars. They came in UPS trucks and U.S. Mail trucks. One group came in a boat pulled by a car. One couple came on an ice-cream truck, another on a Rita's Italian Ice truck. They came in motor homes, a rescue vehicle, a tractor, a drag racer. They came in Hummers and stretch Hummers. They came in convertible Corvettes and Mustang convertibles.

Alyssa Bergman, back at her old school, was a passenger in her father's Camaro, driven by her on-hold boyfriend, Michael Castor. Alyssa's father was waiting in the wings to take the car off Michael's hands and drive it to the safety of his garage.

Lindsey Milroy, with a whole group of Yardley and Newtown friends, came in a conventional limo, of which there were not many. She stepped out of the car in a glimmering blue dress and threw a kiss to the crowd with her left hand. She was radiant. Her hair had never looked better.

One group came in a FedEx truck, and the uniformed driver required signatures before he would release them from the back. Four or five couples, arriving in the back of a giant Ryder moving truck, were low-ered to street level by an automatic lift. One group, dressed as the tropical refugees from *Gilligan's Island,* came on foot. One couple came in a rick-shaw attached to the back of a bicycle. Another came in a rickshaw attached to a team of dogs. Another on a moving mechanical rhino. Another in a cement mixer. Bobby Speer and his girlfriend, Lauren Cognigni, came on the back of their orange-and-black Falcon float.

Bob Costa tried to snag Bobby for a red-carpet interview, like they do on the E! Channel.

"Bob, you know I don't do interviews," the quarterback said.

"Bobby, dude, c'mon—it's for the video yearbook!" Costa pleaded. But Bobby's no meant no.

Alyssa was not such a hard case. Costa put a microphone near her mouth and asked her a series of questions, the longest exchange, by far, they had ever had. He asked about the cardboard cutout of her, which stood nearby. The real Alyssa Bergman was wearing a sparkly ankle-length strapless dress, with long slits on both sides. Costa thought she had never looked better. He saw the in-limbo boyfriend wander off, avoiding the bright lights. It was the first time Costa had ever seen him. Costa felt Michael should be at her side. *He* would have been at her side. Costa had always imagined the boyfriend as an Abercrombie & Fitch model, but no longer. *He's just another Joe Schmoe,* Costa thought. In that moment, part of the Alyssa Bergman mystique died for him.

Matt Fox and his date arrived in a limo. As they stepped onto the red carpet, Fox raised his hands to quiet the crowd.

"The first time I laid my eyes on you, I fell in love with you," the class president said loudly to his date.

Everything stopped and went silent.

Then he said to the crowd, "Tonight is my senior prom. Soon I will be going to college. She will be a senior. I cannot bear to be without her for even one day in my life. That is why tonight—"

He fished a ring out of his pocket, fell to his right knee, and said to his date, Kerin Considine, "Will you be my wife?" She mouthed a yes.

There was shrieking. Mr. Mahoney gave Matt a big congratulatory handshake. The bride-to-be put her hands over her face.

Matt Fox, with the help of his date, had pulled off his best prank of the year.

VIII.

Eight hours cannot go faster. All the sweat and worry, all the shopping and tanning, the tens of thousands of hours devoted to personal beautification projects, all that effort—and the prom went so quickly. It came and went so fast, passing as a favorite song does when it plays on the car radio. The promgoers arrived and checked in. They received their prom favor, a promissory note for a prom-night video. They checked out their metamorphosed school. They danced to the horns and trumpets and searing vocals of the Big House Band, much enjoyed by the dancers. They applauded when the prom king and queen were announced. (The prom queen was Andi Glick, the popular scholar and athlete who had been the added nominee for homecoming queen.) They ate dinner. They went to the hypnotist's show in the auditorium. They danced, kicked off their shoes, and danced some more. When the band was finished, a DJ took over. The gym floor remained packed, and the kids danced to rap and funk, Latin music and classic rock. At one point, the DJ asked "all the sexy people to put their hands high in the air." Everybody on the dance floor put their hands in the air, without shame. One ladies' group, with their dates positioned immediately behind them, stood on a table, shoulder to shoulder. They covered their lower lips with their glistening upper teeth erotically, lifted their chins, tilted their shoulders toward the dancing hordes, and stuck their backsides into the midsections of their dates. Their hands were clenched, and they shook them up and down as if pounding imaginary nails. The gym was steaming.

Dinner was served in the cafeteria, by parents. No, dinner was served in the *dining room*, by anonymous, polite *staff*. The menu was baked ziti, roast beef, chicken marsala, green beans, corn, parsley potatoes. There was a salad course and a dessert table. The drinks menu consisted of iced tea, punch, milk, and coffee. The cups were plastic, but the plates were real china, and the tables were covered with white tablecloths, with candles and flower arrangements every few feet. The air-conditioning was on and the room was cool and smelled like perfume and garlic and melting wax. A few bare-shouldered women put on their dates' tuxedo jackets. It was all very adult.

In places, at least. In the auditorium, where the hypnotist performed, there was mayhem. The hypnotist, a professorial-looking man named Ted Eiferman, had been performing at Pennsbury for nearly twenty-five years, but Hollywood was to be his last prom. He wanted to get out before he got sued for something. The previous year somebody fell off the stage and onto his head while hypnotized, needing thirty stitches. The year before that, a student on some sort of pharmaceutical high could not come out of his hypnosis and was taken to the emergency room. Over the years, the hypnotist felt, the kids at his shows had become more reckless, less inhibited, more willing to try anything.

He gathered a dozen recruits on the stage. "Your eyelids are becoming so tight, so tight, so tight, so tight," he said, and within minutes some of his subjects were sleeping so soundly that they were sliding off their chairs and to the floor. Eiferman had those under his spell responding like zombies to his words, laughing uncontrollably ("as if you are in a movie theater watching the funniest movie you've ever seen") and crying hysterically ("as if you just heard an old woman is about to be evicted from her house"). He had them chasing imaginary butterflies and spotting celebrities in the audience of classmates. He had his subjects wear special glasses that made people appear to be unclothed. At one point two girls under the spell started chasing after a boy in the hallways.

"Whoa, whoa," yelled Mr. Mahoney. "Slow down."

"Get out of our way, we're chasing Justin Timberlake," one of them said while the other shrieked. They never would have addressed a teacher that way under normal circumstances. Matt Fox dismissed the whole show as a hoax made by superb impromptu acting. It was hard to know. Sean Adams, who'd been Alyssa Bergman's escort at homecoming, seemed stuck in a hypnotic state long after the conclusion of the show. But he made an amazing recovery when an EMT flashed a light in his eyes and said he would be taken home right away if he didn't come out of it immediately.

Around eleven o'clock Costa and Lisa Mamzik and two other PHS-TV junior workers, Jesse Beam and Kelley Wilson, broke away from the prom, crept down a pitch-black hallway, and entered Studio 230. They could hear, faintly, the amplified prom music through the studio floor. Kelley and Lisa had sneaked in bags of Burger King food, and the four juniors sat around eating Whoppers and telling stories. They reclined in Mr. Wilson's swivel chairs and spoke of intimate things. "A year from now," Costa said, "that'll be us down there." It was a little memorable moment.

Downstairs, Rob and Stephanie saw Mr. Mahoney, who said, "I'm so glad you guys were able to come. How's the baby?" It was a comment in passing made by a decent man, and it touched them.

While leaving the prom, Michael Castor looked at Alyssa and said something indelible: "Whatever happens, however things turn out, I want you to be happy."

On his way to the prom, Mr. Katz had stopped at his parents' house in Levittown. It was from that house, thirty-six years earlier, that he had left for his own prom. His parents had waved good-bye from the front door as their basketball star son drove off to pick up his date. Five years later, the young couple from the '67 Pennsbury prom was at Emilie Methodist, getting married. Now it was May 2003 and Mr. Katz's father was an old retired military man, left speechless by a stroke. The visiting son, wearing a mint-green tuxedo jacket, brought him a new batch of word-search puzzles. His mother said, "You look nice, Bill," and got out her little camera to snap a picture that she would put into a photo album for posterity.

For the first few hours, Harry Stymiest was nervous and out of sorts. He was at a big school event, and there was no camera on his shoulder. He felt naked. He knew Mr. Wilson had selected some of the most promising PHS-TV talents to work the prom. Still, they were juniors, inexperienced in the ways of taping and the vagaries of TV production. They could not go unsupervised. During the hypnotist's show, Harry noticed that one of the junior cameramen had left his camera running on an unattended tripod. The hypnotized were doing crazy things out of the camera's range—unrecorded action!—and Harry was not pleased. He walked over to the cameraman and quietly admonished him. The cameraman apologized and immediately went back to work. The exchange was a first for Harry—Harry as manager. It made him feel powerful, and it calmed him down.

Bobby Speer detested dancing, but when the first slow song came on, Lauren dragged him out. She had ditched the high heels that matched her stunning dress, and she was dancing barefoot, her head in Bobby's chest. Bobby, his strong chin in her fine hair, thought, *I came with the right girl*. Wordlessly, they danced on.

Lindsey Milroy was spent by midnight. Her racing heart and high-strung nervous system had been operating on overload for nine straight months, and she simply asked her boyfriend to get the car, not because she had some better place to be but because she needed to go home.

At its peak, there were more than sixteen hundred people in the village of Pennsbury on the night of the prom. Nobody noticed that John Mayer had failed to come. By three A.M., when the DJ announced the last dance, there were hundreds of people standing on the gym floor—Harry Stymiest and his date, Kelly, among them—stoned on weariness. The immense doors that led from the gym to the parking lot were now open, and the cool night air poured in. At a bar's final call, there is a sense of hollowness for the lonelyhearts who arrived with hope but find themselves still solo as the lights go up. The prom was different. You came with a partner. For some, the night was a dress rehearsal for a wedding night, right down to the ceremonial sex. For everybody, it was an experiment in adulthood. On the night's final dance, Jeff Heinbach, the rebel who stood up to Congressman Greenwood, danced his first slow dance, in the arms of a junior, the kid sister of the guitar player from Jeff Says No. Her hands were around his neck, and his were on her hips, and they were separated by Jeff's stiff arms right through the final notes. Was Jeff having the time of his life? It did not matter. He was a citizen by choice.

As the Pennsburians left their prom, some of them stopped to give an interview to the man making the prom video. Many of them, without prompting, thanked Mr. Katz, Mr. Minton, Mr. Mahoney, and the Prom Committee for all their work. One senior clutched a phantom Oscar and thanked the Academy. A daughter of Pennsbury said, "I've had the time of my life. Unfortunately, it has to come to an end."

Much, much later, Mr. Minton, still in his red tuxedo jacket, and Mr. Mahoney, still in his black one, were ready to call it a night. Their final task was to lift a gigantic MGM papier-mâché lion into the back of a van too small to accommodate it. They were too groggy to think straight. The sun was rising over the parking lot, rising over where the steel mill used to be. They shook hands and congratulated each other on a prom well done and went home to their wives, to their own children, and to their beds.

Sunday, May 18

I.

The Pennsbury kids didn't view the prom as a single eight-hour dancing shift at the school, with adult supervision. If they had, if that had been the extent of their prom experience, they would have been even more frenzied through the night (if that were possible). The Pennsbury prom had legs; it was a five-day affair. On Friday the kids tended to their bodies. On that third Saturday in May—tradition, tradition!—there was the walk-through during the day and the prom itself at night. Some went to a wee-hours breakfast after the dance. Kelly and Harry Stymiest and his mother went to the Great American Pub and Diner on Route 1 at three A.M., where Harry had a Monte Cristo sandwich and Kelly cheesecake. He got her home at 4:30 in the morning.

Harry, mindful of Kelly's boyfriend, far away in central Pennsylvania and waiting for a prom report, gave her a good-night hug at her front door.

"Thank you for coming."

"Thank you for asking me."

Some of the kids drove to the New Jersey beach towns, but the more common thing to do was go home, get some sleep, and then late on Sunday morning head (as they say in greater Levittown) "down the shore," where they had rooms booked in cheap motels and off-duty summer homes. They stayed Sunday and Monday at the beach and drove home on Tuesday. On the Tuesday after the prom, school was always closed for a teacher workshop day. The five-day prom. A lot can happen in five days.

II.

For weeks Bob Costa had been anticipating not only the prom but also an event scheduled for the day after it. On that Sunday, Bill Clinton, Costa's political hero, flaws and all, was scheduled to speak in downtown Trenton, in an auditorium at the city's war memorial, across the Delaware River from Fairless Hills. Bob arranged for PHS-TV press credentials for himself and a cameraman, and he asked his prom-night sidekick, Lisa Mamzic, if she wanted to hear (and tape) Clinton. She was up for it. She was a fan, too.

At the prom, after the arrival parade and their interview work, Costa had lost track of Lisa. She was a Pennsbury junior who knew how to wear makeup and clothes; she had long, curly hair, expertly maintained, and show-business teeth. She looked like a college junior, or older. Once, Mr. Wilson had sent her to cover minor-league baseball in Trenton for a PHS-TV feature. The Trenton Thunder ballplayers figured she was a genuine grown-up sports reporter and demonstrated their affection by throwing sunflower seeds at her and asking her to come out with them that night.

"But I'm just a junior," she said.

"Yeah, so what?"

"In *high school.*"

This stumped them for about a second until one said, "Yeah, well, so what?"

At the prom she became one of the hypnotist's most wired subjects, dutifully selling popcorn out of her shoe at one point, or that's what she thought she was doing. When she came out of hypnosis, she fell in with a group of her girlfriends and spent most of the night flitting here and there, with no time for Bob. Naturally, this only drew Bob to her more.

On her way to Trenton for the Clinton speech, Lisa passed through the Costa driveway, where she briefly met Dillon Costa, Bob's mother. Dillon saw the whole Lisa package and knew that her son, advanced in many ways but not in others, was overmatched. Lisa looked nothing like a cameraman, even if that was what she was for the night. "If Clinton shakes hands with Bob," Dillon Costa asked her son's assistant, "*please get a picture of it.*" She handed Lisa, who was operating on three hours' sleep (she had gone to one of the many post-prom parties), a disposable camera, in case there was a snapshot opportunity.

All Bob had was an unimpressive-looking press credential, a suit, and a knowing manner. He got right past security, as if he were with the Secret Service, and slipped into the sprawling, packed banquet room where Clinton was eating.

"I'm gonna meet him," Costa said to Lisa.

"No way, you can't just—"

Costa was off.

Clinton was sitting at a round table with a group of New Jersey bigwigs, most notably the governor, Jim McGreevey. Costa put his press credential in his pocket. He walked up to Clinton. He could feel the eyeballs of Clinton's security people on him, but nobody was stopping him. His heart raced. Lisa watched from a distance.

Costa got right beside Clinton, as if he were a waiter, lightly tapped his political hero's shoulder, and said quietly, "Mr. President?" He did not want to call attention to himself.

Clinton was wearing a suit with thick shoulder pads. He was eating a salad. He didn't feel Costa's tapping or hear him. So Costa tapped harder and spoke up. "Mr. President?"

Clinton turned around. Bob extended his right hand. Clinton took Bob's hand with two of his. Bob felt Clinton's big, fleshy, moist palms. They were warm. On his right wrist, the former president was wearing a colorful woven bracelet, the kind kids at Phish concerts wear.

"Mr. President, I'm Bob Costa from Pennsbury High."

"Very nice to meet you, Bob."

"I'm a young Democrat."

"That's what you should be."

Costa could now feel the eyes of the governor of New Jersey on him. Still, nobody was making a move to stop him.

"You should come to our school to give a speech. We'd love to have you."

"That sounds good. Where do you go to school?" Clinton said, still holding on to Bob's hand.

"Pennsbury High."

"Is that in Pennsylvania?"

"Yes. Just over the river from here."

"Are you a leader there?"

"I'm trying to be."

The conversation, about politics and high school life, continued for a full minute, maybe longer. Bob wrapped it up, fearful that he was about to be carted away.

"What's your name again?" Clinton asked.

"Bob Costa."

"Well, that's great, Bob," Clinton said. He let go of Bob's hand. As Bob slowly backed away, Clinton returned his attention to the paying guests.

Bob quickly made his way out of the banquet room. He was flushed with excitement. The rest of the evening raced by for him. Clinton gave a personal speech. He talked about the value of writing one's memoirs, as he was doing. He urged his listeners to do the same, to take stock of the life they had led and to create a record for their heirs. Bob hung on his every word. On his way out, Clinton shook Lisa's hand, one among the throng. Then Bob and Lisa watched as Clinton climbed into the passenger seat of a large white Chevy Suburban with New York license plates. They watched Clinton light an enormous cigar. They watched him drive off.

For a moment Bob, and even the grown-up Lisa Mamzik, looked like two spent kids, glued to the stage door of some downtown arena, the final notes of a monster concert still ringing in their ears.

Monday, May 19

I.

There are dozens of little beach towns along the Jersey Shore, most of them linked by a broad commercial beach boulevard. But Wildwood was by far the most popular beach town for the Pennsbury kids. At least two hundred Pennsbury kids made a pilgrimage there after the prom. Wildwood had several redeeming qualities. It was remote, 120 miles from the high school. It was on an island connected to mainland New Jersey only by a causeway, so no parent could simply pop in, claiming to be in the neighborhood. And it had an abundance of cheap

family-run motels with owners willing to rent to high school kids. The
kids looked for motels where the owners would not freak out if a
drunken poolside toga party suddenly broke out, as long as the drinking itself wasn't public.

Two Wildwood motels proved the most popular. The drinkers stayed
at the Erin Shores Motel, on Atlantic Avenue in North Wildwood, and
the pot smokers stayed at a motel down the street. But it would be wrong
to think there was a great divide, despite what Costa reported in his pot-
smoking story in the *Courier Times*. It was prom weekend and the seniors had come together to drink and smoke and party and lounge about
as one big team. They went off together to get tattoos and body piercings
and they showed off their new additions on the windswept boardwalk.
They played spin the bottle and strip poker and engaged in public neck-
ing and semi-public sex. When two popular girls took part in an inebri-
ated experimental makeout session one night, they were surrounded by
a circle of chanting boys, egging them on.

The sleeping arrangements were a mystery to the parents forward
enough to ask about them, but they made sense to the kids. The motel
registration cards indicated that there were typically two couples per
room. Most rooms had two queen-size beds. Each couple shared a bed,
whether they were sexually involved or not, and there were many who
were not. Kids who found themselves fighting with their dates slept on
the floor in a friend's room. If a couple wanted to have sex, they found
an empty room or kicked everybody out temporarily, locked the door,
had their encounter, and came out eight or ten minutes later. The three
days and two nights at the beach had little to do with romance. It was
mostly about hooking up and hanging out.

II.

Stephanie and Rob were in Wildwood, too, or on its outskirts. They were
staying at the King Nummy Trail Campground, where Stephanie's grand-
father owned a mobile home—a *modular* home—on a small wooded lot.
It was five miles and five decades away from Erin Shores. (At King
Nummy, for instance, there were posted quiet hours.) Stephanie and
Rob were staying there with Katie and Joe, the couple with whom they

shared the comically bad limo. They had driven to Wildwood together. But at King Nummy, the two couples were feuding. Stephanie and Rob felt they were giving in to Katie and Joe on every decision, big (when to leave the prom) and small (where to eat). When Stephanie and Rob bickered about some inconsequential thing—whether the carnival-style ring-toss games on the Wildwood boardwalk were rigged or not—Katie always sided with Rob, and Stephanie and Rob were both irritated by that. (In their defense of one another, Rob and Stephanie each felt the other's love.) Katie and Joe felt that Stephanie was a control freak. In retaliation, Stephanie and Rob stopped talking to them, which was particularly awkward in such tight quarters, deep in the woods, with only one car.

Rob and Stephanie spent as much time as they could on the Wildwood boardwalk, where there was a string of T-shirt stands, pizza parlors, and tattoo studios. They bought a shirt for Luke. Rob was drawn to every barker yelling something like "Special prize for your lady." Stephanie kept pulling on his arm in the opposite direction.

One of their first stops was 24th Street Tattoos. Rob was eager to get his first tattoo. He had turned eighteen two weeks before the prom and now met the New Jersey (and Pennsylvania) age requirement. There were age restrictions for body piercings, too, but Rob had found a way around that years earlier. At thirteen, wanting his ear pierced, he iced up his earlobe and ran a safety pin through the flesh over and over until he had an identifiable hole. Five years later, he had three piercings in one ear, two in the other, and one in his navel. They made him feel unique. His first tattoo, etched into his right bicep, depicted the ancient Chinese symbol for *father*, an elaborate X. Being an eighteen-year-old father set him apart from the crowd even more than his piercings. He liked that.

Each time they walked the Wildwood boardwalk, Rob and Stephanie saw other Pennsbury kids, but nobody stopped to talk. Rob and Stephanie passed kids carrying stuffed toys in arms that bore new tattoos. Some of the boys on the boardwalk were Rob's former football teammates. One of them was a big Pennsbury lineman Rob had no desire to see.

"Whenever I'm around him, all he talks about is how he's doing this and how he's doing that, and then he's like, 'But you can't do that,

Stephens, 'cause you got a kid,'" Rob said to Stephanie when the football player was out of earshot. "I'm like, 'Shut up—I know I have a son.'"

They passed the Erin Shores Motel on their way back to King Nummy. There were Pennsbury kids at the motel pool and hanging over the second-floor railing, their cans of beer hidden behind washcloths. Rob and Stephanie knew them.

"If things were different, I'd be where those kids are now," Rob said. "I'd be another dumb jock."

There did not seem to be envy in his words, not that Stephanie could tell. "I sometimes think it must be fun, going out with a big group like that, going to the diner together," she said. "But then somebody buys a dinner that's three dollars more than yours, and everybody puts in the same amount, and you just end up feeling cheated."

Stephanie had been coming to Wildwood all her life. She'd been on her way there when she called Rob with the news that she was pregnant. Her family had a tradition. When they were getting near the campgrounds, when they were off the highway and on the flat back road lined by scrub oaks and scrub pines, the first person to see the King Nummy sign was to yell out, "I see King Nummy!" The success of the ritual required honesty on the part of its participants. You had to actually see the sign.

"I see King Nummy!" Rob said on the Monday of prom weekend as he and Stephanie were driving back to the campgrounds from the Wildwood boardwalk.

"No you don't," Stephanie said.

"Yes I do."

"No you don't."

Rob gave her an annoyed look and said, "Chill out. I was just joking." They drove on in silence for a half-minute or so.

"I see King Nummy," Stephanie said quickly, when the sign first came into view. "You lose."

Tuesday, May 20

Bobby and Lauren did not go to the shore. (Lindsey Milroy and her boyfriend did, but far north of Wildwood, off by themselves.) Pennsbury's most athletic, famous, and handsome couple had many invitations, but a three-day, two-night shore trip did not fit for them, not with Danny in a hospital bed. Besides, if Bobby didn't go to Brew Crew keg parties, he certainly wasn't going to be part of the Erin Shores party scene. And Lauren had to be in school on Monday, for softball. The day after the prom, Bobby and Lauren went to Six Flags Great Adventure, an amusement park in central New Jersey. The following day Bobby watched Lauren pitch. On Tuesday, when other Pennsbury kids were packing up, bleary-eyed, at the shore, Bobby and Lauren rode with Bobby's grandfather to the duPont Hospital for Children. They both slept the whole way there.

Bobby would have come earlier, but Danny didn't want his brother to see him in his hospital state. The patient had not been out of bed for eight days, and it was only shortly before Bobby's arrival that the tubes had been removed from Danny's throat. He had been put through the wringer, enduring one operation after another. A team of surgeons had built a bladder for Danny out of part of his bowel. They had removed his appendix. They had discovered a testicle in the vicinity of his stomach and taken it out. They had created a tunnel into his new bladder through which they hoped he would someday be able insert a straw and urinate. They had fixed irregularities in his bowel, hopeful that he would someday be able to have unassisted bowel movements. Only with the tubes out and the operations over, only when he was something close to whole again, was Danny ready to see Bobby.

In a few months Danny would be sending Bobby off to college. The timing of the surgery was exquisite. If the operations were successful, and if Danny could learn to use the mechanical devices designed for him, he would be able to lead a more independent life than ever before, just in time for his big brother to begin summer football practice and his new away-from-Levittown collegiate life.

A nurse came into Danny's room while he and Bobby were playing high-speed chess. Lauren was sitting in Danny's wheelchair, watching. The nurse asked who was winning. "Not me," Danny said, and Bobby and Lauren cleared the room silently, without fanfare, knowing the nurse needed to see Danny alone.

Bobby found the children's game Guess Who? in a waiting area, and he and Lauren began playing. They didn't talk about Danny or baseball or softball or college or anything. They were comfortable in the quiet. They were playing to win. Every so often, a child in a wheelchair or on a gurney rolled by on the hospital floors, cool and hard and shiny. Some of the children made awful noises as they came and went, their pained voices filling the corridors. There was a child with a misshapen face, another bald from chemotherapy treatments. Bobby's grandfather, Vernon, looked up from his paperback when the children's tormented cries reached his old, wobbly ears. He saw that Bobby was not scared of these children. He was taking them in with his wide, kind eyes. Bobby knew about pain, his brother's and his own. He played through pain and lived with pain.

Along the way Bobby had found a life for himself, in the cafeteria and classrooms and hallways of his school, and on the bumpy playing fields behind it.

Chapter
Eleven

Reunion

I.

One weekend in the summer after the Pennsbury prom, I went home for my twenty-fifth reunion: Patchogue-Medford High School, class of '78. It was held at a nice restaurant down by the bay, a mile or so off Main Street. At dinner, my wife and I sat with my long-ago prom date and her husband. The ladies compared notes. From what I could glean, my dance moves, so called, were mocked.

In twenty-five years Lienne had changed surprisingly little. She volunteered to organize the thirtieth reunion, certain she could improve the meager turnout. (Only a fool would bet against her.) Her voice was the same, and so was her tone. It seemed her life had unfolded pretty much in accordance with her schoolgirl plans. She continued to wear her hair far below her shoulders, as she had in high school, and her friends from orchestra flocked to her, as they always had. Writing this some weeks after the reunion, it's funny: I can tell you the patterns and colors of sweaters she wore in high school, but I cannot remember what she wore to the reunion. It may have been a dress, or maybe it was a pantsuit. I'm not sure.

When the DJ played the 1970s King Harvest hit "Dancing in the Moonlight," Christine said, "I *love* this song." There is no known spousal defense to those words. I followed her to the empty dance floor.

Everybody here is out of sight
They don't bark, and they don't bite
They keep things loose, they keep things tight
Everybody was dancin' in the moonlight

I cannot tell you what Christine wore to the reunion, either, but the next morning she made Sunday breakfast for our kids in my mother's kitchen, and the plates were deposited in the sink where I was bathed as an infant. Outside of Pennsbury, I can't think of anyone who married their high school prom date. Christine did not go to her high school prom, in California, but she was my date to Hollywood Nights. Better late than never.

I polled some people at the reunion, and there was no one who remembered the Noblemen playing our prom. Nobody was too concerned about the phantom band. The prom did not linger as an event of particular magnitude, although one person told me he had a dream date in mind twenty-five years before but had lacked the nerve to ask her. My classmate who stole the black prom shoes for me from the ROTC supply room could not recall doing such a thing, and I don't believe he was protecting himself. At the reunion he talked openly about how he had run cash in steel briefcases for Oliver North.

Lienne came to the reunion from South Carolina, where she teaches at a university, and I came from Philadelphia, but most of our classmates who were there lived in Patchogue or nearby. The football team was particularly well represented. It was obvious that the players had kept up with one another because they discussed not just vanished plays, meaningful only to them, but also their children's schools, their work traumas, and the state of their golf games. They didn't discuss weighty themes; just their everyday lives. My shoe supplier, who had played football, reminded me that the team was undefeated in our senior year. He said a fellowship had come out of that success, and it was still going strong twenty-five years later.

I imagined the same would be true for the Hollywood Nights crowd at Pennsbury. For the Prom Committee, certainly. They already had a fellowship. But maybe for every last person who was there on that Saturday night in May, when Pennsbury went Hollywood.

II.

In the September after he graduated, you couldn't tell that Harry Stymiest was no longer a Pennsbury student. He was attending Bucks County Community College full-time, but it seemed that he was working for Mr. Wilson and PHS-TV full-time, too. Mr. Wilson was rattling school budgets, trying to pry loose some money so Harry could have a paying job. But with pay or without, Harry was there, reporting almost daily to Studio 230.

Sometimes he'd see his prom date in the school hallways, and he continued to see her every Sunday at Emilie Methodist. Kelly Heich was an eleventh-grader now and in the big house, the building that housed the juniors and seniors. She was a rising star on the debate team.

Her relationship with Harry had changed. They weren't boyfriend and girlfriend. Nothing like it. But they had toured Tullytown in the Fat Fender together, frittered a night away together dancing on the gym floor, gone out to the Great American Diner for a three A.M. breakfast. They were bonded for life. For Harry, Kelly Heich would always be the answer to the question "Who'd you go to your prom with?"

There was one other significant change for Harry: the scale of his meals. No more double orders of fries, no more heaping plates of nachos with cheese, no more multiple cans of Mountain Dew. Harry was on a health kick. He had joined a gym. By Halloween he had dropped three or four pounds.

He saw plenty of familiar faces at Bucks. One hundred and seventy-six of his Pennsbury classmates had enrolled there, including Shawn Ledger. Ledger had not graduated with Lindsey Milroy and Bobby Speer and Rob Stephens and Blair Maloney and the rest of his class in June. Mr. Mahoney flunked him in the final marking period. All Ledger had to do was show up regularly, hand in the work, and take the tests, but he did nothing. He gave Mr. Mahoney no choice. Ledger wasn't worried.

He made up the credit in summer school, but really he was just going through the motions. Did you need a high school diploma to make it in rap? Did you need a two-year degree from a community college? Shawn Ledger didn't think so. What a rapper needed was a life and stories to tell from it. He was collecting those.

After Miss Snyder left Pennsbury, she and Ledger did not cross paths. She had a new job in a different district. She was not looking back. She told me she loved her experiences at Pennsbury as a student, but working there was horrible, and the ISS assignment brutal. She said she would never again live in the district in which she was teaching. In the fall after her departure, the morning show of a popular Philadelphia radio station, WMMR, conducted a contest to bestow the title Miss Philly Girl upon a listener. The contestants, Jen Snyder among them, gathered at Hooters, a restaurant and bar, wearing bikinis. Word of her foray into the world of radio contests made the rounds at Pennsbury, of course. Then she won the contest, and with it a trip to Jamaica for two. The faculty rooms were abuzz about that.

III.

Rob Stephens and Stephanie Coyle were trying to make room for it all: school, work, child-rearing, adolescence, each other. Five months after the prom, in the middle of the first marking period of her senior year, Stephanie, for the first time in her life, was making all A's. How she was doing it, she did not know. On school days she would wake up before five A.M. to get herself ready for the day and take Luke to the family baby-sitter. She left school early to go to work, at the JCPenney portrait studio at the mall. She took the job because it paid $7.25 an hour, $2.10 above minimum wage. She had no idea it was so difficult to get a three-year-old to flash his baby teeth while wearing a cowboy hat.

Rob was a full-time student, too, in an eighteen-month computer-programming course at a Bucks County technical school. It was a for-profit school that recruited students over the radio. Amazingly, the school gave Rob a scholarship to cover half of the $24,000 cost. Rob took out a loan to cover the rest. He had after-school jobs, too. He worked at Toys "R" Us for a while, and then he tried selling window installations, but nothing seemed to stick.

Once Luke had arrived, Stephanie discovered that her Catholicism was more important to her than she had ever realized. As a baby, she had been baptized a Catholic, but she had dropped out of all organized religion before she was a teenager. In the early months of Luke's life, she felt the pull of church for the first time. She wanted Luke to be baptized a Catholic. Stephanie's local church urged her to take a series of weekly classes to learn about Catholic teachings before Luke took his holy bath. Rob, who grew up nominally Protestant but with even less church affiliation than Stephanie, joined her at the classes. He had decided he wanted to be baptized, too.

It wasn't as if Rob had suddenly found God. He had always believed in a deity. It was Catholicism that was the discovery for him, the ritual of it, the order it imposed on a family. He felt that the blanket of a single religion over Stephanie, Luke, and him would make the trio feel like a family, no matter what happened to them in the years to come. Luke's baptism was scheduled for Easter. Rob and Stephanie were looking for godparents. Harry Stymiest, Rob's old friend, was still on their short list.

IV.

Mr. Mahoney and Mr. Minton—Dumb and Dumber, as they called themselves—decided to sign on for one more year together. Mr. Minton was always claiming to be ready to retire from the Prom Committee, and then he always found his way back. Mr. Mahoney's decision seemed irrevocable. He was intent on getting his master's degree. His wife was pregnant with their second child, and his son, Mini Me, required more time. They were looking to move out of Levittown, where they had lived all their lives, and buy a house on the other side of Route 1. Mr. Mahoney really meant it: one and done. It was clear there would never be another Jim Cunningham, able to devote himself to the prom year after year, until the years turned into decades and the decades into a legacy.

Early in the new school, the first Prom Committee meetings went unannounced, in keeping with the custom. Still, a couple dozen girls and a smattering of boys (but very few black kids) found their way to Mr. Mahoney's room during EOP on Wednesday mornings. "You guys have a tough act to follow," Mr. Mahoney said. "Last year's committee was one of the best we've ever had. I know you guys want to outdo them. But you're going to have to work really hard to do it. I think you've got a chance." He was throwing down the gauntlet. It had always worked in the past. He figured he could get one more year out of it.

The new theme was an old classic: Cities Around the World.

V.

At the National Constitution Center, the other guides quickly came up with a nickname for Jim Cunningham: The Scholar.

He had found just the right job for himself. He liked taking the train into Philadelphia with the other morning commuters. He relished working with recent college graduates who were amazed by how much history he knew. He enjoyed wearing the uniform of the interpreters, the khaki pants and the polo shirt with the National Constitution Center logo embroidered on it. He felt so official.

George and Barbara Bush toured the center one night. The center's director wanted his best interpreters on hand, and Mr. Cunningham was called in. No questions, it happened, were directed to him. But he was ready.

Every day at work, he explained something to somebody. People wanted to know why Gouverneur Morris, a delegate to the Constitutional Convention, had a wooden leg, and Mr. Cunningham would provide the answer. He was teaching again.

When he thought about Pennsbury, which wasn't often, he thought about Mr. Katz. "When I returned from my sojourn to Florida, he welcomed me back with a hug," Jim said one day in his first autumn as a retired teacher. He was referring to the nine-week leave of absence Mr. Katz had granted him so discreetly. "He didn't ask me about it. He just welcomed me back."

He considered Mr. Katz a true educator in a time when the profession was dominated by timid bureaucrats. He had few living heroes, but Mr. Katz was one of them.

VI.

Mr. Katz was fifty-four years old when he returned to school in September 2003, four years away from retirement. Four more years would bring him to thirty-five years in the Pennsylvania educational retirement system—and twenty-four years as the Pennsbury principal or an assistant—which would allow him to retire at 87.5 percent of his salary. He didn't know if he'd have a say in who his successor would be. But he imagined that whoever came next would want to keep the prom going. He took his role as the patron saint of the Pennsbury prom seriously.

Sometimes people new to Pennsbury made the mistake of thinking the prom was some sort of nostalgia trip for him. He knew it was not. The Pennsbury prom was onward and upward, always looking ahead and looking to improve. Every year more people came to the walk-through and to watch the arrival parade.

Early in the new school year, Mr. Katz received a call from a young man, a recent Pennsbury graduate. The caller had attended his prom—Mr. Cunningham's swan-song prom, as it happened. His date was from Council Rock. And now, the young man told Mr. Katz, he wanted to return to Pennsbury for a day. He wanted to propose to his prom date in the Pennsbury gym, on the floor where he had danced straight through the night only a few years earlier, when he was a teenager falling in love. (With a yes, he could join the Pennsbury club: "Who'd you go to your prom with?" "My wife.") He sought Mr. Katz's help in securing the gym. He wanted to pop the question surrounded by nothing but empty bleachers and memories.

Mr. Katz would want his successor to know that sort of thing.

VII.

Before Jeff Heinbach, still the front man for Jeff Says No, began his freshman year at Temple, he requested and received a meeting with Jim Greenwood, the congressman. They met for an hour—*one hour*—in an office Greenwood had near the Oxford Valley Mall. It was just the two of them. No mothers, no aides. Heinbach said he got what he wanted: an apology from Greenwood. It wasn't the public apology he had once sought. Still, Greenwood had said he was sorry.

Greenwood was a year away from running for a seventh term. Heinbach told me he would consider voting for him, but that it wasn't very likely.

VIII.

Two months into her freshman year, Lindsey Milroy was calling her mother nightly and having IM conversations with her daily. She had enrolled at West Chester University, she was playing field hockey, and she was thoroughly homesick. She was only an hour away from home, and from her boyfriend, Jamie. Anytime there was a twenty-four-hour gap in her schedule, Lindsey jumped into her fixed-up Mercury Tracer and headed home. "It's a good thing she didn't go to Vermont," her mother said. "She wouldn't have lasted a week."

Lindsey had her heart surgery after the prom and before gradua-tion, and it seemed to change her. The operation had sounded fairly simple. Her cardiologist used the most gentle-sounding layman's terms to explain what they would be doing—eliminating unnecessary tissue that wa. hindering blood flow when her heart was under stress. But Lindsey was unprepared for the stark language in the preopera-tive disclaimers she had to sign, and agitated by the long preamble to surgery. She was surprised and scared when she was told the surgery could take nearly four hours. She asked, "Am I going to die?" She was hysterical. The whole thing was far more arduous and serious than Lindsey had ever guessed it would be. Her mother and father were there for the surgery. Jamie Quinn was, too. He and Lindsey were going strong.

All the worry was for nothing. Everything went fine, and, much to her chagrin, Lindsey was quickly cleared to play sports again. She re-turned to Pennsbury and put on a brave face and told people it was no big deal. But she seemed different: less headstrong, more vulnerable. She kept telling Jamie and her mother and her friends how much she loved them.

She hated West Chester, and she especially hated the field-hockey team. Lindsey felt as though she had no privacy and no freedom. She thought often of her parents and home. It was there, amid the bland uniformity of the Heather Ridge development, that she got through her difficult senior year, the harassment episodes, the breakup with Win, the heart scare. She had always taken home for granted. Then she left and realized there was no place like it.

IX.

Two months into his freshman year and his freshman football season, Bobby Speer felt he had made the wrong college choice. All that effort, all that weighing, all the calls made and received, and in the end he felt he should have done it differently. There were four quarterbacks on the King's College football team: a senior, a junior, another freshman, and himself. Bobby was ranked fourth. He could envision no scenario in which he'd ever become the starting quarterback. He was an in-the-pocket quarterback, one who stood relatively still, protected by a cocoon of linemen as he looked for an open receiver. The King's College offense was designed for a quarterback who threw on the run, a rollout QB. King's College played the kind of offense Kirk had so often talked about, a West Coast–style offense.

The school was good, although Bobby felt that seventy-five minutes of straight lecturing was a poor way to get an idea across. He and Lauren were still boyfriend and girlfriend. It wasn't easy. They were separated by 125 miles, and they had already been through one breakup. But they had gone to the Pennsbury prom together, so could anyone be surprised if they ended up married?

Bobby's goal was still to play professional football and, lacking that, to teach and coach at Pennsbury. Early in his freshman year, he couldn't see how King's College was going to help him reach his goals, and he was thinking of transferring to another school for his sophomore year. To where, he did not know. He knew of no school where his talents and a team's needs would be anything like a perfect match.

X.

It only seemed that Bob Costa had figured out Alyssa Bergman's work schedule at T.G.I. Friday's. On more than one occasion, Costa and a friend drew Alyssa as their waitress. Alyssa called Bob by name and talked to him as if they were equals, which Bob found amusing, because he knew they were not. He always calculated her tip carefully. His goal was to be generous without being excessive. She never received less than 20 percent from him.

Alyssa remained an untouchable to Bob, but she was no longer a mythic figure, as she had been at the height of her Pennsbury fame, when she was the newly named homecoming queen. Prom night, the night Bob saw the on-the-outs boyfriend for the first time, had made her something closer to real. Bob imagined that in ten years she would be a supermodel and he could say he knew her when. But he also recognized the possibility that she'd still be a T.G.I. Friday's waitress.

Alyssa had patched things up with Michael Castor. For a while over the summer they had dated other people, but nothing felt right, and they slipped into the comfort of their old relationship. They were cut from the same cloth—from the same families, practically. They knew it.

In the new academic year, Michael had enrolled at Rider University, over the river from Newtown in New Jersey. He had given up the idea of playing college basketball and was now thinking about following his father (and Alyssa's father) into chiropractic medicine. Alyssa had switched schools, too. She left Bucks County Community for the Bucks County School of Beauty Culture. She hoped to someday open her own beauty salon, maybe even in conjunction with her father's practice. She was looking to become certified in a skin-care technique called microdermabrasion. She felt certain there was a bright future in that.

XI.

The police in Florida found no evidence of a crime being committed in the death of Michael Harris Kosmin, and that only brought more indignation and grief to his family. Mike and Cyndi knew a crime had been committed. A boy, *their* boy, had been killed. A boy who had spent New

Year's Eve playing Scrabble, who had received unsolicited letters fro
MIT, who had turned himself into a hockey player, was dead. Nobody
could tell Mike and Cyndi that no crime had been committed.

Between the police report and that of their own investigator, Mike
and Cyndi felt they had a pretty good idea of what had happened in the
hours before Mike was killed. Through a friend of a friend, Mike wound
up at a private house with, as Cyndi described them, "a bunch of spoiled
rich kids." No adults were in the house. Liquor supplies were abundant,
left over from New Year's Eve. The kids, five or six of them, all in high
school, started drinking cranberry chasers. They drove to a club that was
having an under-twenty-one night. Mike was a passenger. The club's
doorman refused to admit the group because they were visibly intoxi-
cated, including Mike. The group loitered in the parking lot. Just as the
stepfather had presumed months earlier, the reports said Mike got in a
fight with another boy in the group over a girl. Punches were thrown,
and Mike fled, right into Powerline Road and its oncoming traffic.

Mike and Cyndi kept asking themselves what they should have done
to prepare their son for the world of drinking. They were hard on themselves but not irrational. They knew the death of their son had required a
horrid confluence of events for which they were not responsible: absentee parents in houses with open liquor cabinets, hostile teenagers wal-
lowing in boredom, a club that allowed drunk minors to return to a car.

Cyndi and Mike knew their son had died a wrongful death. They
were gathering evidence for a civil suit. They made a vow that the guilty
parties would be identified and forced to pay for their viciousness, so
help them *God*.

XII.

In the new school year, Bob Costa picked up where he had left off. He
was still on the PA system daily, making the morning announcements,
but now he addressed his bleary listeners as Matt Fox once had, as school
president. With the graduation of the one kid ahead of him, Costa was
now the best debater on the Pennsbury forensics team. Maroon 5 had
become something like a fixture on MTV, and at Pennsbury, Costa was
credited for that. Costa's legend was growing with the band's. Maroon 5

was written up in *Rolling Stone* and had appeared on *The Late Show with David Letterman*. The band's first album, *Songs About Jane*, reached the Billboard Top 50. Bob was trying to get the band to play Cities Around the World, the 2004 prom, *his* prom, but he kept that close to the vest. He had learned from his John Mayer experience. When you're trying something audacious, keep it quiet. Mr. Katz was in on it, and that was it. Not even the Prom Committee knew. Bob had the announcement written in his head, for if and when the deal got done.

He was through with John Mayer. Michael McDonald, too. Mayer came out with a new album, *Heavier Things*, in the fall. Bob thought it didn't even sound like the guy who had made *Room for Squares*.

He went to Mayer's summer show in Camden—after working that day as a church janitor, his summer job—planning to write about it for the *Courier Times*. The story would be the evolution of John Mayer, or something like that. Unable to secure an interview, and against his better judgment, Costa accepted McDonald's offer to be placed on the patronizing meet-and-greet list. Costa shook Mayer's hand, and Bob's twin brother, James, snapped a picture. In his ninety seconds with Mayer, Bob reintroduced himself as the guy from Pennsbury High who had tried to get him to play the school prom. He reminded Mayer of the letter he had brought backstage at the Temple concert. Mayer responded with silence, with a blank stare, with . . . nothing.

It was humiliating. Mayer seemed to have no idea what Costa was talking about, and no interest in talking to him. Costa concluded that Mayer had never read the letter and that McDonald had never even *presented* the Pennsbury prom idea. Bob didn't care about the time and the energy he'd spent. That came with the territory. But they had wasted his optimism and the optimism of others, too. Mayer's utter boredom told Bob what he needed to know. Bob vowed never to become like that, on his own little island, surrounded by lackeys, even if he became president of the United States. *Especially* if he became president of the United States.

But you couldn't keep Bob down. He was on PHS-TV. He continued to manage the band 1903, although, recognizing his shortcomings, he gave up his position as the bongo player. He was writing a pilot for a cable show about his forays into the music world. He was still writing for the *Courier Times*, which was now paying him for his pieces, $50 each. Bob's father wondered if his son needed college at all, and Bob didn't think his father was completely joking.

Bob was filling out college applications. He knew that the application forms and his Pennsbury transcripts told a stranger nothing about the richness of his Pennsbury adventure. That felt right to him. He wasn't leading a life to impress people he didn't know. He wasn't trying to get into Princeton. Lawrenceville kids tried to do that. Bob wanted to go to a city school, maybe a Jesuit school in New York or Philadelphia.

In an English class, Bob studied "The Hollow Men," the pensive T. S. Eliot poem with the famously laconic ending:

This is the way the world ends
This is the way the world ends
This is the way the world ends
Not with a bang but a whimper.

But it was two other stanzas that stayed with him:

Between the idea
And the reality
Between the motion
And the act
Falls the Shadow

and

Between the conception
And the creation
Between the emotion
And the response
Falls the Shadow

Bob wasn't scared of the shadow, whatever it was supposed to be: death, sin, distraction, whatever. He figured he could outrun the damn shadow, clunky recovering clubfeet and all. That's what he aimed to do. Overwhelm it with enterprise, with *liveliness.*

Pennsbury was ideas, realities, emotions. It was death, and it was most certainly life. Maybe Bob would have been essentially the same kid had he gone somewhere else, but he didn't think so. Mike Kosmin's mother had Pennsbury exactly right. It was a world. "I've attached myself to Pennsbury," Costa said one October afternoon, dusk nearing. He would go where it went and it would go where he went.

We had met at the Starbucks in Newtown, on the antique borough's lovely old main street. Bob had already checked out the inventory of the funky record shop next door. The malls and the developments and the commuter traffic seemed far away.

It was a typical late-autumn afternoon, chilly and windy, cloudless—wistful. We made the short drive to the Newtown Cemetery and visited Mike Kosmin's grave, which was still waiting for a tombstone. It was marked by fresh flowers and a little autumnal flag, with a pumpkin or something on it. Fresh tufts of grass were coming up through the rich dirt.

"This is it?" Bob said. He was not always cheerful, which made him interesting and believable, and at that moment he was deeply sad. "There's got to be more to it in the end than this, don't you think?"

A short distance away was a stone that caught Bob's eye. He read it once and then again:

It isn't the date on either end that counts,
But how they used their dash

The ditty struck a chord deep within Bob, for its brevity and its insight. It made him want to rewrite Eliot's final stanza:

How will you use your time?
How will you use your time?
Shadow, whimper, bang.
How will you use your time?

He had just turned eighteen. In a few weeks he would be voting for the first time. All he had ahead of him was the prom, graduation, the summer before college, and all the tomorrows that would come after it. The wind was dying with sunset. It was a Saturday night. The school was closed—no debate tournament, no football game, no dance—but the village of Pennsbury was up and running. What Bob would do, he did not know.

Author's Note

The kids saw me all year long, notebook in hand. They knew what I was doing. One day a boy said to me, "The book's gonna be true-life, right?"

"That's right."

"Like real names and everything?"

"Yep," I said. Real names, true-life, real everything.